D1356473

Heterodox Shakespeare

Heterodox Shakespeare

Sean Benson

FAIRLEIGH DICKINSON UNIVERSITY PRESS
Madison • Teaneck

Published by Fairleigh Dickinson University Press
Copublished by The Rowman & Littlefield Publishing Group, Inc.
4501 Forbes Boulevard, Suite 200, Lanham, Maryland 20706
www.rowman.com

Unit A, Whitacre Mews, 26-34 Stannary Street, London SE11 4AB

British Library Cataloguing in Publication Information Available

Library of Congress Cataloging-in-Publication Data

Benson, Sean, 1966- author.
Heterodox Shakespeare / Sean Benson.
Madison : Fairleigh Dickinson University Press ; Lanham, Maryland : Co-published with The Row-
     man & Littlefield Publishing Group, Inc., [2017] | Includes bibliographical references and index.
LCCN 2016058800 (print) | LCCN 2016058891 (ebook) | ISBN 9781683930259 (cloth : alk. paper) |
     ISBN 9781683930266 (Electronic)
LCSH: Shakespeare, William, 1564-1616--Religion. | Religion and drama. | Good and evil in litera-
     ture. | Drama--Religious aspects.
LCC PR3011 .B46 2017 (print) | LCC PR3011 (ebook) | DDC 822.3/3--dc23
LC record available at https://lccn.loc.gov/2016058800

Printed in the United States of America

to Jennifer

Contents

Acknowledgments

I would like to thank Harry Keyishian, director of Fairleigh Dickinson University Press, for his support in bringing this book to press. I am equally indebted to John Mahon, whose generous and careful reading of the manuscript strengthened it at all points. Portions of this manuscript have been read at the annual conferences of the Shakespeare Association of America and the South-Central Renaissance Conference. Among the listeners who offered constructive advice are Irving Kelter, Nancy Bunker, Donald Stump, Christopher Baker, George Klawitter, John Mercer, Frederick Kiefer, Maurice Hunt, Philip Lorenz, and Jason E. Cohen. Any faults that remain are my own. My departmental colleagues, particularly Jonathan Barz and Jessica Schreyer, have listened patiently to some strange ideas about Shakespeare and have enriched my work life with their support.

My research could not have been completed without the continual and timely assistance of the library staff of the Charles C. Myers Library, under the always capable direction of Mary Anne Knefel. John Rush, director of library services, has allowed me generous access to the collection at Emmaus Bible College. I am indebted to a former colleague, Nathan Faries, whose course on zombies and aliens spurred me to begin thinking about zombieism and its potential relationship to *Hamlet*. Chapter 3 could not have been written without the assistance of my philosophy colleague, Paul Jensen, who introduced me to Alvin Plantinga's free will defense to the problem of evil, and whose conversation has enriched my thinking throughout that chapter. I also wish to thank Dawnie Wolfe Steadman, director of the Forensic Anthropology Center at the University of Tennessee, for having directed me to taphonomic studies on the human body. None of my writing gets done without the intellectual enrichment I receive from students in my Shakespeare course; I owe them more than they know. My wife, Jennifer, and our two children, Derek and Gabi, are a continuing source of grace in my life.

Two earlier and shorter versions of chapters 2 and 3 have been previously been published; both are herein used with permission and originally appeared as follows:

"'Like Monsters of the Deep': Transworld Depravity and *King Lear*." *Philosophy and Literature* 37.2 (October 2013): 314–29.

"'Perverse Fantasies'?: Rehabilitating Malvolio's Reading." *Papers on Language and Literature* 45.3 (Summer 2009): 261–86.

I also cite extensively from one particular work:

Hans Urs von Balthasar, *Theo-Drama: Theological Dramatic Theory.* Volume 1: *Prolegomena*. Translated by Graham Harrison. San Francisco: Ignatius Press, 1988. 650 pages. www.ignatius.com. Used with permission.

Finally, I have received several John Stewart Research Awards that aided in my research and writing, and I have also been awarded a sabbatical this year to complete the book. For these awards, and for their ongoing and generous support of my teaching and writing, I wish to express my gratitude to Mark Ward, vice president and dean of the faculty; to Jeffrey Bullock, president; and to the Board of Trustees of the University of Dubuque.

Introduction

Shakespeare and the Church

For the last quarter century, the role of religion in Shakespeare's plays has been vigorously contested. On the one hand, since the advent of the new historicism in America and cultural materialism in England, it has been asserted with growing confidence that Shakespeare's exploration of religious ideas reflects profound skepticism and perhaps even dismissal of the truth claims of revealed religion. Partially in response to such critical demystification, there has been a "turn to religion" in Shakespeare studies,[1] typified by nuanced readings at several removes from early and mid-twentieth century interpretations that located a triumphalist Christianity in the plays. Those earlier readings often assumed that Shakespeare's plays represented a uniform *Weltanschauung* or " world picture,"[2] comprising religious orthodoxy as well. When scholars of a more materialist bent argued that Shakespeare and other playwrights depicted and possibly endorsed radical religious ideas well beyond the confines of orthodoxy, they were able to point to the abiding presence of skepticism and even what Christopher Hill calls the *irreligion* embraced by a sizable number of Shakespeare's contemporaries.[3] The older critical hegemony seemed to creak under the stress of assertions such as Jonathan Dollimore's in *Radical Tragedy*—now in its third printing—that "*King Lear* is, above all, a play about power, property, and inheritance."[4]

This book is the first to propose an accommodation, uneasy as it may initially appear, between these respective sides. For every reader who sees, as Dollimore, *King Lear*'s relentless materialism, still others note that the play's religious complexity seems to suggest that all of life cannot be reduced to the material or to power relations; that the religious has an abiding and irreducible presence in *King Lear* and Shakespeare's other plays. Why, however,

1

must we read the plays one way or the other? This divide in the criticism, though real, obscures the fact that Shakespeare often embeds secular and religious interpretive possibilities within the same play; his doing so is a characteristic feature of his drama. Unfortunately, Shakespeare's plays are routinely viewed as either a part of a movement in early modern theater toward "a secular, even a secularizing, stage," or as profoundly religious, even sacramental, as in the readings of Jeffrey Knapp, Piero Boitani, and others.[5] Those who weigh in on the issue typically do so in terms of a binary opposition: "is, as some have recently claimed, theatre infused with religious content, or does it remain a primarily secular domain?"[6]

It is time to move past such thinking, which has persisted among materialist critics because of their sense of the illusory nature of the religious. As Paul Stevens remarks of recent discussions of the term *secular*, the argument in the West for the inevitable displacement of religion by secularism is not, as has often been assumed, a natural progression or stripping away to the real, but rather a move from one carefully constructed perception of reality to another:

> The secular itself is no longer seen as our natural state—what John Milbank calls "the perennial destiny of the West," always there "gestating in the womb of Judeo-Christianity"—but simply another way of being in the world. Indeed, the secular, so Milbank feels, is "constituted or *imagined*" every bit as much as the religious understandings of things it is supposed to have superseded. It is not simply a process of stripping away or desacralizing, but one of active construction.[7]

Shakespeare actively constructs both secular and religious understandings of his playworlds. I will demonstrate this most fully in the final two chapters on *Hamlet*, arguing first for a renewed secular reading of it as a godless, bleak, even apocalyptic world where the soul is either nonexistent or dead, and human life is animated by pure mechanistic forces. The subsequent chapter argues that *Hamlet* also invites a modern theological interpretation and examination of the inwardness or conscience of a person (Hamlet's in particular) in relation to the divine. Shakespeare's willingness to explore all aspects of religious and secular life, often simultaneously, is a mark of his tremendous intellectual range. His art is in an important sense *heterodox* because it reveals a willingness to explore ideas that were "not in accordance with established beliefs and religious doctrines" (*Oxford English Dictionary*); Shakespeare's writing—irrespective of his own precise confessional position[8]—is undoctrinaire, probing, seemingly without boundaries. The boundaries of orthodoxy were contested and even shifting at times during the Reformation, as we shall see in the discussion of ghosts in chapter 4.

The modern critical split, however, remains firmly entrenched. Richard McCoy is among the more recent to argue that Shakespeare's plays are thoroughly secular: "arguments made for a theological significance and sacramental purpose for Shakespeare's plays are mistaken."[9] McCoy is aware of the many critics—David Bevington, Debora Shuger, Huston Diehl, Maurice Hunt, and Jeffrey Knapp, to name a few—who argue that Shakespeare's plays wrestle with issues of deep theological moment. I take exception neither to those who argue for the secularism of the plays nor to those who stipulate a deeply religious sensibility in them; my own reading has been informed by both sides. It is not that Shakespeare is a relativist—far from it, I will argue—but he does allow competing beliefs about ultimate reality to coexist and vie for interpretive center stage.

When Edgar leaves to fight for the restoration of Lear's kingdom, Gloucester's language is couched as a blessing: "Grace go with you, sir!"[10] With their decisive defeat following immediately, Edgar returns to inform Gloucester of his need to flee, only to be rebuffed: "No further, sir. A man may rot even here" (5.2.8). Gloucester appears hopeless: he seems to experience not the divine grace he had wished for his son only moments ago, but its absence. Edgar then reminds his father of the need for resignation that can be read equally well in stoic or Christian terms (or both): "Men must endure / Their going hence, even as their coming hither; / Ripeness is all" (9–11). Gloucester's response—"And that's true too"—is not to make a typical move made in secular criticism; that is, to invalidate the divine intimations of his earlier reference to "grace" and embrace instead a nihilistic reading of the moment. It may be true that life is merely a matter of rotting somewhere, but the compactness of Gloucester's later reply—"And that's true too"—allows for the additional possibility that he recognizes a benevolent universe despite his own suffering and benighted human condition. Edgar had earlier tried to persuade him of this on Dover cliff (4.6.73–74), and the effect is here palpable but not complete. Remarkably, Gloucester privileges neither the religious nor a resolutely materialist—even godless—view: both exist together in the moment as possibilities, with neither as a certainty.

The history of criticism attests to the many perfectly valid religious, as well as secular, readings of the same plays. To argue that *any* theological (or, alternatively, secular) understanding of Shakespeare's plays is mistaken is unnecessarily dismissive and reductive of the plays' rich complexities. Moreover, the division between the secular and the religious is to some extent artificial and arbitrary, as critics on both sides of the issue would agree. For some secularists, religion is merely a mask, or an illusion, or something (seen in its most charitable light) that can be explained by the quotidian material. A secular understanding of the world reads the religious out of it, often by means of demystifying or explaining away the numinous in favor of the phenomenal. To the religious mind, on the other hand, nothing is outside God's creation, which includes the material, and thus a religious understanding also attempts to encompass all of life. For Stevens, and as I will argue for

Shakespeare as well, the religious and the secular are competing contingencies. Shakespeare recognized, as we all do, distinctions between the sacred and the profane and appears to have been genuinely interested in both rather than invalidating one in favor of its opposite.

What I propose then is a modified—or rather, unsynthesized—Hegelian understanding of the plays, one that was first hinted at by Germaine Greer:

> Shakespeare was not a propagandist; he did not write plays as vehicles for his own ideas. Rather he developed a theatre of dialectical conflict, in which idea is pitted against idea and from their friction a deeper understanding of the issues emerges. The resolution which is reached is not the negation of the conflict, but the stasis produced by art.[11]

Unlike Jean-Christophe Mayer, I do not regard Shakespeare's art as a hybridization of competing religious faiths,[12] but rather as an examination, often without a definitive resolution, of competing contingencies. With Greer, I do not see Shakespeare as a propagandist but as someone who advances a thesis (the religious), explores its antithesis (the secular), and explores the two in such a way not as to hybridize them but to consider them alongside one another in what Greer describes as the stasis of Shakespeare's art. I would call it the ekphrasis of Shakespeare's art, as it is a moving tableau along the religious and secular continuum, oscillating back and forth without negating either position. It is true that a play such as *King Lear* at times comes close to the possibility of a godless universe, but this remains only a possibility, one that Shakespeare counters by providing, within the play itself, a contingent world where God not only exists but can be regarded as benevolent toward his creation.

The secular/religious pendulum swings back and forth in the plays. David Bevington has captured this nicely in his recent discussion of the deep religiosity in *Hamlet*, noting nonetheless that Horatio's final speech points to a revisionist history, a competing and alternative secular understanding of what has just happened in the play. After quoting Horatio's account of "accidental judgments, casual slaughters" (5.2.383–7), Bevington writes

> This is the secular humanist speaking, and it sorts well with the dramatic voice in *Julius Caesar*, *King Lear*, and other tragedies of the Jacobean period that explore the daunting prospect of a world that is presided over not by a benign overseeing deity who makes sure that every smallest event in our lives is ultimately meaningful, but by unforeseen accidents, "casual" violence.[13]

Shakespeare explores questions of religious belief, nonbelief, and unbelief with an eye to the contingencies entailed by each of them. His openness or complementarity, what Keats called *negative capability*, suggests a willingness to explore the possibility in *Lear* that we inhabit a godless universe indifferent to human suffering. Equally and contradictorily, the play also opens the possibility that we live in a universe with a personal God who cares for humans even in the midst of their suffering. As I will discuss in chapter 3, human suffering can be viewed as the theistic price of free will. In the end, Shakespeare is neither a mere debunker of religious orthodoxies nor their unquestioning champion. In fact, religious inquiry in his plays is capacious enough to encompass the heterodox, to tolerate religious dissent and radical belief, and even to explore on stage the real possibility of God's nonexistence.[14]

There is no mistaking Shakespeare's investigation of ideas and phenomena that are, from the Church's perspective—be it Catholic or Reformist—heterodox and even unorthodox.[15] The walking dead, as I will argue, are in the margins of Shakespeare's plays, even though the idea of the corporeal yet soulless dead returning from their graves to harry the living is an idea the possibility of which is officially denied by the Church. This is not to suggest that church dogma is antithetical to inquiry; dogma represents (despite animadversions against it) inquiry's culmination, not its foreclosure from the outset. Francis Bacon recalls Pontius Pilate's skepticism in the face of Jesus: "What is truth? said jesting Pilate, and would not stay for an answer."[16] Shakespeare's artistic patience allows him to consider an array of contingent truths—what Leibniz called *possible worlds*—whose cosmologies conform to the range in beliefs of his characters. What has not been discussed at length is his ability to embed both religious and secular, sacred and profane, readings within the plays. Yet such a move would have seemed natural, fitting even, to a dramatist whose plays were routinely performed on professional stages and, as I will demonstrate in chapter 1, in churches as well. The secular and religious were a part of Shakespeare's theatrical world, and it should hardly surprise us that each receives serious and sustained treatment in his work.

This book attempts in part to document the mutual dependence and even synergy between Shakespeare's plays and the Church. Even if Shakespeare were not a Christian, which I think unlikely (more on this in the conclusion), this does nothing to prevent his exploration of agnosticism, atheism, materialism, and other challenges to theism. In fact, I will argue that it is precisely Shakespeare's theism that fosters the bracing heterodoxy—the fearlessness of religious and philosophical inquiry—that so characterizes his plays. He was intensely interested in what radical believers and even the most skeptical unbelievers thought. Shakespeare's thoroughgoing exploration of religious belief leads him to examine figures and ideas well outside the primrose path of Christian orthodoxy. His drama thus engages quite broadly with the religious beliefs and practices of his contemporaries, believers and nonbelievers alike.

On a concrete level, his plays envision the Church as a physical presence: the staunch local parish church that served as a center of religious and social life. The church building served both as an imaginative backdrop and as a physical site—the playing space—for performances when the early modern theatrical companies toured the provinces. Moments in *Twelfth Night* and *Hamlet* take on a special poignancy in light of the reality of church performances. Yet the plays also cast a critical eye at the theology of the Church, with characters offering serious challenges to, perhaps even refutations of, its doctrines, and of theism itself. I have neither the wish nor the ability to deny the plausibility or legitimacy of secularist readings of Shakespeare's plays, as he clearly contemplates in his work both radical religion and the possibility of a godless universe. The converse of such theological skepticism is his representation of a sustained theism and the embrace of the Church by the body of believers who constitute its membership. For every Iago, there is a Desdemona. Shakespeare's drama thus runs the gamut from fervent belief to dismissive unbelief, yet even in the most theologically stark moments he also remains attentive to possible correspondences between action on his stage and God's action in the world as recorded in the gospels.

Commenting on Bottom's synesthetic garbling of 1 Corinthians 2:9, "The eye of man hath not heard, the ear of man hath not seen, man's hand is not able to taste, his tongue to conceive, nor his heart to report what my dream was" (*MND* 4.1.209–12), Stephen Greenblatt writes, "this is the joke of a decisively secular dramatist, a writer who deftly turned the dream of the sacred into popular entertainment."[17] Such transformation is unmistakable, and yet theology, which takes as its object the real,[18] has enough substance, even if it is sometimes only of things unseen (see Hebrews 11:1), for Bottom's dream to be more than merely a dream of the sacred. Yet Greenblatt is surely right to point to this latter possibility: the sacred as possible chimera. Shakespeare's dramatic interest in such contingencies is real and far-reaching. We can get an initial glimpse of that reach by looking at the response to the religious from a few of Shakespeare's heterodox scoundrels, as well as their more pious counterparts.

Consider first *As You Like It*'s Duke Frederick. He usurps his brother's dukedom; banishes both father and daughter, the savvy Rosalind; attempts to have Orlando murdered; and uses the power of the state to confiscate Oliver's house and lands. Frederick is, by any estimation, a tyrant. To that end, we discover late in act 5 that he has learned the whereabouts of his brother and has levied "a mighty power" "purposely to take / His brother here and put him to the sword" (5.4.155–57). His purpose turns awry, however, with his sudden conversion—whether we like it (as the title suggests) or not:

And to the skirts of this wild wood he came,

That apprehends no further than this world,

And squar'st thy life according. Thou'rt condemned;

But, for those earthly faults, I quit them all,

And pray thee take this mercy to provide

For better times to come.—Friar, advise him;

I leave him to your hand. (5.1.490–97)

His earthly crimes are pardoned, but there is no evidence that Barnardine cares any further than this world, and squares his life accordingly. Shakespeare later recycles this aspect of Barnardine's character in *The Winter's Tale*'s Autolycus, who explains that he engages in petty trickery rather than more serious (capital) crimes: "Gallows and knock are too powerful on the highway; beating and hanging are terrors to me." Concerned about temporal punishment, he gives no thought to the future, including, quite possibly, to the hereafter: "For the life to come, I sleep out the thought of it. A prize, a prize!" (4.3.28–31). Autolycus chases after trifles while he remains steadfastly indifferent to any heavenly prize (or punishment) that might be his. His apathy, like that of Barnardine, is at one end of a spectrum with Frederick's radical conversion at the other.

Consider, too, Prospero's valedictory lines in *The Tempest*:

And my ending is despair,

Unless I be relieved by prayer,

Which pierces so that it assaults

Mercy itself, and frees all faults.

As you from crimes would pardoned be,

Let your indulgence set me free. (Epilogue 15–20)

The opposition between the impenitent Barnardine and the remorseful magus, whose "every third thought" is now his grave, could hardly be greater (5.1.315). The stirrings of conscience, of a mortality that makes him think of his finitude, of life *sub specie aeternitatis*, touches Prospero in a way it never does Barnardine, unless one wants to read the latter's final silence as a miraculous transformation from sloth to conversion. The play, however, gives no evidence of it, and the Duke's imploring him to reform suggests any change has yet (if ever) to come about.

Barnardine's slothful disinterest in the spiritual also diverges from a more malignant strain seen in characters such as Edmund and Iago, both of whom come to an implicit, if not explicit, denial of the Christian faith. Consider, for instance Edmund's famous profession of faith: "Thou, Nature, art my goddess; to thy law / My services are bound" (*Lr.* 1.2.1–2). In his edition of the play, David Bevington glosses Nature as "the sanction that governs the material world through mechanistic amoral forces,"[19] an apt description of Edmund's deism or of his social Darwinism—in either case, a far cry from Christianity's traditional understanding of a personal God who loves his creation and for whose sake, as Hamlet remarks, "there is special providence in the fall of a sparrow" (5.2.217–18). Edmund does, however, relent— "Some good I mean to do, / Despite of mine own nature" (5.3.248–49)— even if his belated attempt to save the life of Cordelia, whose execution he had ordered, fails. Is his deathbed repentance a sign of some sort of religious conversion, or merely the belated stirrings of his conscience, in spite of his admittedly perverse nature? The play never resolves this question, and resists any sort of pat religious answer.

If Edmund relents, Iago never wavers in his malice. He announces his destructive intentions: "I am not what I am" (*Oth.* 1.1.67), an inversion of God's declaration of his creative goodness and absolute being: "I am that I am" (Exodus 3:14). Iago's implicit repudiation of the Christian faith is steadfast, so much so that Othello looks to see if he has perhaps the devil's own cloven feet, and also calls him a "demi-devil" (5.2.309). Othello and a few critics wish to read Iago allegorically, or even anagogically, but he seems to embody a motiveless malignity, to use Coleridge's phrase, that is all too human. As Augustine remarked in his discussion of the problem of evil, all of God's creation is intrinsically good: "it was made clear to me that thou madest all things good . . . whatsoever is, is good."[20] The evil of Iago's destructive impulses stands in contrast not only to God's creative goodness but also, on a human level, to Desdemona's. She works to restore Cassio to his lieutenancy, even though doing so undoes her in Othello's eyes, and likewise strives to placate her husband's wrath, even in her famous death scene. Before her demise, when Othello first confronts her for her alleged infidelity, he asks, "Swear thou art honest," to which she responds with no hesitation, "Heaven doth truly know it" (4.2.40). Later in the scene, Othello reiterates the charge:

Are not you a strumpet?

DESDEMONA No, as I am a Christian.

If to preserve this vessel for my lord

From any other foul unlawful touch

Be not to be a strumpet, I am none.

OTHELLO

What, not a whore?

DESDEMONA

No, as I shall be saved.

Desdemona's performance as a type of patient Griselda is firmly and explicitly grounded in her affirmation of the Christian faith and its strictures, recorded in the Decalogue and elsewhere, proscribing adultery.

Edmund and Iago teeter on the brink of an atheism that allows them to act in light of this life only. Iago's "Virtue: A fig! 'Tis in ourselves that we are thus or thus" (1.3.322–23) rejects the Catholic doctrine of the divinely infused (cardinal) virtues—faith, hope, love—in favor of a no-holds-barred approach to life. Iago and Edmund freely commit mortal sins—murder, for instance—that so bedevil Macbeth, who initially expresses his willingness to forgo the next life for this: "that but this blow / Might be the be-all and the end-all!—here, / But here, upon this bank and shoal of time, / We'd jump the life to come" (1.7.4–7). Yet he recognizes the Faustian nature of his bargain:

For Banquo's issue have I filed my mind;

For them the gracious Duncan have I murdered,

Put rancors in the vessel of my peace

Only for them, and mine eternal jewel

Given to the common enemy of man. (3.1.66–70)

Despite his recognition of the parlous state of his soul—"mine eternal jewel"—he asks the men he would have assassinate Banquo and his son, "Are you so gospeled / To pray for this good man and for his issue"? (89–90). Neither he nor they are so gospeled. *Macbeth* is a study of a man who fully recognizes the negative commandment against murder. His final line, "And damned be him that first cries, 'Hold, enough!'" (5.8.34), appears to reject any limitations, divine or temporal, on his will or actions. Like Desdemona,

Macbeth recognizes the spiritual consequences of his actions. Unlike her, he is willing to accept those consequences if he can achieve power in this life.

That question is also put to Desdemona as she discusses the possible adultery of some wives:

DESDEMONA

Wouldst thou do such a deed for all the world?

EMILIA

Why, would not you?

DESDEMONA

No, by this heavenly light!

EMILIA

Nor I neither by this heavenly light;

I might do't as well i'th' dark.

DESDEMONA

Wouldst thou do such a deed for all the world? (4.3.66–70)

Desdemona's answer to her own rhetorical question is an unequivocal no, and she frames it, as usual, in light of her religious faith. Emilia nonchalantly responds that she might well do such a thing—"who would not make her husband a cuckold to make him a monarch?" (78–79)—but when she is faced with the evidence of her husband's treachery, she reveals it and stops his rise to power, even though she recognizes that he will kill her for her refusal to keep silent (5.2.204).

What this all suggests, of course, is that Shakespeare's engagement with the Church—theology, conversion, disbelief, the inner promptings of the Holy Spirit, skepticism—is as varied as the spiritual lives of persons. In some ways, Shakespeare's corpus constitutes an early modern dramatic equivalent of William James's *The Varieties of Religious Experience*. Whatever Shakespeare's own religious commitments, the Church with its claims to truth and ultimate meaning was of importance to his artistry and to the culture in which he lived. I have to this point largely avoided a discussion of religion within the three plays that form the core of this book—*Hamlet*, *Twelfth Night*, and *King Lear*—to show just how varied is the range of and response to the religious in Shakespeare's entire corpus. His plays continually explore the religious alongside more mundane phenomena, as should be expected from a writer of his breadth and complexity. In a commentary on *Measure for Measure*, Geoffrey Bullough long ago suggested the range of Shakespeare's mixing of the sacred and the profane:

> Shakespeare here shows himself rather the *anima naturaliter Christiana* [soul of the natural Christian] than the exponent of particular Christian doctrines, though it is wrong to limit his religious ideas to wellings up from an unconscious heritage, in view of . . . pervasive references to Christian teaching. Rather the Christian heritage is blended in a wide pattern of humane ethics which allows of inconsistencies, touches of pagan feeling, bawdiness, delight in crooked ways.[21]

Shakespeare, whose language is the most concrete, as well as the most sublime, of dramatists, traverses almost all of life's experiences, including the religious, which enjoys an abiding presence in his work. Indeed, the thousands of biblical allusions in the plays—not to mention his use of liturgical and other theological references—far outpace his use of any other single source. Perhaps this should not be a surprise since the Church offered ultimate meaning to its parishioners and was at the center of much of their social lives as well.[22]

Despite various Protestant as well as Catholic and crypto-Catholic readings of the plays, Shakespeare is not a religiously sectarian artist who can readily be identified as such in the same way that a writer such as Ben Jonson can. Given Shakespeare's emphasis on the need for forgiveness, reconciliation, divine and human love—what Park Honan calls the "profound religious and moral sense that underlies Shakespeare's urbanity"[23]—Christianity does color his thought, but the religious is always reflected through the aestheticism of his art. One of his distinctive traits is his "confessional invisibility,"[24] and to read Shakespeare as a sectary is to pigeonhole a writer whose intellect ranges from orthodoxy to religious radicalism and other outliers on the religious spectrum. He explores the walking dead in *Hamlet*; puritanism, both its excessive asceticism as well as the need to tolerate such belief, in *Twelfth Night*; and in *King Lear*, the distinct possibility of philosophical nihilism and religious atheism. Whether this latitudinarianism was a mark of deeply felt religious belief or lack thereof, the fact remains that his work is broadly ecumenical rather than partisan. This breadth allows Shakespeare to engage theological questions in ways that still speak to believers and nonbelievers alike. Puritanism, for instance, was a phenomenon that intrigued him for its ascetic articulation of the Christian faith, and quite possibly for its increasing opposition to his profession, especially when plays, as we will see in chapter 1, were routinely performed on church property. It is true that he lampoons puritan characters including Falstaff,[25] but he also takes the abstemiousness of a Malvolio seriously and gives him his due. Shakespeare was similarly interested in the concept of Christian resurrection, and staged in his drama recognition scenes where long-separated characters appear to each other to have come back from the dead.[26] His use of biblical motifs and language at such moments is well understood.

Conceptually, this book falls into two halves; what unifies them is the textual analysis—close readings—of the religious language that surfaces in the plays. The first half of the book examines Reformation theology in *Twelfth Night* on its own early modern terms; the other half uses modern approaches—philosophy of religion, cultural criticism, and theological aesthetics—to offer three new interpretations of *Hamlet* and *King Lear*, the two plays at the epicenter of Shakespeare studies. Chapters 1 and 2 examine early modern religious belief and practice: the practice of professional companies' using local parish churches as performance venues; and the competing beliefs of *Twelfth Night*'s Malvolio and his antipuritan opponents. The second half of the book—chapters 3 through 5—examines atheism, the walking dead, and the religious promptings of Hamlet's conscience, respectively. The final chapter of the book applies to *Hamlet* the theological aesthetics of Hans Urs von Balthasar, an astute reader of Shakespeare's plays and arguably the most important Catholic theologian of the twentieth century. This book explores both the heterodoxy and orthodoxy of Shakespeare's thought, from his willingness to consider the possibility that God does not exist to his probing of the relations between human beings and the divine, what Balthasar calls "theo-drama."

To give the book clarity and focus, I decided early to concentrate on three plays: *Twelfth Night* (chapters 1 and 2), *King Lear* (chapter 3), and *Hamlet* (chapters 4 and 5). Each of them is an exploration of heterodoxy in one way or another, either in terms of conformist Reformation thought or in the challenge that my arguments present to established approaches to the plays. The first and fifth chapters question settled views on the performances of plays and of characters in them. Chapter 1 concerns the local parish churches that literally served as outlying performance venues for the traveling theatrical companies. This chapter is the first to show the extent to which local parishes hosted the traveling professional troupes on their premises, often in disregard of official—civic and ecclesial—opposition. Although the Queen's Men and every other professional troupe performed routinely and repeatedly in churches during the latter half of the sixteenth century, we have largely lost sight of this tradition. To be sure, there was indeed a general movement in the staging of plays from the church to the professional London playhouses, but plays never left the churches altogether, and the longstanding vitality of churches as performance venues has been overlooked.

The secularization theory of early modern English performance practice has been with us at least since 1850 when Emerson declared, "We have to thank the researches of antiquaries, and the Shakespeare Society, for ascertaining the steps of the English drama, from the Mysteries celebrated in churches and by churchmen, and the final detachment from the church, and the completion of secular plays."[27] Shakespearean drama is the apotheosis of Emerson's Transcendentalist vision, yet if one examines the performance history of early modern plays, it quickly becomes evident that they did not move in any simple or unidirectional way from the church to the (secular) stage. Chapter 1 uses the existing *Records of Early English Drama (REED)* volumes to offer a new historicist reading based on the records of church performances and the references in *Twelfth Night* that tantalize us with the play's awareness of such stagings. I suggest that the circulation of social energy, to borrow Greenblatt's phrase, included the Church and its relationship with the social lives of parishioners, which included everything from enjoying rowdy church ales to attending the touring companies' plays. This chapter suggests that performing the plays on stages and in churches was standard practice, and corrects any staging history that would insist on a simple secular/religious divide.

Chapter 2 demonstrates that Shakespeare's alleged satire of Malvolio and puritanism is instead a probing investigation of the religiously motivated persecution of one's opponents. Doing a close reading of Malvolio's reading of Maria's letter in 2.5 of *Twelfth Night*, I suggest that what really is at issue in his reading is the theological debate over textual exegesis. Can a lay person, the Reformers asked, read and interpret scripture according to one's own lights, or must one rely on a tradition as well as approved authorities? Who legitimates one reading or reader, and on what authority does one disqualify the interpretation of a heterodox figure such as the puritan Malvolio? Malvolio's hermeneutics are—*pacé* the consensus view among professional Shakespeareans—thoroughly vindicated. In interpreting Malvolio as at once an astute reader and a sympathetic figure, this chapter examines Shakespeare's willingness to probe the doctrines and tolerance of his religiously conforming peers.

Chapter 3 is a philosophy of religion essay, challenging the widely held assumption that *King Lear*, bordering on philosophical nihilism as it certainly does, also constitutes a proof of the nonexistence of God. As to this last point, I argue that *Lear* allows for the possibility that a good and just God exists amidst the bleakness of its playworld. My reading is thus heterodox within the critical consensus, and I use analytic philosophy to discredit the view that *Lear* inevitably presents a godless or godforsaken world. While such a reading is plausible—the darkness is unmistakable in *Lear*—there is nothing that compels us to read the play only in this light, and an abundance of evidence points in the other direction. The chapter adapts Alvin Plantinga's free-will defense to the problem of evil—his argument that for humans to be truly free in their actions, the possibility exists that they will in their creaturely freedom nonetheless choose evil. In other words, if Shakespeare takes human freedom seriously, then even in the world of *King Lear* it is not logically possible for him to suggest (as many critics insist he does) that there is any contradiction between the abundance of moral evil and the existence of a good and loving God.

Chapter 4 is another turn to heterodoxy, in this case popular folk beliefs in the living or walking dead who, surprisingly, also dot the landscape of Shakespeare's plays, particularly *Hamlet*. Few scholars have discussed this recurrent interest of Shakespeare's, yet it raises tantalizing religious and philosophical questions about human existence. The chapter is in part a cultural critique, opening with a discussion of the current vogue for zombieism and Shakespeare's oblique, if nonetheless real, relation to it. The plays reveal his interest in folk beliefs about what happens to the body after death. Shakespeare does not give us zombies *per se*, the term having been invented only in the nineteenth century, but he does rely on popular legends to explore the possibility of corpses returning from their graves. These folk beliefs suggest physical revenants not only can walk about churchyards at night but also stalk and harry the living. To be sure, these are not the resurrected bodies of the saints, restored with glorious bodies and minds (or souls) fully intact, but something more sinister and even subhuman.

Shakespeare could have easily dismissed such folklore as nonsensical or superstitious, just as he could have dismissed notions of hobgoblins or the figures of Ariel and Puck. He was, however, one of what Philip Rieff called "the older symbolists who saw in what there is that which is,"[28] a writer who saw, by means of the mundane, realities beyond them. Shakespeare makes good dramaturgical and aesthetic use of such imaginative possibilities. What is most surprising is how Shakespeare uncannily anticipates our current interest in the living dead, and I offer a reading of Old Hamlet as a corpselike figure. Although he is traditionally represented as a ghost, the play is decidedly ambivalent about his existential and ontological status, and recent zombiesque adaptations of Shakespeare's plays explore this possibility to the point of excess. I want to bring some scholarly scrutiny to bear on this trend, and to offer some modest direction so as to avoid the campy parodies that have recently made their way to stage and screen.

Chapter 5 analyzes *Hamlet*, a play that has been thoroughly psychologized and secularized in modern readings, in light of Hans Urs von Balthasar's twentieth-century aesthetics. Hamlet's pronounced religious language has been interpreted since Nietzsche as a sign of neurosis, and I want to ground his language, as well as the problem of his interiority, in a theological approach. In my view, Hamlet's problem is not his thinking *per se*, but his thinking through of his relationship to the divine. He repeatedly speaks the language of the Church because he is a believer struggling with the proper course of action he should take in his life—revenger, martyr, scourge, pacifist? The play reveals not so much the conscience of the king, as Hamlet would hope, but his own conscience wrestling with a divine call that he seeks to discern and to which he can surrender, becoming like Duke Frederick, a religious radical in the Machiavellian world of Danish realpolitik.

Taken together, the five chapters that follow are meant to shed new light on well-established positions in Shakespearean criticism: the secularizing hypothesis of early modern staging; Shakespeare's distaste for and intolerance of puritanism; his embrace of religious nihilism in *King Lear*; the ontological status of the ghost of Old Hamlet; and the idea of Hamlet as a secular revenger. As I will suggest in Chapter 1, Shakespeare's plays come close to the theological realm, even as they preserve their appropriate aesthetic distance from it. *King Lear* and *Hamlet* both offer the distinct possibility of a world devoid of God, one where there is no theo-drama but rather human beings in a cosmos utterly indifferent, if not openly hostile, to their well-being. Shakespeare's engagement with the religious is capacious enough to consider the potential of God's nonexistence—even as he points to the no-less-real possibility of God's abiding presence in the midst of *King Lear*'s seeming bleakness. In *Hamlet* he similarly directs us to the possibility of the prince's searching for and finding God's voice in the face of his death, which he realizes has already been scripted and is thus inevitable. *Twelfth Night* points to the hatred and internecine struggles between coreligionists who share neither the same fine points of doctrine nor ideas as to how one should live in the world. Amid such mutual antagonisms and contestation over what it means to be orthodox, Shakespeare's theater explores various heterodox positions that reveal his theater is not so much church-haunted, as has been suggested, as it is church-inspired. His is existential theater, concerned with the here and now, whose reach nonetheless extends to the metaphysical. In this way, his concern for the lives and beliefs of people, including parishioners who saw his plays in their local parish churches, is enacted in "secular" drama that is simultaneously compatible with the divine drama of the Church.

NOTES

1. Ken Jackson and Arthur F. Marotti, "The Turn to Religion in Early Modern English Studies," *Criticism* 46, no. 1 (Winter 2004): 167–190.

2. E. M. W. Tillyard, *The Elizabethan World Picture* (New York: The Macmillan Company, 1944).

3. Christopher Hill, "Irreligion in the 'Puritan' Revolution," in *Radical Religion in the English Revolution*, ed. J. F. McGregor and Barry Reay (Oxford: Oxford University Press, 1984), 191–211.

4. Jonathan Dollimore, *Radical Tragedy*, 3rd ed. (New York: Palgrave Macmillan, 2004), 197.

5. The quotation is from Jeffrey Knapp, *Shakespeare's Tribe: Church, Nation, and Theater in Renaissance England* (Chicago: University of Chicago Press, 2002), 1; Piero Boitani, *The*

Gospel according to Shakespeare, trans. Vittorio Montemaggi and Rachel Jacoff (South Bend: University of Notre Dame Press, 2013). On the secularity of the plays, see in particular Anthony B. Dawson, "Shakespeare and Secular Performance," in *Shakespeare and the Cultures of Performance*, ed. Paul Yachnin and Patricia Badir (Burlington, VT: Ashgate, 2008), 84.

6. Dawson, "Shakespeare and Secular Performance," 83.

7. Paul Stevens, "Hamlet, Henry VIII, and the Question of Religion: A Post-Secular Perspective," in *Shakespeare and Early Modern Religion*, ed. David Loewenstein and Michael Witmore (Cambridge & New York: Cambridge University Press, 2015), 232; John Milbank, *Theology and Social Theory: Beyond Secular Reason*, 2nd ed. (Oxford and Malden, MA: Wiley-Blackwell, 2006), 9, italics from Milbanks. See also Debora K. Shuger, *Habits of Thought in the English Renaissance: Religion, Politics, and the Dominant Culture* (Toronto: University of Toronto Press, 1997), 24.

8. On this point see in particular David Scott Kastan, *A Will to Believe: Shakespeare and Religion* (Oxford: Oxford University Press, 2014), chap. 2.

9. Richard C. McCoy, *Faith in Shakespeare* (New York: Oxford University Press, 2013), xii.

10. William Shakespeare, *The Tragedy of King Lear*, 5.2.4. All subsequent references to Shakespeare's works will be indicated parenthetically in the text and, unless otherwise noted, will be from David Bevington, ed., *The Complete Works of Shakespeare*, 7th edition (Boston: Pearson, 2014).

11. Germaine Greer, *Shakespeare: A Very Short Introduction* (Oxford: Oxford University Press, 2002), 23.

12. Jean-Christophe Mayer, *Shakespeare's Hybrid Faith: History, Religion and the Stage* (Basingstoke & New York: Palgrave Macmillan, 2006).

13. David Bevington, "The Debate about Shakespeare and Religion," in *Shakespeare and Early Modern Religion*, eds. David Loewenstein and Michael Witmore (Cambridge & New York: Cambridge University Press, 2015), 35.

14. On this point, see also Michael Witmore and David Loewenstein, introduction *Shakespeare and Early Modern Religion*, eds. Loewenstein and Witmore (Cambridge & New York: Cambridge University Press, 2015), 11.

15. For the purposes of this book, I will typically not make a distinction between Reformist and Catholic understandings of orthodoxy unless there are differences between them on specific issues, as is evident in their treatment of purgatorial spirits—one of the subjects of chapter 4. I use *orthodoxy* to refer to the Christian church (hereafter Church) broadly understood and the traditional understandings shared by most Christian denominations. I use *heterodoxy* and *unorthodoxy* to refer to divergences (e.g., the idea that god does not exist) from these normative beliefs. I am less concerned here with denominational differences, real as they are, within Christendom than I am with distinctions between secular and Christian accounts of reality.

16. Francis Bacon, *The Essays* (New York: Heritage Press, 1944), 9.

17. Stephen Greenblatt, *Will in the World: How Shakespeare Became Shakespeare* (New York: W. W. Norton, 2005), 36.

18. Hans Urs von Balthasar, *Theo-Drama: Theological Dramatic Theory*, volume 1: *Prolegomena*, trans. Graham Harrison (San Francisco: Ignatius Press, 1988), 26.

19. Bevington, *The Complete Works of Shakespeare*, 1212n.

20. Augustine, *Confessions and Enchiridion*, ed. and trans. Albert Cook Outler, vol. 7, Library of Christian Classics (Philadelphia: Westminster, 1955), 148.

21. Geoffrey Bullough, ed., *Narrative and Dramatic Sources of Shakespeare*, vol. 2 (New York: Columbia University Press, 1958), 417.

22. Alison Shell, *Shakespeare and Religion* (London: Arden Shakespeare, 2010), 4.

23. Park Honan, *Shakespeare: A Life* (Oxford and New York: Oxford University Press, 2000), 50.

24. Alison Shell, *Shakespeare and Religion*, 235.

25. Kristen Poole, *Radical Religion from Shakespeare to Milton: Figures of Nonconformity in Early Modern England* (Cambridge & New York: Cambridge University Press, 2000), 32–44.

26. Sean Benson, *Shakespearean Resurrection: The Art of Almost Raising the Dead* (Pittsburgh: Duquesne University Press, 2009).

27. Ralph Waldo Emerson, "Shakespeare; Or, the Poet," in *Shakespeare in America: An Anthology from the Revolution to Now*, ed. James Shapiro (New York: Library of America, 2014), 112.

28. Philip Rieff, *My Life Among the Deathworks: Illustrations of the Aesthetics of Authority*, ed. Kenneth S. Piver, vol. 1 (Charlottesville and London: University of Virginia Press, 2006), 26.

Chapter One

Shakespeare in the Church

Much scholarship in the last hundred years has been devoted to exploring the cultural and theatrical shift from medieval church drama to the professional stages in London. What we have lost sight of, however, is the abiding presence of the local parish church as a performance venue throughout the period. Even the eminent stage historian Andrew Gurr gives scant attention to the practice, merely offering a corrective that is as damning as the usual indictment of the Church's antitheatricalism:

> The hatred of plays and playgoing that boiled up out of English churches from the 1570s onwards was far more positive and considered than we think it now. It was much more than a knee-jerk reaction by puritans to ordinary people getting pleasure. Behind their diatribes sat a real fear of illusion, a revulsion against the deliberate dishonesty and pretense that theatre is based on. [1]

Although playgoing was anathema to some in the Church, it would be a mistake to universalize the sentiment. We must weigh it against the mounting counterevidence of the parish churches' longstanding role in allowing plays, both religious and secular, to be performed on their premises. This chapter will examine in particular the Church's embrace and accommodation of traveling theatrical troupes.

While the evidence of this routine and continuing performance history is fragmentary at best—much of it was simply lost or never recorded—what we do have suggests that the number of church performances by local and touring companies in the century before 1620 is somewhere between the low thousands and (roughly) ten thousand. Even if one errs on the conservative side, the practice of using local parish churches as theatrical venues by the traveling companies is an important and neglected piece of stage history. We have long assumed and taught to students a standard (and secular) view of the traveling theater companies' modus operandi: "Actors traveled from town to town performing in the halls of great houses, in inns, or on temporary platforms set up in town squares."[2] This is true as far as it goes, but it overlooks the vital role that churches filled as sites for play performances throughout the early modern era.[3] With the development of the London playhouses in the late sixteenth century, it has long been believed that the movement from the churches to the professional stages steadily increased and was unidirectional. To the contrary: the early professional companies, perhaps especially Shakespeare's, took full advantage of the opportunity to perform in various local churches. The indisputable use of churches to stage thousands of touring performances suggests that the putative opposition between Church and professional theater was to some extent a minority opinion at odds with the reality of early modern staging practice. Until recently knowledge of this continuity in church performance had long been buried in churchwardens' accounts; its recovery should revitalize our understanding of early modern performance history.

Presciently inaugurating the twentieth century of Shakespeare studies, E. K. Chambers in 1903 suggested that the gradual secularization of drama in late medieval and early modern England comprised shifts from Latin to the vernacular, from "sung drama of the liturgies to spoken drama of the great cycles," and

> from the interior of the church to its precincts, to the graveyard or the neighboring market-place. This must have been primarily a matter of physical necessity. The growing length of the plays, the increasing elaboration of their setting, made it cumbrous and difficult to accommodate them within the walls.[4]

Yet contrary to Chambers's position, as the late John Wasson noted by the close of the twentieth century, "it is now apparent that drama did not necessarily pass from the church to the marketplace and elsewhere."[5] While it is true that acting companies on tour used town halls and guildhalls more than any other venue,[6] it is by no means certain, as Gurr asserts, that "if the town hall was not available an inn would be used."[7] Wasson suggests, to the contrary, that "if the guild-hall was not available or if the village had none, the church was the obvious alternative."[8]

Perhaps we need not argue over an abundance of riches: guildhalls, inns, and churches were the most prominent spaces among the many venues used by both provincial and London-based companies. Churches have received less attention, however, even though as early as 1984 Wasson was able to identify "some sixteen villages and towns where the church seems to have been the normal place for professionals."[9] Paul Whitfield White has further observed that, far from dwindling away, as has been suggested,[10] parish drama was flourishing and even increasing in many parts of the country[11] — perhaps for good reason:

> the normal choir screen of a medieval church would have provided an almost ideal stage façade. There would be the doorways to the north and south aisles or chapels for exits and entrances, and the larger centre entrance to the choir in case a bed or throne were needed, and there would be the rood loft in case an actor needed to appear "above" or "on the castle walls."[12]

A further problem with Chambers's proposal of a linear evolution away from the use of churches was the scarcity of suitable playing space in the provinces. As a matter of necessity, clerical, folk, and professional actors frequently shared the same venues. Both provincial and London professional companies toured throughout the country on a regular basis along established routes, both as a matter of longstanding custom and of economic survival.[13] They did so with the support of intersecting "patronage networks"—royal, aristocratic, civic, commercial, and ecclesiastical.[14] Far from being a minor hiatus from performing in their home area, tours in the 1570s by the renowned Earl of Leicester's Men, for instance, "were a carefully planned major part of their life as a company."[15] Indeed, the earl used his company not for his own personal entertainment, but to advertise his status throughout the country.[16] Its successor in the 1580s, the Queen's Men, spent at least as much time on tour as they did in London,[17] and their experience was typical of other professional and amateur troupes as well. Indeed, under Elizabeth the suppression of certain forms of community drama, in particular the old medieval (Catholic) religious drama,[18] meant that the traveling companies could fill a prominent theatrical void left in local parish churches.

With the help primarily of the *REED* project, I want to extend Wasson's argument and demonstrate that the touring companies often, even routinely, performed in churches, churchyards, and in adjoining church real estate. The records indicate that their doing so was widely, though by no means universally,[19] accepted as an extension of the Church's formative role and ministry in the day-to-day lives of parishioners. Wasson, Rosalind Hays, C. Edward McGee, Mark Pilkinton, Mary Erler, and the other *REED* editors note and discuss in their respective volumes the use of churches by the traveling companies. This chapter, the first summary of its kind, shows just how extensive the practice was of using churches to stage professional drama.

In addition, Shakespeare's theater—the aptly titled *Twelfth Night* in particular—subtly and repeatedly registers its awareness of the Church first as a physical and spiritual presence in the lives of parishioners, as well as a performance site for the touring companies. Since the time of Chambers, literary scholars have been arguing that the Church and the early modern stage are in competition with and therefore at odds with one another, that they are fundamentally incompatible. Stephen Greenblatt has famously argued for the theater's cooptation and evacuation—the hollowing out—of the religious on Shakespeare's stage.[20] In his 2005 biography, for instance, Greenblatt writes

> Shakespeare began his life with questions about his faith, his love and his social role. He had never found anything equivalent to the faith on which some of his contemporaries had staked their lives. If he himself had once been drawn toward such a commitment, he had turned away from it many years before. To be sure, he had infused his theatrical vision with the vital remnants of that faith. . . . throughout his career, Shakespeare altogether scrapped the piety that marked the plays he saw in his youth.[21]

Greenblatt ingeniously reads Shakespeare's appropriation of the pious plays he saw in his youth as a kind of secular expropriation, and Greenblatt is not alone. As David Scott Kastan has remarked, "in one influential understanding" among literary critics, the early modern theater acts "as a surrogate for a Church that no longer satisfies the affective needs of many people." Yet it did satisfy the affective and other needs of countless parishioners, as the *REED* documents amply attest. The sociology of materialist criticism, as Kastan notes, offers a secular and secularizing account: "It is a view of Shakespeare seen through the lens of Max Weber. The disenchantment is that of the teller rather than that of the tale."[22] I want to let the records speak for themselves. This chapter also takes as its related subject *Twelfth Night*'s invocation and celebration of the Church as potential playing space and as a source of continuing vitality and meaning in the lives of early modern persons.

The touring companies performed in a variety of places, indoors and out, large enough and willing to accommodate them, in everything from taverns and streets to markets, great houses, and churches. Yet Wasson notes, tellingly, that "every village in England had a parish large enough to hold all the inhabitants and almost none had any more suitable acting space."[23] As partial as these records inevitably are, they nonetheless amply bear out Wasson's findings. St. Eustachius' Church in Tavistock, Devon records payments to the Queen's Men in 1561–1562 as well as to the Earl of Warwick's troupe in 1572–1573.[24] Churchwardens' accounts list payments for players in St. Guthlac's Church, Lincolnshire, which was used as a performance venue by the Earl of Worcester's Players and other troupes in the 1570s.[25] Players performed in St. Mary's Church, Long Sutton from 1542–1573, including a twelfth day performance (January 6) in 1561–1562.[26] The Earl of Arundel's Players performed in the late fifteenth century on several occasions in St. Mary's, the lone parish church in Rye, Sussex;[27] the King's Players performed at St. Olaf's Church in tiny Poughill, Sussex, in 1550–1551.[28] Unfortunately, from our perspective the accounting of these performances is frustratingly efficient and often enigmatic:[29] "Item paied to the lorde of arundelles Pleyeres that played in the Chirche iiij s. viijd."[30]

To date only a handful of the titles of plays performed by the touring companies have been preserved. White has argued that post-Reformation churches allowed drama only of "an explicitly Reformation nature."[31] This may have occasionally been the case in provinces such as Norwich where officials exercised tight civic and religious control over plays, but there is, for instance, a record of a knightly romance (definitely not a Reformation play) performed by a local parish in Methley during "Whitsun week, 13–16 June 1614."[32] It is also reasonable to assume that the traveling companies performed their repertories, which were usually a mixture of contemporary and classical fare.[33] Performing their repertories would have saved valuable rehearsal time, as "old" plays became new when the provincial and London-based troupes were outside their home areas. In 1635–1636, a "certeyne company of Roguish [i.e., provincial] players" received payment of £1 to perform Massinger's *A New Way to Pay Old Debts* at Skipton Castle in the Yorkshire village of Londesborough, and "on the same date Adam Gerdler of York is paid 5s to play a part in *The Knight of the Burning Pestle*."[34] Unlike most record keepers, the anonymous scribe writing the Bristol Mayors' Audits in the 1570s was unusually expansive, even providing the titles of a few plays offered by the traveling companies: *The Court of Comfort* (1577–1578); *The Red Knight* (1575–1576), performed by the Lord Chamberlain's Players;[35] and *Myngo* (1577–1578), performed by Leicester's Men.[36] Mark Pilkinton adds that "notes on three other plays—which may in fact be titles—include 'what mischief workith in the mynd of man,' 'the Queen of Ethiopia' (both in 1577–1578), and 'quid pro quo' (1578–1579)."[37] Moreover, on August 1, 1592, Edward Alleyn, principal actor for the Admiral's Men, wrote a letter from Bristol to his wife, Joan Woodward, whom he affectionately calls "mouse," in which he mentions his "being redy to begin the playe of hary of cornwall."[38]

In addition, Barbara Palmer has located a Star Chamber case involving a 1609/10 Christmastide tour by Sir Richard Cholmley's North Yorkshire troupe. Before being arrested at Gowlthwaite Hall, the West Riding home of recusant Sir John Yorke, Cholmley's company "offered Sir John a choice of four plays: *The Travailes of the Three English Brothers . . . Pericles . . . King Lear . . .* and *The Play of St. Christopher*."[39] Unless one wants to argue that these are all crypto-Catholic plays—a dubious argument—their performance at Gowlthwaite Hall suggests that the repertoire was a decisive factor in determining which plays the touring companies presented. Thus, the growing body of anecdotal evidence we have suggests that a play such as *Twelfth Night* (ca. 1600) would have been performed on tour by the Queen's Men, and later by the Chamberlain's/King's Men, as part of their normal touring repertory.

Despite Gurr's claim that "in all towns the largest indoor venue for playing was the town hall or guildhall,"[40] the local parish church was often an equally capacious and viable performance space. The sometime playwright Anthony Munday famously inveighed in 1580 against the practice of allowing plays to be performed in churches "so that now the Sanctuary is become a players' stage."[41] Such antitheatrical voices in the period led Chambers and others to assume a growing incompatibility between the professional players and the use of churches as theatrical venues. Writing midcentury, Bernard Spivack remarked that the early modern theater "gradually freed itself from its homiletic purpose, whereby it was essentially the dramatized exemplum of a sermon, and acquired autonomous life and justification as dramatic spectacle. The stage ceased to be a pulpit or the audience a congregation."[42] But as Knapp countered, "there is no reason to assume with Spivack that if a play were not a sermon it could not be religious, or that if the stage were not a pulpit the audience could not be a congregation."[43] Knapp's point is well taken but largely metaphorical; he wants to claim, with Ben Jonson, that even in the London playhouses, playwrights can "steer the souls of men."[44] I wish to literalize Knapp's comment by suggesting that in the recurrent church performances of plays the audience would in fact have been the congregation. The divide between church and stage would have been unworkable for Shakespeare and his contemporaries because, as Mary Erler remarks, "church and civic theatrical worlds, company and parish, were close and drew upon the same body of performers, artisans, and entrepreneurs."[45]

We have long known that churches sponsored and prepared for the material necessities of staging local plays,[46] as well as a variety of para-dramatic entertainment: traveling musicians, minstrels, dancers, bear- and bull-baitings, puppet plays, and so on.[47] What has largely been overlooked until the *REED* editors' scrupulous attention to churchwardens' accounts—the primary source of information—is the equally ready and frequent accommodation of acting companies in local parish churches. In Devon alone, only 45 of 430, or about ten percent, of parish records survive from the period, but 60 percent of these show evidence of drama.[48] It is not hard to extrapolate from these numbers, and the anecdotal evidence of church performances is abundant and growing with each *REED* volume. In Aldeburgh, Suffolk (1573–1574), "The earl of Leicester's men played in the church."[49] In Beaminster, churchwardens' accounts for 1591–1593 note "that there were stage players played in our parshe Churche."[50] Ian Lancashire similarly finds records of the presence of visiting players in the church in Doncaster, Yorkshire, in 1575,[51] while in Lenton, Nottinghamshire, Lord Berkeley's Players drew attention to themselves because they were said to be "fighting in the church" on 19 November 1580.[52]

In their study of Dorset, Hays and McGee offhandedly reveal a view often forgotten or explicitly denied today that was widely accepted in Shakespeare's time: the local parish church was considered to be as much a public space as a market square or town hall:

> public meeting places were the normal venue for performances by travelling companies from outside Dorset and sometimes for local players as well. Such meeting places included the churches of Poole (1551–2), Lyme Regis (1558–9, 1567–8, 1568–9), Beaminster (1591–3), Bloxworth (1589), and Bere Regis (1599).[53]

Likewise, according to the *REED Patrons and Performances Website*, the Queen's Men alone gave at least 401 performances outside of London between 1558 and 1603. They seem to have had no qualms about making use of the interior of churches. The church in Bewdley, Hereford, records a performance they gave in 1572.[54] They also "may have played" at Norwich cathedral in 1583 on the troupe's visit to the city, and their presence is noted in the cathedral records for both 1584 and 1585.[55] Payments were similarly made to them for having performed in the church of St. Mary's, Sherborne in 1571–1572.[56]

In fact, the Queen's Men were in Dorset on an almost yearly basis from 1588 to 1603, and St. Mary's seems to have been a particularly receptive venue, indoors and out, for the Queen's Men, as well as for an array of other companies.[57] Sherborne was a market town with no town charter or town buildings such as a guildhall. The church and its other buildings were at the center of town life, supporting the town's local tradition of theater, as well as the traveling companies. In addition, as Sally-Beth Maclean and Scott McMillin observed, "in towns or villages where civic buildings were lacking, troupes are known to have made use of church houses" such as the one adjacent to St. Mary's, which "John Dier and his interludes" rented in 1567–1568, and for which the Queen's Men paid two shillings to use in both 1597–1598 and 1598–1599.[58] Performances took place in a room on the second floor, which in the sixteenth century was open to the roof rafters. Its length (116 feet) and width (19 feet) were equally capacious, and the room retains to this day a fireplace at one end and a long row of windows on the south side.[59]

Local and touring troupes, however, did not restrict themselves to the interior of churches—and for good reason: the exterior of a church was more ambiguous space than "the clearly sacred space" of the interior.[60] The churchyard could thus more readily accommodate drama less openly devotional than mystery and other religious plays. Weather permitting, open-air performances also afforded players and audiences alike more room.[61] The churchyard was used for plays at least as early as 1311 in Shaftesbury,

Dorset,[62] and, despite Siobhan Keenan's claim that churchyard performances "were rare,"[63] there is mounting evidence of them. Churchyards were the sites of theatrical performances in Arnesby, Leicestershire (April 1510); Bath, Somerset (1491–1492); Beverley, Yorkshire (ca. 1220); Bungay, Suffolk (1566-156[7?]); Bury St. Edmunds, Suffolk (1197); Rye, Sussex (1477); Shrewsbury in both 1515 and 1577–1578; and the Queen's Players in 1589–1590 in the college churchyard at Gloucester Cathedral.[64] This, again, is only a small sample of the extant records.

Churchyards were especially desirable for larger summer audiences, and they had the advantage by the sixteenth century of usually being walled and thus "permitting a degree of audience regulation and facilitating the collection of money from spectators."[65] Receipts for churchyard performances at St. Katharine Cree in 1567 suggest an average of 110 people in attendance[66] —not large by the standards of professional playhouses, but enough to pay the bills. Again in Sherborne, St. Mary's collected money "from spectators standing on the leads of the church roof" as well in as the churchyard, and also rent from Thomas Fuller in 1573–1574 "for the ground in the churche yarde upon the playe Daye."[67] In 1603–1604, a man was cited for vandalism for having cut down two elm trees in a churchyard to make a scaffold "for a play in Sherborne called Corpus Christi play."[68] Churchyard productions could be quite elaborate: the town of Morebath constructed a city in its churchyard for a performance in 1540.[69] Interludes and pageants, including two for Mary I as part of her coronation procession through London on September 30, 1553, were performed in churchyards.[70] The churchyard was a particularly hospitable venue because people regularly gathered there for all sorts of activities; it functioned, along with the church proper, as a center of communal life. In Coventry, "the city center was virtually a large churchyard, dominated on one side by the Benedictine Cathedral and Priory of St. Mary."[71]

All of church property seems to have been fair game for performances. In King's Lynn, Norfolk (1445–1446), a play was performed in "the hall of St George's and St Trinity's (on the eve of 6 January.)"[72] The "chaster plays of Plautus and Terence" were taught in the Free Grammar School in Bury St. Edmunds, Suffolk; these and other plays were performed in the abbey there in the twelfth and thirteenth centuries, as well as in the "prior's hall and chamber" in 1506–1507, 1520–1521; and again by visiting players in 1530–1531.[73] In London, players rented Trinity Hall from St. Botolph for performances from 1557–1568.[74] Vicarages were used as well by players in Plymouth and elsewhere.[75] As in Sherborne, churchwardens' accounts for Wimborne Minster show receipts for renting their church house to players on at least three separate occasions in the 1570s and 1580s. The church house at Stratton, Cornwall, was similarly rented to various entertainers, including traveling players, from 1522–1562.[76]

Such evidence is not to say that the social uses to which English churches were put did not run into considerable official, often *ex post facto*, opposition. Loitering in the churchyard was common, if frowned upon: in 1599 Bishop Cotton chastised those "who do sit in the streetes, churcheard, or in any tavern, Inne or Alehouse, upon the Sundayes."[77] Too much idleness could lead to raucous goings-on. Parishioners themselves were known to "fight or braul within your church or churchyard."[78] In Great Hale, Lincolnshire, two men came before a church court in 1608 "for suffering the churchyard to be prophaned by divers persons *yat* baited a bull therein" with dogs.[79] There were similar impeachments for scandals created by using the churchyard for cockfighting, jousts, beauty contests, soccer, tennis, and for the drunkenness associated with church ales.[80] As odd as it may sound for some of these para-dramatic activities to take place on church property, they indicate how intimately the Church was involved—occasionally against its will—in the social lives of its parishioners, meeting religious as well as more basic, even primal, needs. The Stratford guild buildings, for instance, included the construction of ten almshouses for the relief of the poor.[81] Everything from cockfighting to almsgiving suggests the range of the Church's reach in the early modern era.

So widespread was the practice of using churches for social events that the standard injunction in the visitation articles forbade anyone "to come unreverently into the Church or Churchyard, and there to dance or play."[82] In 1637, Bishop Skinner warned against allowing a church or chapel to be "prophaned by any Playes."[83] It is true that by the 1630s opposition to the staging of plays in churches was bringing the practice to a halt. Churchwardens' accounts for Halstock, Dorset, record in 1634, "There have bin some games or playes used in the Churchyard which now upon admonicion ar now left of."[84] Traveling players in heavily puritan areas such as Plymouth and Barnstaple were repeatedly paid *not* to perform because of objections to the prophaneness of nonliturgical drama, and the practice was adopted elsewhere.[85] The mayor of Bristol, for instance, gave twenty shillings in 1632–1633 "to a company of players to bee ridd of them."[86] Yet the visitation articled issued by Bishop Skinner and others were written for conforming, Church of England parishes, and thus it would be a mistake to suggest that only puritans objected to the use of churches as performance space, or that all puritans were antitheatricalists.

Moreover, one ought not to give too much credence to official proclamations, particularly those of Church of England authorities. In her study of the West Riding, Palmer notes that "the church's injunctions, prohibitions, excommunications and punishments seem to have been ignored on a regular basis by almost everyone everywhere."[87] The Protestant clergyman John Northbrooke, curate of St. Mary Redcliffe, Bristol, and a dedicated antitheatricalist, had to concede in 1577 (even as he was scandalized by it) that people "shame not to say and affirm openly . . . that they learn as much or more at a Play, than they do at God's word preached."[88] To be sure, Chambers and his successors noticed a gradual passing of drama from the churches to the London stages; from this they inferred that references to churches and church practices were vestigial, church-haunted relics of a bygone theatrical era. But this does not hold when *Twelfth Night* and Shakespeare's other plays were written. Many of them reflect and touch upon the longstanding use of churches, churchyards, priories, abbeys, church houses, as well as converted church properties such as the former medieval monastery of Blackfriars. What Chambers could not see without the evidence of the *REED* volumes was the ongoing symbiosis between the traveling theatrical companies and the Church.

In *Twelfth Night*, Shakespeare points not backward with nostalgia to a church-haunted theater but to a present-day theater that is vitally and professionally connected to the ministry of the Church and to the lives of its parishioners. "Shakespeare and his contemporaries," as Knapp has persuasively argued, "were capable of envisaging their profession itself—their acting and playwriting—as a kind of ministry."[89] A Puritan could complain in 1572 of a minister's rushing through service so that he and his flock could attend "heathnishe dauncing for the ring, a beare or a bull to be baited . . . or an enterlude to be plaied, and if no place else can be gotten, it must be done in the church."[90] His frustration at the church's serviceability was shared by comparatively few, and the ongoing practice of the companies' using churches for performances suggests his position was actively opposed by clergy and parishioners alike. In a variety of ways, including the use of church property to stage plays, "the interplay between social and religious activities was often intricate."[91] The Church attended to the social needs of its members, bringing them into community under its auspices. There can be little doubt, too, that parishioners' shared social activities, including the production and viewing of plays, constituted a bond that informed their sense of fellowship as a corporate body of believers. In light of this use of church space as a performance venue by locals and, especially for my purposes, by the touring companies, let us turn to *Twelfth Night*, a play curiously self-conscious about the companies' staging of plays on church property.

I have argued to this point against the standard view of the early modern church and theater as acting in opposition to one another, and indeed as constituting one instance of the religious and secular divide. I want to demonstrate now how Shakespeare tantalizes us, first in a little-remarked passage in *Twelfth Night,* and then in several other plays, with the potential for staging his plays on church property. In Shakespeare's drama, one frequently senses the imaginary and real presence—the proximity and even ubiquity—of the local parish church. Act 3, scene 1 of *Twelfth Night* opens with a seemingly ephemeral exchange, one of those moments where, as Dr. Johnson argued, Shakespeare's love of punning becomes the "golden apple for which he will always turn aside from his career, or stoop from his elevation."[92] Yet in addition to its verbal play, the exchange tantalizes us with a glimpse into early modern staging practice:

VIOLA Save thee, friend, and thy music. Dost thou live by thy tabor?

FESTE No, sir, I live by the church.

VIOLA Art thou a churchman?

FESTE No such matter, sir. I do live by the church, for I do live at my

house, and my house doth stand by the church.

VIOLA So thou mayst say the king lies by a beggar if a beggar dwell near

him, or the church stands by thy tabor if thy tabor stand by the church. (3.1.1–10)

Beneath the laughter Feste's punning evokes, the passage hints at the relations among the Church, players, and the local parish communities. Most editors, following Pope, consider act 3, scene 1 a continuation of the gulling scene (2.5) in Olivia's garden, and thus place it there as well. This is reasonable, as the Edenic, paradisiac echo is carried into Viola's opening salutation, "Save thee, friend"—the contraction of the traditional greeting, "God save thee." She invokes a similar blessing on his music (line 1), but when she asks whether he lives by means of his tabor—a jester's stock-in-trade—he seems to deny it by interpreting the question in spatial, domestic, terms: "No, I live by the church." His answer, wonderfully compact, opens several vistas of interpretation that have gone largely unnoticed except for a brief comment from Knapp: "In *Twelfth Night*, wit lives 'by' the church—that is to say, it pursues a ministry that lies in a determinedly approximate and equivocal relation to the church."[93] Let us begin with that equivocation. Against the odds, one can read the line in a pious light as Feste's professing the Christian faith, of affirming Viola's wish that God save him and grant him the gift of eternal life as a member of the Church universal. He is, in this reading, spiritually sustained—lives by—the Church. This interpretation is unlikely, however, given what we know of Feste, but it may nonetheless be an ironic adoption of the language of the Church, which he later parodies as Sir Topas the curate. On the other hand, Feste could equally well be alluding to his performances, like those of traveling minstrels and other performers, who used their tabors and other instruments to entertain in churches and church-

yards. He makes his living, in other words, by means of the church as performance space for his antics.

Shakespeare offers us an intriguing third possibility as well. When Viola
asks, "Art thou a churchman," Keir Elam in the Arden 3 *Twelfth Night*
suggests that her "question is ironically superfluous, since Feste is presumably wearing jester's motley."[94] Indeed, Viola was in Feste's presence two
scenes earlier to hear one of his songs, followed by his jesting with Orsino
concerning payment for services rendered (2.4.49–78). She even tells him a
few lines later, "I saw thee late at the Count Orsino's" (3.1.33). Thus, Viola
knows not only who Feste is, but also how he makes his living—specifically,
that he is no member of the clergy. The irony of her question is thus multifac-
eted. Her question gestures toward his possible religious faith, since Feste
has already proclaimed to "live by the church." He denies the seeming seriousness of Viola's question—"No such matter, sir"—and redirects it to his
domicile. But his use of "no such matter" is slippery: the phrase can simply
mean "no," as if to say that he is not a cleric. "No such matter" can also mean
"quite the contrary,"[95] as if to suggest, more subtly and suggestively, a denial
of faith. This is a much darker possibility. Feste then goes on quickly to
explain that his house is adjacent to the church, but the mundaneness of his
reference (his use, in other words, of "by" as a simply preposition of place
rather than, as Viola hints, as the truncated form of the prepositional phrase
meaning "by means of") suggests that mere physical proximity may be his
only connection to the church. Feste's seemingly prosaic excursus on the
physical proximity of his house to the church may belie his deeper nonbelief.

The dramatic irony of Viola's question further manifests itself when Feste
becomes a churchman—a curate for the purpose of catechizing and then
mockingly exorcising the imprisoned Malvolio. Feste claims that his clerical
impersonation is not so bad, as he is not "the first that ever dissembled in
such a gown" (4.2.5–6). His own dissembling carries over to much of the
play—he's a professional at it, after all. But on a deeper level, Feste is the
antithesis of a churchman because of his deep-seated desire to have "the
whirligig of time bring in his revenges" against Malvolio (5.1.369–70). Although the use of *churchman* to refer to "a member or supporter of an
established church" only dates in the *Oxford English Dictionary* from 1612,
it is reasonable to believe that Viola's question points more to Feste's personal belief or unbelief in the teachings of the Church than to what she
already knows is his nonexistent standing in the ecclesiastical hierarchy.

In reading seven types of ambiguity[96] into Feste's language—a move
sanctioned by his own adroitness at using "a sentence" as "a cheveril glove to
a good wit" (3.1.10–11)—we arrive at yet another, this time a latent and
metatheatrical, possibility in his "I do live by the church":

At several points in the comedy Shakespeare toys with awareness of the *mise-en-scène* in progress: the most explicit of these moments is Fabian's affirmation . . . that "If this were played upon a stage now, I could condemn it as an improbable fiction" (3.4.123–4). . . . it raises a laugh from the real audience, amused by the irony of Fabian's apparent lack of knowledge of where he is (but also by the suspicion that really he does know).[97]

Elam assumes that Fabian speaks his lines in a professional playhouse, and in many performances, this would undoubtedly be the case. But given the continual need for the companies to tour, it could not always have been so, and when *Twelfth Night* was performed on church property, as it almost certainly was, Feste's "I do live by the church" serves as pointedly a metatheatrical moment as Fabian's comment about performing the play upon a professional stage. His use of the subjunctive mood ("If this were played upon a stage now") underscores uncertainty of the *mise-en-scène* in each new performance—his "now" is continually renewed, be it on stage, in a guildhall, inn, or church. Feste's comment contains even more riches in its wonderful polyvalence, underscoring both physical and metaphysical dimensions of the Church within the metatheatrics of his line.

Throughout his career, Shakespeare saw his plays performed at court; in the Globe, Blackfriars, and other professional theaters; in the Inns of Court, including the Lord Chamberlain Men's performance of *Twelfth Night* 2 February 1602 at the Middle Temple; in town and guildhalls; in taverns and great houses; and without question in and around churches, especially in the provinces. On church property, "I do live by the church" serves as pointedly a metatheatrical reminder as Fabian's comment about performing the play upon a professional stage. Notice, too, how the Church also enjoys a carefully imagined presence as a physical structure in the play. Olivia implores Sebastian

If you mean well,

Now go with me and with this holy man

Into the chantry by. There, before him,

And underneath that consecrated roof,

Plight me the full assurance of your faith. (4.3.22–26)

In his film version of the play (1999), Trevor Nunn employs a real chantry and cuts to it so that Olivia's words do not constitute mere imagination. One need not have a church nearby in order to perform the play, but Feste's line acquires a special piquancy if delivered on church property, or even near one, which would not be difficult in London or the provinces, given the ubiquity of English churches. At most, Feste would only have to point or nod his head in the direction of the nearby church; at the least, he already is on church property.

That he lives by the church also serves as a wry metatheatrical comment from the actor playing Feste on the economic realities of early modern touring practice. As we have seen, churches in the early modern period were the site of a wide array of civic activities irrespective of official animadversions. In 1569, John Jewel, bishop of Salisbury, warned against allowing "disguised persons," "dauncers, minstrels," or others to come into the church "with scoffes, iestes, and ribauldrie talke."[98] Admonitions against "iestes" would by default seem to exclude professional jesters such as Feste. Yet players, jesters, and other performers made their living in part by performing in churches, and "the church's need for money and the players' need for space often intersected to mutual advantage."[99] Indeed, as Alexandra Johnston remarks, church drama was "a fundamental part of the economy of every parish."[100] In Tewkesbury, Gloucestershire, for instance, three plays in 1600 were staged in the abbey itself in order to finance "a new stone battlement on the top of the abbey tower."[101] Stage plays were similarly performed in the church house in Tintinhull, Somerset, in 1451–1452 to raise parish funds money.[102] In 1529, a civic license was granted to the church of St. Katharine Cree in London "for the profight of their Chirche"[103] Fundraising performances in London churches before the establishment of the professional playhouses were also common:[104] the Church of All Hallows on London Wall received a license in 1528 to build a new aisle; receipts from a play performed therein constituted its single largest source of income for the year. To fund a new roof in 1530–1531, St. Botolph without Aldersgate rented its churchyard to theatrical entrepreneur Henry Walton.[105] In Lincolnshire, too, several parishes used plays throughout the sixteenth century to raise funds for the continuing upkeep of their churches.[106] Although the *REED* volumes generally exclude records of wrestling matches, parishes also used them in order to raise funds: "In 1394 during an episcopal visitation canons complained that the dean of Lincoln Cathedral sponsored wrestling matches in the cathedral close, in the bishop's palace."[107] Wrestling matches apparently took place in churchyards in Exeter in the thirteenth century,[108] and they were also paid for out of churchwarden's accounts at St. Lawrence, Bristol, in the sixteenth century.[109] Indeed, the church that did not use theatrical and other para-dramatic entertainment for fundraising would have been the exception rather than the rule.

Feste's comment is thus doubly metatheatrical. First, it can refer to his making a living as a jester performing in a church. St. Mary's, for instance, the parish church in Chagford, Sussex, records having made payment for "the Iesteres shooes" in 1587–1588.[110] A carving in Chalk Church, Kent, depicts "an acrobat and a jester with a drinking pot—probably actual performers at a church ale."[111] A jester's presence in the church, proscribed as it was by some higher clergy, would not have been unusual. But as an actor, à la Fabian's comment about playing upon a stage, he could equally well be referring to his profession as a player (i.e., the actor playing Feste) making his living by performing on church property in front of parishioners and other paying spectators. Feste and Viola's exchange highlights the potential and sometimes real synergy between the touring companies and the church, and this possibility is revisited in the recognition scene in 5.3 as well.

The Church's historic receptivity to drama is well known: professional theater emerged from liturgical and folk drama, both of which were performed in and sponsored by churches. The Church was and remains its own theater, the mass constituting, in Chambers' wry comment, "an essentially dramatic commemoration of one of the most critical moments in the life of the Founder."[112] The ceremonies of Holy Week, which stretched from Palm Sunday to Easter, were the high point of the late medieval church year. Among this cluster of services was the "highly dramatic ritual," as Eamon Duffy calls it, of the Palm Sunday procession, which began with a mass that started inside the church but then progressed outside with palms for a sacred reenactment of Christ's entry into Jerusalem.[113]

Given her own theatrical turn of mind, it is no surprise that one Easter day "in her contemplation" the mystic Margery Kempe (1373–ca. 1440) envisions in its dramatic historicity the moment when Mary Magdalene meets the risen Christ outside the empty tomb (John 20.11–17):

> Mary, not knowing who he was, all enflamed with the fire of love, replied to him, "Sir, if you have taken away my Lord, tell me, and I shall take him back again."
> Then our merciful Lord, having pity and compassion on her, said, "Mary."
> And with that word she—knowing our Lord—fell down at his feet, and would have kissed his feet, saying, "Master."
> Our Lord said to her, "Touch me not."[114]

A few lines later, Margery repeats Christ's admonition to Mary, "Touch me not," the *noli me tangere* topos invoked in Viola's charge to Sebastian, "Do not embrace me" (5.1.247) in the midst of their own discovery scene late in the play.[115] As Balthasar points out, Shakespeare conflates the secular recognition scene with the unmistakable suggestion of the Resurrection: "He takes the risk of portraying the return from the realm of the dead as a pure gift to those in mourning. In these self-contained plays the Christian resurrection from the dead becomes the reappearance of those believed dead."[116] The echo of the biblical phrase in Viola's "Do not embrace me" would only be more poignant when the play was performed in a church.

"It is even more splendid at the end of *The Winter's Tale*," writes Balthasar, "when the statue of the dead Hermione comes into sight, the guilty Leontes stands thunderstruck before the 'masterpiece' that seems to breathe, and Paulina promises him even greater things if he will rouse up his 'faith.'"[117] Church and theater alike point to "things unseen," as the apostle Paul remarks, in order to imagine possibilities and realities beyond our sight.[118] Paul's namesake, Paulina, admonishes her auditors, "It is requir'd / You do awake your faith" (5.3.94–95)—faith in the theater alone, as Richard McCoy argues, but a performance of *Twelfth Night* in or near a church points to religious faith as well, as does the allusion to the Epiphany in its title. Paulina's comment refers, after all, to the resurrection of the seemingly dead Hermione. What more powerful context for her call for a renewed faith could there be than a church as a performance venue? She even declares the aptness of such a setting, telling her auditors they can either leave the church in disbelief or remain and be astounded by the quasi-miraculous resurrection of Hermione she is about to effect: "Either forbear, / Quit presently the chapel, or resolve you / For more amazement" (5.3.85–87). Both Feste's and Viola's religiously inflected language points to the possibilities of staging plays in the church or on its adjacent property.

Shakespeare's plays frequently register their awareness of the church as a physical structure and tantalize us with the idea of a church as a possible performance venue. It is no accident that Hermione's resurrection takes place in a chapel. For his part, Falstaff declares his repentance to come: "An I have not forgotten what the inside of a church is made of, I am a peppercorn, a brewer's horse. The inside of a church!" (*1H4* 3.3.7–9). One senses the heightened comic effect of his lines if they were delivered in a church. He would in such performances literally be speaking to the choir. Even when recited in a professional theater, which often competed with churches by having performances on Sundays, one sees the aptness of his preacherly irony: it is as if he ventriloquizes Munday, Philip Stubbes, Stephen Gosson, and other antitheatricalists.

Likewise, *Romeo and Juliet* sets its famous last scene, the double suicide of its star-crossed lovers, in a churchyard, with the first watchman declaring, "The ground is bloody; search about the churchyard," followed later by the third watchman's "Here's Romeo's man. We found him in the churchyard" (5.3.172, 182). The play reminds us that churchyards were (and still are) typically used as cemeteries. When the play was first performed, churchyards had relatively few surface obstructions—small headstones, wooden crosses—in comparison to the large monuments that only became common later in the seventeenth century.[119] *Romeo and Juliet* need not have been performed in a churchyard qua graveyard, but it was ideally suited for such a performance, and the prospect would no doubt have appealed to the traveling companies. The equally famous gravedigger scene in *Hamlet* (5.1) is also understandably set in a churchyard. Young Mamillius, too, only begins to tell his sad winter's tale of "a man" who, like Feste, "dwelt by a churchyard" (*WT* 2.1.29–30). It is this sense of sobriety in regards to churches and church-yards that carries over into and is transformed into comedy by *Twelfth Night*, the title and action of which invoke the Feast of Fools, the use of boy bishops, and other festivities associated with Epiphany.[120]

Although the church remained a venue for theatrical performances well into the seventeenth century, there is the possibility that, along with religious vestments and other props, the vitality of the church was simply expropriated for the professional stages and thus emptied of its religious content. Such a secularist account, however, is up against growing evidence that the relation-ship between Church and theater was rather more complicated and symbiotic than antagonistic. Shakespeare's life was officially rounded by the Church: his christening was recorded on April 26, 1564, in the baptismal register of Holy Trinity Church, Stratford-Upon-Avon, and his burial—his gravestone now located in the chancel near the altar—is likewise recorded in the Strat-ford parish on the same date in 1616. His life in the theater was similarly encompassed by church structures. In the market town of his birth, the Strat-ford Guildhall was where Shakespeare was educated, as well as the "almost certain location for performances by visiting players," which included per-formances by Lord Strange's Men, the Queen's Men, and Leicester's Men in 1573–1574 and 1576–1577, any of which the young Shakespeare may have seen.[121] As with many of the guildhalls in which the traveling players per-formed, the Stratford Guildhall had its origins in the church, having been founded as the Guild of the Holy Cross.[122] The guild complex of buildings, which included the Guild Chapel, was the center of the town's administrative and religious life, attending to both the spiritual and practical needs of its parishioners.[123]

At the close of his career, too, from 1608 onward Shakespeare's plays were performed in Blackfriars, the converted Dominican priory that served as home to the King's Men. What is one to make of a Blackfriars' perfor-mance of *Cymbeline* when the eponymous king extends mercy to the penitent Iachimo: "Kneel not to me. / The power I have on you is to spare you; / The malice towards you to forgive you" (5.5.421–23); or of Prospero's valedicto-ry couplet, "And my ending is despair, / Unless I be relieved by prayer" (Epi. 15–16)? The rich religious resonance of such lines becomes more poignant in light of their being spoken in a former church space. When Hermione returns from seeming death after sixteen years, is there, again, a more fitting space for her quasi-resurrection from the dead than a priory, even a converted one such as the Blackfriars? It was professional theatrical space, but its name, as with the permanence of the brick and mortar, associates it indelibly with its former use. Such use matters. One purpose of this book is to underscore the once-living context of Shakespeare's plays in their routine staging on former church property such as Blackfriars, as well as in the local parish churches, when the companies were on tour. Even secular buildings such as the merchant Guildhall of St. Mary's, Coventry, constructed in 1342 and named in honor of the Priory of St. Mary, was used as a performance space for the Lord Admiral's Men, the Queen's Men, the Earl of Sussex's Men, and some fifty other traveling companies from 1574–1640.[124] The guildhall was a secular building, but even here its name and architecture do not escape the influence of the Church. Marcus Lynch, the current manager of St. Mary's Guildhall, remarks, "Whilst the basic architecture of the Guildhall is essentially that of a baronial hall of the period, there is a high degree of ecclesiastical iconography in the decorative elements, partly reflecting the highly religious principles of the guild, but also the experience of the masons and other craftsmen who would previously have been working on great religious buildings."[125]

The professional English stages were mundane sites—the antitheatricalists considered them dens of profanation. Critics have long understood the tendentiousness of such arguments, yet literary scholars in particular have largely accepted the implicit church/theater binary Stubbes and Gosson posited. The position is less tenable the more one recognizes how extensively local parish churches were used for the staging of professional plays. Much criticism has been rightly devoted to Shakespeare's and other playwrights' opportunistic use of the London stages to craft new dramatic fare. But why should we assume that Shakespeare gave no thought to the prospect and reality of performing his plays on church property? The last scene of the early *Comedy of Errors* is set before a priory where another of Balthasar's "miracles of earthy love" occurs in the abbess Angela's reunion with her husband and rediscovery of her lost son—"such nativity," she calls it, glancing at Christ's birth (5.1.407). The priory underscores a living context of these plays, and church staging lends such moments a piquancy the London stages, for all their imaginative and real inventiveness, could not match.

From London where St. Paul's Cathedral dominated the skyline to the local parishes in the provinces, church spires were readily visible: "The spire of Shakespeare's church—the Church of the Holy Trinity—," wrote Nathaniel Hawthorne in 1863, "begins to show itself among the trees at a little distance from Stratford."[126] Even when a play was not performed on church property, the church remained a commanding physical structure, its presence never far from English consciousness: "I've a good eye, uncle," remarks Beatrice, "I can see a church by daylight" (*Ado* 2.1.76–77). Beatrice's line should remind us that even though I have concentrated on *Twelfth Night*, it is merely one of a number of plays whose language tantalizes us with the proximity of a church. Why, asks *As You Like It*'s Jaques rhetorically, must people laugh at his folly? "The 'why' is plain as way to parish church"

(2.7.52). Such comic levity stands in contrast to the melancholy strain in sonnet 73—a haunting reminder of the iconoclasts who defaced English Churches after the dissolution. "That strain again" with its "dying fall" (1.1.4) surfaces intermittently throughout *Twelfth Night*, and thus it is with Feste's comment that he "doth live by the church"—perhaps that is, after all, his only connection to it. But even that line seems less church-haunted than church-inspired, and it is this lighter refrain that is celebrated rather than hollowed out in *Twelfth Night*. These more festive references to the church sprinkle the play: In response to Sir Andrew's boast that he is an excellent dancer, Toby exhorts him, "Why dost thou not go to church in a galliard and come home in a coranto?" (1.3.124–26). Feste, too, begging for more money from Orsino, asks for "a good tripping measure, or the bells of Saint Bennet" (5.1.34–35), reminding his patron of almsgiving in general and specifically of the London parish church of St. Bennet Hithe, which was located just across the Thames from the Globe Theatre.

As Sylvia Gill notes, "There are many references to the old religious ways in Shakespeare's work,"[127] and Shakespeare appears to take an irenic stand against those who, like Malvolio, would hollow out the old practices. As we shall see in chapter 2, Shakespeare has sympathy for Puritans, especially when they become the objects of religious ridicule and persecution. But their asceticism in regard to old practices such as church ales and the use of churches as theatrical space for touring troupes—activities that promote social cohesion—appears to run afoul of his professional interests, as well perhaps of his personal tastes. The performance of plays in churches was a longstanding practice, part and parcel of the good fellowship the church attempted to promote among its parishioners. The Church, after all, was not separate from the social fabric of English life, but embraced both its glory and its occasional raucousness. Shakespeare demonstrates how the community came together at festivities centered on the church calendar. His *Twelfth Night* celebrates the role of religious practice in the lives of early modern persons, and in doing so suggests a mutual dependence and synergy between the Church and the stage.

Finally, as a coda to this chapter, one can readily extrapolate from the sociologist Peter Berger's work on the "redeeming laughter" of comedy to the natural receptivity of a church for the staging of a play such as *Twelfth Night*. As with the Church's pointing to a world yet to come, Berger notes that "the comic, at its most intense, as in folly, presents a counterworld, an upside-down world."[128] From *Lysistrata* to Erasmus's *Praise of Folly* to the modern absurdist drama of David Ives, comedy presents precisely such topsy-turvy worlds. *Twelfth Night*'s inversion begins by signaling the misrule associated with the Feast of Epiphany on January 6, and the idea is picked up at the outset of act 4:

FESTE Will you make me believe that I am not sent for you?

SEBASTIAN Go to, go to, thou art a foolish fellow. Let me be clear of thee.

FESTE Well held out, i'faith! No, I do not know you, nor am I not sent to you by my lady to bid you come speak with her, nor your name is not Master Cesario, nor this is not my nose, neither. Nothing that is so is so. (4.1.1–8)

Feste envisions a counterfactual world in which he neither knows Cesario, nor has been sent for him, nor even knows his own identity: "this is not my nose, neither." He uses a *reductio ad absurdum* to satirize what he believes to be Cesario's pretense of not knowing him: if this be so, then "nothing that is so is so." Feste refuses to relinquish the hard facticity of the world he knows, a world in which, *inter alia*, wrongs are remembered and revenged: "But do you remember?" he asks Malvolio, "'Madam, why laugh you at such a barren rascal? An you smile not, he's gagged.' And thus the whirligig of time brings in his revenges" (5.1.374–77). Yet Feste also knows that Christianity offers a counterworld to the *lex talionis*:

FESTE Good Madonna, why mourn'st thou?

OLIVIA Good fool, for my brother's death.

FESTE I think his soul is in hell, madonna.

OLIVIA I know his soul is in heaven, fool.

FESTE The more fool, madonna, to mourn for your brother's soul, being

in heaven.—Take away the fool, gentlemen. (1.5.63–69)

For a moment, he recognizes the Pauline insight that "the wisdom of this world is foolishness with God" (1 Cor. 3:19), but he much prefers, as we are about to see in chapter 2, an eye-for-an-eye mentality. Feste's foolishness is the wisdom of this world.

NOTES

1. Andrew Gurr, *The Shakespearean Stage, 1574–1642*, 4th ed. (Cambridge & New York: Cambridge University Press, 2009), 7.
2. David Bevington et al., eds., *English Renaissance Drama: A Norton Anthology* (New York: W. W. Norton, 2002), xiii–xiv.

3. Alexandra F. Johnston, "'What Revels Are in Hand': The Parishes of the Thames Valley," in *English Parish Drama*, ed. Alexandra F. Johnston and Wim Hüsken (Amsterdam and Atlanta, GA: Rodopi, 1996), 100.

4. E. K. Chambers, *The Mediaeval Stage*, vol. 2 (London: Oxford University Press, 1903), 90 and 79.

5. John M Wasson, "The English Church as Theatrical Space," in *A New History of Early English Drama*, eds. John D. Cox and David Scott Kastan (Columbia University Press, 1998), 35; Elza C. Tiner, ed., *Teaching with the Records of Early English Drama* (Toronto: University of Toronto Press, 2006), xv.

6. Siobhan Keenan, *Travelling Players in Shakespeare's England* (Basingstoke: Palgrave, 2002), 24–25; John M Wasson, *REED. Devon* (Toronto: University of Toronto Press, 1986), xvi.

7. Andrew Gurr, *The Shakespearian Playing Companies* (Oxford: Oxford University Press, 1996), 40.

8. Wasson, *REED. Devon*, xxvi.

9. John M Wasson, "Professional Actors in the Middle Ages and Early Renaissance," in *Medieval & Renaissance Drama in England*, ed. J. Leeds Barroll, vol. 1 (New York: AMS Press, 1984), 7.

10. Glynne William Gladstone Wickham, *Early English Stages, 1300 to 1660.*, vol. 3 (New York: Columbia University Press, 1959), 60–61.

11. Paul Whitfield White, *Theatre and Reformation: Protestantism, Patronage, and Playing in Tudor, England* (New York: Cambridge University Press, 1992), 135.

12. Wasson, *REED. Devon*, xxvi.

13. Barbara D. Palmer, "Playing in the Provinces: Front or Back Door?," *Medieval & Renaissance Drama in England* 22 (January 2009): 83.

14. Suzanne R Westfall, "'The Useless Dearness of the Diamond': Theories of Patronage Theatre," in *Shakespeare and Theatrical Patronage in Early Modern England*, ed. Paul Whitfield White and Suzanne R Westfall (Cambridge & New York: Cambridge University Press, 2002), 19–21.

15. Alan Somerset, "'How Chances It They Travel?': Provincial Touring, Playing Places and the King's Men," in *Shakespeare Survey*, vol. 47, 1994, 52.

16. Andrew Gurr, *The Shakespearean Stage*, 39.

17. Westfall, "'The Useless Dearness of the Diamond'," 35; Scott McMillin and Sally-Beth MacLean, *The Queen's Men and Their Plays* (Cambridge: Cambridge University Press, 1998).

18. Diarmaid MacCulloch, *The Later Reformation in England, 1547–1603*, 2nd ed. (New York: Palgrave, 2001), 114.

19. On antitheatrical appeals to the godly, see in particular Peter Lake and Michael Questier, *The Anti-Christ's Lewd Hat: Protestants, Papists and Players in Post-Reformation England* (New Haven: Yale University Press, 2002), 425–82.

20. Stephen Greenblatt, *Shakespearean Negotiations: The Circulation of Social Energy in Renaissance England* (Berkeley: University of California Press, 1988), 125; *Renaissance Self-Fashioning: From More to Shakespeare* (Chicago: University of Chicago Press, 1984).

21. Stephen Greenblatt, *Will in the World: How Shakespeare Became Shakespeare* (New York: W. W. Norton, 2005), 388, 35.

22. David Scott Kastan, *A Will to Believe: Shakespeare and Religion* (Oxford: Oxford University Press, 2014), 8–9.

23. Wasson, "English Church," 25.

24. Wasson, *REED. Devon*, 279.

25. James Stokes, ed., *REED. Lincolnshire* (London: British Library and University of Toronto Press, 2009), 257.

26. Ibid., 226.

27. Cameron Louis, ed., *REED. Sussex* (Toronto: University of Toronto Press, 2000), 53, 55, 57.

28. Sally L Joyce and Evelyn S Newlyn, "REED. Cornwall," in *Dorset/Cornwall* (Toronto: University of Toronto Press, 1999), 505.

29. Peter H. Greenfield, "Parish Drama in Four Counties Bordering the Thames Watershed," in *English Parish Drama*, eds. Johnston and Hüsken, 8–9.

30. Louis, *REED. Sussex*, 57.

31. White, *Theatre and Reformation*, 138.

32. John M. Wasson, "A Parish Play in the West Riding of Yorkshire," in *English Parish Drama*, eds. Johnston and Hüsken, 149.

33. Keenan, *Travelling Players in Shakespeare's England*, 57–8; Gurr, *The Shakespearian Playing Companies*.

34. Palmer, "Playing in the Provinces," 86, 99.

35. Mark C Pilkinton, ed., *REED. Bristol* (Toronto: University of Toronto Press, 1997), 112.

36. Ibid., 115.

37. Ibid., xxxiv.

38. Ibid., 143–44.

39. Barbara D. Palmer, "Playing in the Provinces," 69; Alison Shell, *Shakespeare and Religion* (London: Arden Shakespeare, 2010), 107.

40. Gurr, *The Shakespearian Playing Companies*, 40.

41. Anthony Munday, *A Second and Third Blast of Retrait from Plaies and Theaters* (New York: Garland Publishing, 1973), 78.

42. Bernard Spivack, *Shakespeare and the Allegory of Evil* (New York: Columbia University Press, 1958), 59. Quoted in Jeffrey Knapp, *Shakespeare's Tribe: Church, Nation, and Theater in Renaissance England* (Chicago: University of Chicago Press, 2002), 119.

43. Knapp, *Shakespeare's Tribe*, 119.

44. Ben Jonson, *The Staple of News*, ed. Devra Rowland Kifer (Lincoln: University of Nebraska Press, 1975), prol. 23.

45. Mary Carpenter Erler, ed., *REED. Ecclesiastical London* (Toronto: British Library and University of Toronto Press, 2008), xxxvi.

46. See, for instance, Ian Lancashire, *Dramatic Texts and Records of Britain: A Chronological Topography to 1558* (Toronto: University of Toronto Press, 1984), 277; Hays and McGee, eds. *REED. Dorset*, 126, 259–65.

47. Lancashire, *Dramatic Texts*, 120.

48. Wasson, *REED. Devon*, xxi.

49. Lancashire, *Dramatic Texts*, 77.

50. Hays and McGee, *REED. Dorset*, 121.

51. Lancashire, *Dramatic Texts*, 123.

52. Ibid., 166.

53. Hays and McGee, *REED. Dorset*, 39.

54. Lancashire, *Dramatic Texts*, 84.

55. McMillin and MacLean, *The Queen's Men and Their Plays*, 60, 42–43; David Galloway, ed., *REED. Norwich 1540–1642* (Toronto: University of Toronto Press, 1984), 70.

56. Hays and McGee, *REED. Dorset*, 266.

57. Ibid., 42.

58. McMillin and MacLean, *The Queen's Men and Their Plays*, 76–77; Hays and McGee, *REED. Dorset*, 41, 272.

59. C. Edward McGee, "Church House, St Mary's, Sherborne," email to the author, February 3, 2013; Keenan, *Travelling Players in Shakespeare's England*, 53.

60. Hays and McGee, eds. *REED. Dorset*, 38.

61. Keenan, *Travelling Players in Shakespeare's England*, 61.

62. Hays and McGee, *REED. Dorset*, 320.

63. Keenan, *Travelling Players in Shakespeare's England*, 60.

64. Lancashire, *Dramatic Texts*, 77–108, 257–65; Keenan, *Travelling Players in Shakespeare's England*, 45, 54; Audrey Douglas and Peter Greenfield, eds., *REED. Cumberland, Westmorland, Gloucestershire* (Toronto: University of Toronto Press, 1986), 311.

65. Keenan, *Travelling Players in Shakespeare's England*, 55.

66. Erler, *REED. Ecclesiastical London*, xxxviii.

67. Ibid., 38, 269.

68. Hays and McGee, *REED. Dorset*, 273.

69. Lancashire, *Dramatic Texts*, 228.

70. Ibid., 212, 219.

71. R. W. Ingram, *REED. Coventry* (Toronto: University of Toronto Press, 1981), xv.

72. Ibid., 162.

73. Ibid., 91–92.

74. Lancashire, *Dramatic Texts*, 216.

75. Wasson, *REED. Devon*, 244.

76. Joyce and Newlyn, *REED. Cornwall*, 400, 521–22.

77. Hays and McGee, *REED. Dorset*, 115.

78. Ibid.

79. Stokes, *REED. Lincolnshire*, 77.

80. Ibid., 99, 337, 409; Keenan, *Travelling Players in Shakespeare's England*, 63; Wasson, *REED. Devon*, 329; Erler, *REED. Ecclesiastical London*, xliv.

81. Kate Giles and Jonathan Clark, "The Archaeology of the Guild Buildings of Shakespeare's Stratford-upon-Avon," in *The Guild and Guild Buildings of Shakespeare's Stratford: Society, Religion, School and Stage*, ed. J. R. Mulryne (Burlington, VT: Ashgate, 2012), 154–56.

82. Erler, *REED. Ecclesiastical London*, 8; Hays and McGee, *REED. Dorset*, 113, 115.

83. Hays and McGee, *REED. Dorset*, 113.

84. Ibid., 210.

85. Patrick Collinson, "Elizabethan and Jacobean Puritanism as Forms of Popular Religious Culture," in *The Culture of English Puritanism: 1560–1700*, ed. Christopher Durston and Jacqueline Eales (New York: St. Martin's Press, 1996), 43; Wasson, *REED. Devon*, xiii, 47, 50.

86. Pilkinton, *REED. Bristol*, 235.

87. Barbara D. Palmer, "'Anye Disguised Persons': Parish Entertainment in West Yorkshire," in *English Parish Drama*, eds. Johnston and Hüsken, 81–2.

88. John Northbrooke, *A Treatise Wherein Dicing, Dauncing, Vaine Playes or Enterluds With Other Idle Pastimes Etc. Commonly Used of the Sabboth Day, Are Reproved* (1577), ed. Arthur Freeman (New York: Garland, 1974), 66.

89. Knapp, *Shakespeare's Tribe*, 9.

90. Walter Howard Frere and C. E. Douglas, eds., "An Admonition to the Parliament," in *Puritan Manifestoes: A Study of the Origin of the Puritan Revolt* (New York: Burt Franklin, 1972), 29.

91. R. N. Swanson, *Church and Society in Late Medieval England* (Oxford and New York: Basil Blackwell, 1989), 257–58.

92. Samuel Johnson, in *The Yale Edition of the Works of Samuel Johnson*, ed. Arthur Sherbo, vol. 7 (New Haven: Yale University Press, 1968), 74.

93. Knapp, *Shakespeare's Tribe*, 175.

94. Keir Elam, ed., *Twelfth Night*, 3rd ed. (London: Arden Shakespeare, 2009), 251n.

95. *Oxford English Dictionary*, s.v. "matter."

96. William Empson, *Seven Types of Ambiguity*, 2d ed. (New York: New Directions, 1947).

97. Elam, *Twelfth Night*, 87–88.

98. *Ibid.*, 114.

99. Erler, *REED. Ecclesiastical London*, xxxvi.

100. Johnston, "'What Revels Are in Hand': The Parishes of the Thames Valley," 101–02.

101. Lancashire, *Dramatic Texts*, 273; Greenfield, "Parish Drama in Four Counties Bordering the Thames Watershed," 108.

102. Ibid., 276.

103. Erler, *REED. Ecclesiastical London*, 227.

104. Ibid., xxxvii.

105. Ibid.

106. Stokes, *REED. Lincolnshire*, 436.

107. Ibid., 431–32.

108. Wasson, *REED. Devon*, 318.

109. Pilkinton, *REED. Bristol*, 29–31.

110. Wasson, *REED. Devon*, 56.

111. J. G. Davies, *The Secular Use of Church Buildings* (London: SCM Press, 1968), 48–49.

112. Chambers, *The Mediaeval Stage*, vol. 2: 3.

113. Eamon Duffy, *The Stripping of the Altars: Traditional Religion in England, c.1400–c.1580* (New Haven: Yale University Press, 1992), 25.

114. Margery Kempe, *The Book of Margery Kempe*, trans. Barry Windeatt (New York: Penguin Classics, 2000), 238.

115. Sean Benson, *Shakespearean Resurrection: The Art of Almost Raising the Dead* (Pittsburgh: Duquesne University Press, 2009), 53–58; Yu Jin Ko, "The Comic Close of Twelfth Night and Viola's Noli Me Tangere," *Shakespeare Quarterly* 48.4 (December 1, 1997): 391–405; Cynthia Lewis, "Soft Touch: On the Renaissance Staging and Meaning of the 'Noli Me Tangere' Icon," *Comparative Drama* 36.1/2 (Summer 2002): 53.

116. Hans Urs von Balthasar, *Theo-Drama: Theological Dramatic Theory*, volume 1: *Prolegomena*, trans. Graham Harrison (San Francisco: Ignatius Press, 1988), 384.

117. Ibid.

118. Benson, *Shakespearean Resurrection*, 13.

119. David Dymond, "God's Disputed Acre," *Journal of Ecclesiastical History* 50, no. 3 (July 1999): 467; Keenan, *Travelling Players in Shakespeare's England*, 54–55.

120. Douglas and Greenfield, *REED. Cumberland, Westmorland, Gloucestershire*, 28, 130.

121. J. R. Mulryne, "Professional Players in the Guild Hall, Stratford-upon-Avon, 1568–1597," in *Shakespeare Survey*, ed. Peter Holland, vol. 60 (Cambridge: Cambridge University Press, 2007), 1–4, 20–22.

122. Ibid., 14; Sylvia Gill, "Reformation: Priests and People," in *The Guild and Guild Buildings of Shakespeare's Stratford*, ed. Mulryne, 35–41.

123. J. R. Mulryne, "Introduction," in *The Guild and Guild Buildings of Shakespeare's Stratford*, ed. Mulryne, 2.

124. Ingram, ed., *REED. Coventry*, 313–444.

125. Marcus Lynch, email to the author, December 19, 2012.

126. Nathaniel Hawthorne, "Recollections of a Gifted Woman," in *Shakespeare in America: An Anthology from the Revolution to Now*, ed. James S. Shapiro, Library of America 251 (New York: The Library of America, 2014), 153.

127. Gill, "Reformation: Priests and People," 51.

128. Peter L. Berger, *Redeeming Laughter: The Comic Dimension of Human Experience* (New York: Walter de Gruyter, 1997), 207.

Chapter Two

"Perverse Fantasies"?

Rehabilitating Malvolio's Reading

Given the affinity between Church and theater, including the accommodation of the touring troupes by local parish churches, we ought to be able to see its expression in the comedies where reconciliation, as in the Church, is a fundamental goal. Yet in *Twelfth Night*, as in the problem comedies, conciliation proves elusive, and critics of the play have pointed to the nearly irreconcilable differences between Malvolio and his detractors. What most divides them, interestingly enough, is hermeneutics, and it is now in fact a commonplace notion that Malvolio's reading of Maria's letter in 2.5 of *Twelfth Night* satirizes the Puritans' approach to interpreting the Bible. The play's first audiences even seem to have appreciated the joke: in his diary of a Candlemas performance at the Middle Temple on February 2, 1601, John Manningham singled out the gulling of Malvolio as "a good practice."[1] Manningham further defined a Puritan as "such a one as loves God with all his soul, but hates his neighbor with all his heart."[2]

While perhaps more sympathetic, modern critics still routinely attribute Malvolio's interpretation of Maria's letter to "his complete isolation from reality."[3] In his introduction to the play, David Bevington, a perceptive and sympathetic reader of the religious dynamics in Shakespeare's work, nonetheless offers the standard view of Malvolio as a solipsistic reader: "He tortures the text to make it yield a suitable meaning, much in the style of Puritan theologizing."[4] In this chapter, I want to challenge that critical orthodoxy, and I will do so by demonstrating how the play offers its own critique of conformist antipathy to nonconformist—specifically Malvolio's—hermeneutics, which are alleged to be so heterodox as to be damnable. The play brings Malvolio's reading back within the interpretive pale, demonstrating

45

that it is eminently reasonable despite his opponents attempts to asperse his hermeneutic method.

To be sure, Malvolio is a flawed character: he "taste[s] with a distempered appetite" and is, as Olivia says, "sick of self-love" (1.5.90–91). It is this self-love that leads him—so goes the argument—to identify himself as the letter's addressee. Malvolio is austere, a killjoy of others' fun, and an egregiously bad reader who deserves, in the eyes of Toby and his cohort, imprisonment and a mock exorcism that borders on psychological and physical torture. They punish him not only for his hostile sobriety, but also, and more immediately, for his reading of Maria's letter, an act that critics, as well as his antipuritan detractors in the play, consider misreading on a grand, even delusional, scale.[5] This consensus on Malvolio's alleged misreading, however, is in need of serious revision: his hermeneutic, far from being the mark of Puritan excess, is actually quite astute.

Malvolio is a religious outlier in Olivia's household, identified by Maria as being "sometimes a kind of Puritan" (2.3.140). His detractors attack him for reading as a Puritan would, yet Shakespeare takes pains to rehabilitate Malvolio's reading. First, while his reading may seem to fulfill the stereotype or caricature of Puritan exegesis, Malvolio is in reality a shrewd interpreter of the kind of language that Olivia, were she really in love with him, would (and later most certainly does) use. Maria wrote the letter, but its style is Olivia's. Second, Malvolio reads as a textual pragmatist who does not believe that texts are self-interpreting; they cannot, in other words, be understood apart from social contexts, including oral ones, available to corroborate or invalidate his reading of the letter. He repeatedly makes use of those contexts. Malvolio has been much maligned for believing he is the letter's addressee, but this is scarcely a mistake: it is written specifically for him and to him in everything but the use of his name—and Maria virtually dangles that before him too.

In addition, Shakespeare uses Malvolio's reading as a way of touching on the Reformation dispute over hermeneutics—"the art of understanding texts"[6]—yet at the same time he expands the notion of textuality to include the "text" of the body. Once Shakespeare establishes that people can also be "read" or interpreted, he suggests a striking parallel between Malvolio's reading of the letter and Sebastian's and Viola's "reading" of each other's identity in the play's recognition scene. While brother and sister reunite and marry others, Malvolio is excluded and purports to seek revenge. But the difference in their respective ends owes nothing to the respective quality of their readings (they are nearly indistinguishable) and everything to a misreading of Malvolio as one who pursues "perverse fantasies" in lieu of a careful hermeneutic.

REFORMATION HERMENEUTICS, REFORMATION VIOLENCE

The writing and reading of letters is a prominent feature of *Twelfth Night*'s design. At Toby's exhortation to "taunt [Cesario] with the license of ink" (3.2.44–45), Sir Andrew writes a letter so inept—"excellently ignorant" (3.4.188)—that Toby ignores it and improvises a challenge by way of mouth. Similarly, once he is imprisoned, Malvolio asks Feste to "help me to a candle, and pen, ink, and paper" (4.2.81–82), thinking that Olivia will need no hermeneutic rigor to make sense of his plain style. He is mocked to the end, however, with Feste telling Olivia that he only belatedly brought Malvolio's letter to her because "as a madman's epistles are no gospels, so it skills not much when they are deliver'd" (5.1.287–88). He then reads the letter, presumably in deranged fashion, eliciting Olivia's "How now, art thou mad?" (293). His reply, "No madam, I do but read madness" (294), signals his intention to render Malvolio's letter unintelligible. Even under ideal circumstances—never the case in *Twelfth Night*—hermeneutics is always susceptible to the possibility of misreading.

Because of Maria's duplicitous intention "to make," as Manningham noted, "the Steward beleeve his Lady widdowe was in love with him,"[7] Malvolio's perusal of her letter would seem to offer the play's quintessential example of misinterpretation. The letter's cryptic, quasi-evocation of his name—"M. O. A. I. doth sway my life" (2.5.107)[8] —tantalizes him: "what should that alphabetical position portend? If I could make that resemble something in me!" (118–20). Malvolio desperately wants to find his name in the anagram, which is, as the philosopher Hans-Georg Gadamer notes, a legitimate hermeneutical tactic: the reader "must not try to disregard himself and his particular hermeneutical situation. He must relate the text to this situation if he wants to understand at all" (340, 324). The temporal and historical situations are part of what Gadamer describes as the reader's *horizon*: "Such horizons constitute the interpreter's own immediate participation in traditions that are not themselves the object of understanding but the condition of its occurrence."[9] Malvolio relates the text to his situation, but his critics (again, both those inside and outside the play) would have us believe that he carries this hermeneutic to an absurd extreme.

As noted, Malvolio's reading of the letter also has an inescapable Reformation context. In the midst of act 2, Toby tells Malvolio, after the latter interrupts his drunken merrymaking, "Art any more than a steward? Dost thou think because thou art virtuous there shall be no more cakes and ale?" (2.3.112–13). Implicit in Toby's seemingly offhand comment about such festive imbibing is deep-seated religious antagonism. His use of cakes and ale is no accident: they were, as Elam observes, "the food and drink traditionally associated with church festivities such as saint's days and holy days (like Twelfth Night), and as such particularly unpalatable to ceremony-hating 'Puritans' like Malvolio."[10] Maria's indistinct comment, "sometimes he is a kind of Puritan," indicates that Malvolio may be a Puritan or at the least act like one. Yet his puritanism (not just his asceticism) is fairly well established in the literature.[11] Peter Milward remarks, Malvolio "is described by Maria as 'a kind of Puritan,' which means—for all the learned reservations of commentators—still a Puritan, if not quite so extreme as the Brownists."[12] Even if Malvolio's puritanism remains somewhat indistinct, Maria and her confederates believe that he certainly reads like one. Maurice Hunt remarks, "juggling the alphabetical letters of [M. O. A. I.] to suggest his own name reflects conformists' accounts of Puritans willfully twisting the literal sense of biblical passages to create meanings justifying their narrow beliefs."[13] Yet, as we shall see, it is not at all clear that Malvolio actually juggles the letters in M. O. A. I.; audiences almost always think he does because his adversaries in the scene tell them as much. By having others describe him as "a kind of Puritan" and allege that he twists the meaning of the letter, Shakespeare raises the issue of Reformation hermeneutics with its long history, one that I need only briefly rehearse here.[14]

In 1546 the Catholic Council of Trent took up the gauntlet first thrown down by Luther and Tyndale, declaring that no person, lay or otherwise, "must, relying on his own judgment . . . dare to interpret Holy Scripture by twisting it to his own personal understanding."[15] The statement was clearly a response to, and caricature of, the Protestant push for vernacular translations so that the laity could read without priestly mediation or guidance. The martyrologist John Foxe was one of countless evangelicals to reciprocate in kind: in interpreting scripture, the Catholic clergy were said in his *Actes and Monuments* (1570) to "darken the right sense with the mist of their sophistry . . . wresting the Scripture unto their own purpose, contrary unto the process, order, and meaning of the text."[16] Over seventy years later, Milton in *Of Reformation* (1641) felt free to level Foxe's charge against "these devout Prelates" in the Church of England who "for these many years have not ceas't in their Pulpits wrinching, and spraining the text."[17]

Yet in England by the turn of the seventeenth century, the hermeneutical debate had largely shifted away from Protestant reformers and Catholics (Henry's break from Rome lay, after all, three generations in the past) to the daily, internal struggle between conforming members of the Church of England and various nonconformists, Puritans among them.[18] *Of Reformation* nicely illustrates the shift in emphasis to a clash within Protestantism itself. Even as early as 1542–1543, the English statute "An Acte for the Advancement of True Religion" warned of "seditious" persons [i.e., nonconformists] who through "their perverse froward and malicious minds, wills, and intents, [intend] to subvert the very true and perfect exposition . . . of the said Scripture, after their perverse fantasies."[19] It is no stretch of the imagination to say that Toby and his coconspirators view Malvolio's desire of marrying the Countess Olivia as a "perverse fantasy" abetted by the tortuously self-serving interpretation that they believe he brings to the letter.

As James Simpson comments, "in the Reformation, modes of reading became the criterion of institutional inclusion and exclusion—exclusion of all the evangelical's obvious enemies [Jews and Catholics], but also, more interestingly, of other evangelical readers."[20] *Twelfth Night* contains a "whole pack" of those who oppose Malvolio's hermeneutical method (5.1.378); they see to it that there are spiritual consequences for his alleged misreading. He is bound "in hideous darkness" (4.2.30), then both catechized and exorcised by Sir Topas, a curate whose treatment recalls that of Doctor Pinch in *The Comedy of Errors:* "Mistress, both man and master is possess'd: / I know it by their pale and deadly looks. / They must be bound and laid in some dark room" (*Err.* 4.4.92–94).[21] Maria even pronounces his excommunication: "Yond gull Malvolio is turn'd heathen, a very renegade; for there is no Christian that means to be sav'd by believing rightly can ever believe such impossible passages of grossness" (3.2.69–73). Shakespeare's etymological rendering of "orthodoxy" as "believing rightly" is at the heart of Maria's charge: Malvolio is a heretic and reads as such. If hermeneutics is, as Friedrich Schleiermacher defined it, "the art of avoiding misunderstandings,"[22] Malvolio is a bad reader, or a Puritan, which from a conformist perspective is much the same thing.

Although Malvolio's puritanism has been the subject of much discussion, less attention has been paid to the religious affiliation of the other Illyrians. Anthony Nuttall claims there is no "factional grouping" in the play,[23] an untenable assertion in light of Sir Andrew's exclamation, upon learning that Malvolio is "a kind of puritan," "O, if I thought that, I'd beat him like a dog!" (2.3.140–41). Andrew never explains his antipathy to puritanism, yet it is clearly evident and an important reason they all close ranks against Malvolio.[24] The other Illyrians are neither Puritans nor Catholics; they belong, as Hunt, Milward, and others have demonstrated, to the world of official (conforming) Protestantism.[25] This may sound odd given the setting in the quasifictive Illyria, yet as Marjorie Garber remarks of the play's geography, "I am presuming here that Illyria = England, following the custom of other Shakespearean plays."[26] Moreover, Northrop Frye noted that Shakespeare frequently used "spatial anachronism, in which Mediterranean and Atlantic settings seem to be superposed on top of each other."[27] One can otherwise scarcely explain Andrew's later expressed preference, "I had as lief be a Brownist as a politician" (3.2.30)—Robert Browne (1550–1633) having founded the separatist Puritan sect in 1581. Maria and her cohorts evince antipuritan disdain for Malvolio and his ilk, especially for his reading of the letter, which confirms for them their worst suspicions of his puritanism. One could say of Maria (or of any in her circle) that she is, to use her own indistinct formula, "sometimes a kind of conformist."

And what was it about Puritan hermeneutics that conformists opposed? Tyndale himself encouraged a presentist, personal application of scripture among his evangelical readers: "As thou readest therefore think that every syllable pertaineth to thine own self."[28] Malvolio does this, to be sure, and it is this alleged egoism that rendered Puritans vulnerable to charges leveled by James I, among many others, that they pursued perverse fantasies while reading.[29] Thomas Hobbes acerbically quipped, "After the Bible was translated into English every man, nay, every boy and wench that could read English, thought they spoke with God Almighty and understood what he said."[30] For his supposedly heretical reading—what Hunt calls "the arbitrariness of Malvolio's willful interpretation"[31] —Malvolio finds himself imprisoned. Behind his jailers' antics lies a cold reality: English heretics were routinely sentenced to one-month prison sentences; a recidivist faced either burning or the threat of having "his body to be committed to perpetual prison."[32] As Simpson notes, Reformation hermeneutics "unleashes an aggression and, not infrequently, a violence between different groups of evangelical readers themselves."[33] Toby and company imprison Malvolio for his supposed misreading, but their supposal turns out to be their own willful misinterpretation of Malvolio's careful reading of the letter.

MALVOLIO'S READING

The twelfth night of the play's title conjures the Feast of Fools (*festum fatuorum*), whose festive inversion of social hierarchies would be fully realized in Illyria if the countess were to marry her majordomo. Instead, Malvolio is left out, deservedly so in the eyes of some critics: "Malvolio's absurd and egotistical reading"[34] represents what J. L. Simmons and David Willbern regard as "a fall from grace which is not only personal and social, but has spiritual resonance as well."[35] Though this is the consensus view, it hinges rather precariously on the assumption that Malvolio misreads the letter. As Nuttall comments, "Scholars and commentators may strain to explain how very unpleasant Malvolio is so that we can feel less bad about the way he is treated."[36] And just how unreasonable is it for him to attribute the language of the letter to Olivia? Are Maria's self-described "impossible passages of grossness" inconsistent with how Olivia actually speaks?

The first thing to notice is that although the letter does not use Malvolio's name, the clues it provides render doing so virtually unnecessary: "thou art made if thou desir'st to be so; if not, let me see thee a steward still, the fellow of servants, and not worthy to touch Fortune's fingers" (2.5.155–56). To whom else could her use of "steward" refer? It is of course one of many false trails meant to mislead him. Yet even with the reference to "steward," the absence of his name ought to give Malvolio pause—as, in fact, it does: "If this should be thee, Malvolio?"; "what should that alphabetical position portend?" (118–20). His questions indicate that he does not leap immediately to conclusions. Malvolio will ultimately believe that he is the addressee, but only after a careful—recursive—reading of the letter in its entirety.

Second, Olivia acknowledges that Maria's handwriting is "much like the character of her own" (5.1.346), yet Maria also possesses the unerring ability to imitate Olivia's idiolect. "Be not afraid of greatness" and "thou art made if thou desir'st to be so" may sound like "impossible passages of grossness," as Maria characterizes them, but they bear striking resemblance to the language Olivia actually uses. Aristotle might describe the language of the letter as a "likely impossibility":[37] impossible to believe one actually speaks like that, but on closer inspection it proves true, given what we know of Olivia. Late in the play she exhorts Cesario, whom she thinks she has just married, "Fear not, Cesario, take thy fortunes up; / Be that thou know'st thou art, and then thou art / As great as that thou fear'st" (5.1.146–48). This is how she really speaks to one she loves, and it is precisely the style of Maria's letter. The letter's cryptic salutation is similarly consistent with what Malvolio knows about her language: "'To the unknown belov'd, this, and my good wishes':—her very phrases!" (90–91). Is this just wish fulfillment on his part? Hardly. When Olivia sees the letter at the end of the play, Malvolio challenges her, "Write [differently] from it, if you can, in hand *or phrase*" (5.1.332, italics mine). She can only "confess" the truth of the remarkable mimicry (346). Thus, Malvolio, far from egregiously misreading the letter, astutely begins to locate Olivia's voice in its cadences.

Third, notice the letter's multiple exhortations: "be not afraid of greatness. Some are born great, some achieve greatness, and some have greatness thrust upon 'em. Thy Fates open their hands, let thy blood and spirit embrace them. . . . Go to, thou art made if thou desir'st to be so; if not, let me see thee a steward still" (2.5.144–47, 155–56). It is as if the letter takes its cue from Olivia's repeated commands to her beloved Cesario: "Be not afraid, good youth" (3.1.131); "Get you to your lord" (1.5.279); "let him send no more" (280); "Hold little faith" (5.1.171). Olivia commands nearly everyone: "Open't and read it" (Feste at 5.1.288); "Read it you, sirrah" (Fabian, 301); "See him deliver'd, Fabian, bring him hither" (315). So consistent is Shakespeare's representation of Olivia that he reveals her imperiousness in her very first utterance: "Take the fool away" (1.5.38). Opening lines are often quite revealing in Shakespeare's plays.

Likewise, Maria's letter neatly captures Olivia's use of the imperative mood: "Cast thy humble slough"; "be opposite with a kinsman"; "let thy tongue tang with arguments of state"; "put thyself into the trick of singularity" (3.4.68–72). Her language puts Malvolio in the mood, both figuratively and grammatically: "Go off, I discard you. Let me enjoy my private. Go off"; "Go hang yourselves all!" (89–90, 123). He, too, appropriates Olivia's language in anticipation, he hopes, of their union. Although Malvolio imagines the match even before he reads the letter (2.5.23–80), he is scarcely the perverse fantasist his detractors make him out to be—a Puritan who reads according to his own lights. But this is merely a caricature of Puritan hermeneutics[38] and of Malvolio's actual reading practice as well. Tyndale and Luther, for instance, both rejected "private interpretation" in favor of reading guided by the Holy Spirit, which they argued would lead believers into all truth. Not only does Malvolio rely on the clues that the letter provides, he also has recourse, as we have seen, to the riddling language that Olivia actually uses when she speaks to Cesario: "To one of your receiving / Enough is shown" (3.1.120–21).

Perhaps to offer a counterweight to the bias of the antipuritans in the scene, Shakespeare rehabilitates Malvolio's reading of the letter before it even begins: "Maria once told me she did affect me, and I have heard herself come thus near, that should she fancy, it should be one of my complexion" (2.5.23–26). Malvolio's recounting of Maria's statement is of course hearsay, but there is no evidence in the play that he misremembers (quite the opposite, in fact [2.2.5–11]) or, worse, lies about what others have told him—even Toby concedes that he is "virtuous" (2.3.114). One cannot, however, trust Maria, but even if Olivia made no such statement to her, it does not change the fact that Maria's allegation serves as one piece of evidence to persuade Malvolio that Olivia might affect him. Maria could also make such a claim with clever impunity: "affect" can refer either to loving someone—the definition Malvolio wishes were true—or merely "to have affection for or liking" someone, which, as both Maria and Malvolio both know, is at the very least how Olivia feels toward him.[39]

Olivia keeps to herself while she is in mourning, yet she is typically in Malvolio's company and is quite solicitous about his health when he later appears cross-gartered before her: "Let some of my people have a special care of him. I would not have him miscarry for the half of my dowry" (3.4.62–63). Maria later corroborates Olivia's offer of half her dowry: "My lady would not lose him for more than I'll say" (3.4.104–05). Maria's hesitancy to state such a large amount almost certainly indicates her unwillingness to admit just how highly Olivia regards Malvolio. Everything she does indicates her trust in him. As Olivia's steward, Malvolio is in control of the domestic affairs of her household; if he were as inept as Manningham and others have thought, how has he risen to this important managerial position? Olivia entrusts him with multiple household responsibilities, all of which he seems to accomplish with dispatch (e.g., 1.5.297–305; 2.2.16).[40] Her willingness to give up half her dowry—a dowry reserved for marriage, it is worth noting—indicates that Olivia almost certainly does affect, though not love, him.

Even more intriguing is Malvolio's recounting of Olivia's having told him that "should she fancy, it should be one of [his] complexion." Since Olivia is not present to verify that she actually made the statement, this is another bit of hearsay—yet it, too, has the ring of truth, of authenticity, about it. The statement is elusive, evasive even: she may not fancy anyone, but if she were to, having a "complexion"—a word that can refer to one's appearance, skin color, even temperament[41] —similar to that of Malvolio would be the sine qua non of her attraction. The entire comment is noncommittal and, strikingly, as cryptic as (and certainly in the style of) Maria's letter: it again maps Olivia's idiolect. To indicate that there is something about his complexion she finds attractive is an odd statement for Olivia to make in Malvolio's presence unless she absolutely trusts him. Yet Malvolio does not leap to conclusions; he wonders, quite understandably, "What should I think on't?" (2.5.28). There is no indication in the play that Olivia actually loves Malvolio, but he clearly aspires to the match, and it is not unreasonable for him to regard her statement as giving him hope. Her remark about his complexion is cryptic, neither refusing nor accepting him as a possible match—in pointed contrast to her repeated refusals of Orsino.

As if that weren't enough initial evidence, Malvolio tells us that "she uses me with a more exalted respect than anyone else that follows her" (2.5.26–28). Olivia's later concern for him when he is cross-gartered corroborates the claim. Her last line in the play, "He hath been most notoriously abus'd" (5.1.379), is further evidence of her sympathy. Together, these three pieces of evidence, all of which he considers before he discovers the letter, offer an intriguing prelude to his subsequent reading of it. Olivia's remark that she might marry someone of Malvolio's complexion tantalizes him, but it is in the end as indefinite as the letter's lack of a named addressee. Malvolio certainly fantasizes about a future marriage to her, but he also clearly does not yet believe with certainty that she loves him. He only fantasizes in soliloquy; when he is around Olivia he is all business. Toby calls him "an overweening rogue" (2.5.29) for the supposed presumptuousness of his perverse fantasy, but it is not unreasonable (and quite human) in light of what Malvolio has heard from and about her, as well as from her own behavior toward him. Then, after considering such evidence, to receive a love letter written in what appears to be Olivia's hand, in her distinctive style, is to confirm for him—with such "clear lights of favor," as he later says (5.1.336)—that her earlier uncertainty about falling in love has been settled in his favor.

When Malvolio then picks up the letter, his reading of the tantalizing anagram could potentially be quite self-serving: "M. O. A. I. This simulation is not as the former; and yet, to crush this a little, it would bow to me, for every one of these letters are in my name" (2.5.139–41). Malvolio wishes that he could "crush" the letter, perhaps crinkling the paper so as to transpose the "A" and the "I," but there is no indication that he ever does so, literally or figuratively. Instead, he notes that the arrangement of the letters "suffers under probation" (128), unlike the many other parts of the letter that "simulate" his person with "no obstruction" (117–18)—Maria's use of "let me see thee a steward still" is a good example. Even his use of "crush" registers a possible awareness that he would be doing some violence to the text if he were to make the letters correspond to the order of those in his name. Malvolio is also correct that the letters are in his name, and almost certainly rearranged as they are in order to induce him to transpose them. Without question, he wishes he could "crush" it "a little," but instead of doing so, he simply moves on to the remainder of the letter. Given the other overwhelming evidence identifying him as the addressee, Malvolio probably does think, on some level, that the anagram is not inconsistent with the letter's cryptic style—and he is correct. Nonetheless, he indicates his uncertainty or wariness about positively connecting M. O. A. I. to his name.[42]

Shakespeare teases us with the *possibility* that Malvolio might crush the letters and thus fulfill the caricature of Puritan solipsism, but again there is no evidence that he actually does so. Given Shakespeare's famed complementarity, his ability to play both sides of an issue, it is no surprise that the issue is unresolved in a delicate balance, one that gets lost before the repeated ejaculations of Toby and his confederates, all of whom believe that Malvolio's application of the letter to his situation is a perverse and self-serving fantasy. Having drawn their conclusion about his reading before it ever takes place—"I know this letter will make a contemplative idiot of him," Maria declares (2.5.19–20)—they offer their derisive running commentary with such effectiveness that audiences have a difficult time being guarded in their appraisal of Malvolio's reading. In effect, the confederates function as early modern talking heads, eavesdropping pundits who tell us what to think of Malvolio's reading as it unfolds. Yet they are hardly nonpartisan observers.

In wishing to portray Malvolio in the worst possible light, Maria acknowledges only her ability to mimic Olivia's handwriting: "I can write very like my lady . . . we can hardly make distinction of our hands" (2.3.159–61). What she fails to mention is her equal facility at ventriloquizing Olivia's linguistic style. Maria downplays the full extent of her imitative prowess, saying she has written "some obscure epistles of love" (155–56) full of "impossible passages of grossness"—passages that are, if one cares to notice, entirely consistent with Olivia's idiolect. Moreover, Maria flatly contradicts herself. On the one hand, she claims her missive contains such grotesque ideas—the wearing of yellow stockings, for instance (3.2.71)—that no reasonable interpreter could take them seriously. Yet she assures her cohorts that "by the color of his beard, the shape of his leg, the manner of his gait, the expressure of his eye, forehead, and complexion, he shall find himself most feelingly personated" (155–58). In their antipuritan contempt, Maria and the others want to see Malvolio as someone who twists any writing to suit his purposes and then studiously avoids additional evidence that might invalidate his interpretation. A careful reader—a textual pragmatist—would examine such evidence, but this is, again, precisely what Malvolio does. Everything in the letter and everything he knows about Olivia's speech patterns, what she has told him, and what she may well have told Maria about him, points to the conclusion that Malvolio reaches. And he hardly jumps to that conclusion: rather, "each circumstance / Of place, time, fortune, do cohere and jump" (5.1.251–52). The lines are Viola's, and, as we shall see, she and Sebastian later mimic Malvolio's hermeneutic circumspection.

How then is there such near-unanimity in seeing Malvolio as such a bad, self-serving reader? Why have we, in fact, misread him? In our own defense, we can say that his foes' animadversions throughout act 2, scene 5 incline us to adopt their self-serving interpretation of his hermeneutic method. They are far from charitable, however; Malvolio's use of both written and oral contexts is surely the mark of a conscientious reader. It is even, ironically enough, part of conformist, High Church, tradition.[43] Maria and the others disregard all evidence to the contrary and insist that his reading deserves whatever punishment the "whirligig of time" brings in. They look after him—not quite as Olivia had intended—with "a special care" (3.4.62). Talk about misreading. "Antipuritans," writes Patrick Collinson, "constructed an image of the godly as pharisaical, hypocritical, proud and divisive."[44] Such caricature is little more than "the projection onto the polemically defined other" of aspects they would rather not look at too closely in themselves.[45]

Having said this, there are indeed two possible flaws with Malvolio's hermeneutic. The first occurs when, appearing before Olivia cross-gartered and speaking to her in the language of the letter (3.4.14–63), he does not trust the evidence of her confusion and incredulity. But everything he knows about her and has read in the letter confirms for him that she is merely acting in public as if there is nothing between the two of them. Such indirection, even outright denial, is also evident in her speech to Cesario, whom she does love: "Be not afraid, good youth, I will not have you" (3.1.131). Second, Maria tells us that Olivia "detests" yellow stockings and cross-gartering (2.5.198–200). Malvolio flatly contradicts her: "She did commend my yellow stockings of late, she did praise my leg being cross-gartered, and in this she manifests herself to my love" (166–68). Ought we to believe that Maria speaks the truth here and that Malvolio is either lying or delusional? While Malvolio is prone to fantasizing about a prospective relationship with Olivia, he scarcely conjures things out of thin air as Maria does the love letter. Why should we accept Maria's word over Malvolio's when her duplicity is abundant while Malvolio's probity is acknowledged even by his detractors?

Garber suggests that Maria's contradiction of Malvolio's claim makes "it clear that Olivia was only being polite."[46] This, however, would be distinctly out of character for her. Olivia reproves Feste when he displeases her; has little time for Toby's nonsense; is repeatedly gruff with Cesario; and rebuffs Orsino's importunities with dispatch, telling him on the last of these occasions, "If [your suit] be aught to the old tune, my lord / It is as fat and fulsome to mine ear / As howling after music" (5.1.102–04). She had no problem, again, telling Malvolio that he is "sick of self-love" (1.5.90–91), and her continual use of imperatives is scarcely the height of polite discourse. Still, it is possible that she may dislike the fashion and have nonetheless commended Malvolio's wearing of it; alternatively, Maria may actually be falsifying Olivia's real approval of such attire. Because the event happened before the play opens and is only briefly related, it is impossible to determine with any certainty why Olivia had apparently praised Malvolio, or what she really thinks of his clothing.

We don't even know that Olivia objects to his cross-gartering when he later appears clothed in this fashion before her. It is humorous for audiences to see such bright colors on Malvolio, and this alone may merely surprise Olivia. Maria and the others tell Olivia that Malvolio is mad, and this as much as his unusual behavior in the scene convinces her that something is amiss. We assume that Olivia objects to his yellow stockings, but she never says so; all we have to rely on is Maria's word for it, which, again, contradicts what Olivia had told Malvolio. What we do know for certain is that Malvolio is *not* delusional: Maria is well aware that Olivia had commended his outfit—why else would she enjoin him in the letter, "Remember who commended thy yellow stockings, and wish'd to see thee ever cross-garter'd" (2.5.153–54)? Maria uses that piece of information, once again, to make him identify himself as the letter's addressee. It is similarly clear that Malvolio is not distorting the letter, but testing it against the oral context of what Olivia had said to him. He is, indeed, feelingly personated in the letter.

Malvolio knows, too, that a marriage between social unequals is possible—"the Lady of the Strachy married the yeoman of the wardrobe" (2.5.39–40).[47] Toby can't believe that Olivia would marry a mere steward, but she is prepared to marry Cesario, who is also a servant. And Toby himself, of course, marries Maria. In similarly good Saturnalian fashion, Olivia is no respecter of class: she is not afraid of marrying down or of disowning and virtually kicking her uncle out, as Malvolio, the steward, informs Toby (2.3.95–101). Despite this evidence of the reality of marriage between social unequals, all that Toby can envision while eavesdropping on Malvolio's reading is his own perverse fantasy of wrath: "Fire and brimstone!" (50); "Bolts and shackles!" (56); "Shall this fellow live?" (62); "I'll cudgel him" (133). Maria's "I can hardly forbear hurling things at him" (3.2.81) illustrates why she will be such an apt mate for Toby, joined as they are, morally speaking, at the hip. But as Stephen Booth remarks, against the weight of critical opinion and with his usual eye for detail, "The credentials of and in that letter are awfully convincing. The letter gives Malvolio plentiful and persuasive evidence that Olivia loves him. . . . Sherlock Holmes himself would accept Maria's letter as a love letter from Olivia to Malvolio."[48] In the end, poor Malvolio is shut out not by the purported inadequacy of his reading but by the malicious sport of his coreligionists.

SEBASTIAN AND VIOLA'S "READING"

The attention paid, and censure given, to Malvolio's supposed misreading can lead us to overlook similar charges of misreading that characters level against one another. What is remarkable is how Shakespeare continually glances at Reformation hermeneutics as a way of framing the issue.[49] When Cesario claims that Orsino's love for Olivia is the first "chapter" of his heart, Olivia responds, "O, I have read it; it is heresy" (1.5.225–28)—the same charge lodged against Malvolio for his reading. The play's subtitle, "what you will," is an apt subtitle for a play about interpretive willing—here Orsino wills himself into a potential marriage to Olivia, even though she never gives him (as she had Malvolio) the least bit of encouragement. Feste, too, twice "catechizes" others on the proper hermeneutic approach: Olivia is taught to believe she should not mourn because her brother's soul "is in heaven" (1.5.38–69), while Malvolio is nonsensically instructed in how not to "dispossess the soul of [his] grandam" (4.2.20–61).[50] And when Olivia calls Feste a fool, he disclaims against her misreading of him: "Misprision in the highest degree!" (1.5.55).

Hermeneutic miscues, or even the mere allegation of such, are potentially dangerous. Violence often ensues, including the physical harm that comes not only to Malvolio, but to Toby and Aguecheek (5.1.190–97), as well as the threatened executions of Antonio (60–72) and Cesario (117–30). That the play is a comedy suggests, generically at least, the possibility of eventually making intelligible sense of the world in which one lives; the continual misunderstandings nonetheless underscore the need to exercise hermeneutic care. To the extent that things can be made well, the play points to a kind of hermeneutics writ large wherein words and other visual markers such as the body require careful examination. Strikingly, the play suggests that the act of reading encompasses texts such as Maria's letter but also the text of the body, as in the "text" that lies in Orsino's heretical bosom (1.5.223–28).

Later, in response to Cesario's question, "what manner of man is [Andrew]?" Fabian answers, "Nothing of that wonderful promise, to *read* him by his form, as you are like to find him in the proof of his valor" (3.4.264–66, italics mine). The passage suggests the difficulty of reading accurately on the basis of form.[51] Earlier, Olivia had told Cesario that he also misinterprets her: "Under your hard construction must I sit" (3.1.115). Shakespeare thus makes explicit what he does implicitly throughout the play: he textualizes persons so that they can be "read" or interpreted, as in his adversaries' insistence that Malvolio's cross-gartering must be interpreted as madness.[52] Reading others by their form is everywhere: Cesario and Andrew each comically misreads the other as a ferocious adversary (3.4); Olivia (4.3) and Feste (4.1) mistake Sebastian for Cesario; Antonio mistakes Cesario for Sebastian (5.1); Orsino mythologizes Olivia as a nubile Diana and thus misreads woman and goddess alike (1.1.18–22); and Sir Andrew, a knight, misinterprets Olivia, a countess, as being within his marital ambit. He also mistakes Toby for a friend, only to receive Toby's vicious "Will you help?— an ass-head and a coxcomb and a knave, a thin-fac'd knave, a gull!" (5.1.205–06). Misreading, be it books or people, is serious business, and nowhere is this more evident than in the play's recognition scene.

When Viola and Sebastian finally share the stage in 5.1, they each must discover who the other one, a mirror image, really is. This is no easy task: she is in disguise and he has had great trouble interpreting events throughout the play. He does not, after all, know who Olivia is, why she thinks she knows him, or why she wants to marry him. To complicate matters, each believes the other to have died in the shipwreck. Seeing Cesario, his apparent double, Sebastian fumbles at comprehending:

Do I stand there? I never had a brother;

Nor can there be that deity in my nature

Of here and everywhere. I had a sister,

Whom the blind waves and surges have devoured.

Of charity, what kin are you to me?

What countryman? What name? What parentage? (5.1.226–31)

Sebastian examines the text of Viola's physical body. His repeated questioning, including the verbalizing of his own hermeneutic, imitates Malvolio's own piecing together of the letter. The similarity should tip us off that this scene functions as a clever if subtle reprise of Malvolio's reading of the letter in 2.5.

The siblings' mutual appearance confuses them and everyone else on stage; like Malvolio, they cannot simply rely merely on the surface of the text—the appearance of the body—before them. "A hermeneutically trained consciousness," as Gadamer remarks, "must be, from the start, sensitive to the text's alterity"[53] —sensitive, that is, to what the text says, not forcing it to mean, as the title blithely offers, "what you will." Disguised as Cesario, the text of Viola's body is as cryptic to Sebastian—as hard to read—as Maria's letter was to Malvolio. Yet because Cesario looks just like Sebastian—"One face, one voice, one habit, and two persons" (5.1.216)—one can see in Sebastian's questioning the same desire of Malvolio to make the tantalizing M. O. A. I. "resemble something in me!" Yet the transvestite Cesario gives neither no more nor no less appearance of being Viola than M. O. A. I. does of being Malvolio; Cesario is and is not Viola. Likewise, Sebastian both is and cannot be the dead brother Viola lost.

Sebastian quickly realizes that even though Cesario is nearly identical to him in appearance, he can be neither Sebastian—"Do I stand there?"—nor an identical twin—"I never had a brother" (226). He similarly rules out the divinity that could make possible his simultaneous appearance in two places: "Nor can there be that deity in my nature / Of here and everywhere" (227–28). Sebastian's hermeneutical "questioning of things"[54] forces him by default to consider his fraternal twin sister, but having presumed that she, "Whom the blind waves and surges have devoured," died at sea, the possibility of her resurrection from the dead appears just as implausible as the other alternatives already dismissed. His only apparent recourse, given her resemblance to him, is to consider whether she is potentially part of his extended family: "what kin are you to me? / What countryman? What name? What parentage?" (230–31). It is a wrong road, but the questions are sufficient to test and correct his hypothesis.

Viola, too, must read against the countervailing presumption of her brother's death at sea:

Of Messaline; Sebastian was my father;

Such a Sebastian was my brother too;

So went he suited to his watery tomb.

If spirits can assume both form and suit,

You come to fright us. (232–36)

Viola must first rule out the appearance of a wraith. Stirring somewhere in her mind must also be the recollection that Antonio's recent mistaking of her for Sebastian had made her entertain the possibility of Sebastian's survival: "Prove true, imagination, O, prove true, / That I, dear brother, be now ta'en for you" (3.4.375–76). In addition, the mention of places and names begins to persuade Sebastian: "Were you a woman, as the rest [i.e., of the evidence] goes even, / I should . . . say, 'Thrice welcome, drowned Viola!'" (5.1.239–41). After such concerted effort, stichomythia leads to quick resolution:

VIOLA: My father had a mole upon his brow.

SEBASTIAN: And so had mine.

VIOLA: And died that day when Viola from her birth

Had numbered thirteen years.

SEBASTIAN: O, that record is lively in my soul!

He finished indeed his mortal act

That day that made my sister thirteen years. (242–48)

Their recourse to family history is the mark of textual pragmatism: they confirm their suspicions with information outside the "text" of the other's body, in part because those texts, as in the case of Malvolio's letter, are hardly self-explicating.

Viola closes the exchange with a final caution that they not jump to false readings: "Do not embrace me till each circumstance / Of place, time, fortune, do cohere and jump / That I am Viola" (251–53). Her tantalizing allusion to the "*Noli me tangere*" topos derives from Christ's words to Mary Magdalene in the gospel of John: "Touch me not: for I am not yet ascended to my Father."[55] *Twelfth Night* fittingly commemorates the Resurrection as it re-creates another, a near-resurrection from the dead that requires a careful hermeneutic, an imaginative suspension of disbelief, and perhaps even a modicum of faith that one can read signs in the world and make intelligible sense of them.[56] The scene is yet another of those Balthasarian "miracles of earthly love" in which "the Christian resurrection from the dead becomes the reappearance of those believed dead."[57] This too could be condemned as an improbable fiction (3.4.129–30) were it not performed, as it must have been on more than one occasion, in a church where such a miraculous recognitions scene would have reminded audiences of the architectonic recognition scenes of the Church, the Epiphany and—here especially—the Resurrection. Sebastian and Viola's minor recognition scene is one of Aristotle's improbable but possible events, and when the play was performed in a church, then the moment is subtly juxtaposed to what for the Church is the impossible but probable event of the Resurrection itself.[58]

Yet does Sebastian and Viola's hermeneutic care stand in contrast to Malvolio's reading? The answer is an emphatic no. Viola warily acknowledges that their interpretation of events may prove illusory; for now, however, they show themselves willing to accept the provisionality of their reading and to adjust it, if necessary, in time. Sebastian and Viola have recourse to the "text" of the other person, which, because Viola is cross-dressed, is as

misleading as the text of Maria's letter was to Malvolio. Viola promises to
dispense with her "masculine usurp'd attire" (5.1.250) so that she can be
correctly interpreted as a woman. Malvolio had changed his clothes, too, so
as to confirm to Olivia that he understood the letter's injunctions, but no such
joyous union with Olivia awaits him, in stark contrast to the reunion between
the twins. To their advantage, Viola and Sebastian can test their reading with
and against one another, testing each other's history against their mutual
presumption of the other's death. Moreover, they read without Toby, Feste,
Maria, and Fabian commenting disparagingly on their efforts to make sense
of what they see. Malvolio tests the letter with every available resource he
has, and reads it correctly as being addressed to him, but he has the disadvan-
tage of having Toby and the others actively working to distort his reading of
the letter, as well as audiences' perceptions of his hermeneutic care. The
letter also commands Malvolio not to be tentative but, instead, to usurp the
clothing and the role of Olivia's presumed beloved.

Nuttall trenchantly observes

> The jokers assume that Malvolio will be caught by the chance of social climb-
> ing. In fact he is caught by something more elementary, by the thought that he
> is loved. There is a subtle pathos in the fact that this inadequate human being,
> so deficient in warmth towards others, should still be vulnerable at this point.
> Suddenly we see, Malvolio is human.[59]

Malvolio wants as desperately to be loved as Sebastian and Viola each wants
to believe that the other has survived the shipwreck. Shakespeare points not
to Malvolio's bad reading but to the difficulties of interpretation: one can do
one's best and still get it wrong, especially in the face of the malevolence of
others. Manningham has bequeathed us a longstanding tradition of misreading Malvolio as a gull worthy of being duped, but he is every bit as careful a
reader as Sebastian and Viola. Malvolio has some faults, but even in this
regard Shakespeare rehabilitates him: Fabian confesses that they wrote the
letter "Upon some stubborn and uncourteous parts / We had conceiv'd
against him" (5.1.361–62). Malvolio may be stubborn and uncourteous, but
their "conceptions" of him may well be worse than he really is.[60] Thus,
instead of reading Malvolio as one who is imprisoned because of his tortuous
reading, we ought to regard him as one who, despite his careful hermeneutic,
is tortured for it.

Torture is not too strong a word for it, as both Toby and Feste's dogged
pursuit of Malvolio's borders on sociopathy. At one point, however, Toby
seemingly relents of the whole business of Malvolio's imprisonment and
exorcism over, telling his coconspirators, "I would we were well rid of this
knavery" (4.2.67–68). He recognizes it as the low form of entertainment it is,
on a par with bear- or bull-baiting, only worse because they are practicing on

a human being. Toby's belated compassion, however, is self-interested: "If he may be conveniently delivered, I would he were, for I am now so far in offense with my niece that I cannot pursue with any safety this sport to the upshot" (68–71). He argues for Malvolio's manumission, but only because Toby is so worried about offending Olivia that he can't carry his inhuman treatment of Malvolio to its conclusion, represented in his mind as a mere sporting event. With the exception of Malvolio, the game is well understood by all: as Toby and Maria come to witness the exorcism, Feste laconically notes, "The competitors enter." Were it not for being caught, they would torture Malvolio for sport, and in seeming perpetuity if they could.

TWELFTH NIGHT AND COMEDY

Finally, let us return briefly to the argument from chapter 1 concerning the routine practice of staging Shakespeare's plays in parish churches. Aside from the practicability of doing so when the companies toured the provinces, churches were uniquely amenable as performance venues for comedies. Moreover, as Berger remarks, comedy presents a world without real pain; real suffering opens onto the tragic, whereas comedy holds pain in abeyance. Thus,

> *Etsi Deus non daretur* [Even if God does not exist], every instance of the comic is an escape from reality. . . . The real world of empirical existence must in the end reassert itself; the counterempirical world of the comic must be seen as an illusion. Comedy is fundamentally counterfactual; tragedy reveals the hard facticity of the human condition. But as soon as all of this is perceived in the light of faith—*etsi Deus daretur*—the assertions of reality and illusion are reversed. It is the hard facts of the empirical world that are now seen as, if not illusion, a temporary reality that will eventually be superseded. Conversely, the painless worlds of the comic can now be seen as an adumbration of a world beyond this world.[61]

Comedies need not make this leap of faith into the religious—Berger allows for secular comedy, comedy "in a lower key"—but seen through the eyes of religious belief, aided and abetted by a (naturally) sympathetic staging in a church, the comic "presents not an illusion, but a vision of a world infinitely more real than all the realities of *this* world."[62] In this higher key, Sebastian and Viola's recognition scene points to "one manifestation of a sacramental universe . . . contain[ing] visible signs of visible grace."[63] Again, one need not read the play this way, but in the light of faith, which is precisely what its title seems to call for, and what staging *Twelfth Night* in a church encourages among its parishioners, "the comic becomes a great consolation and a witness to the redemption that is yet to come."[64] The upside-down world of comedy finds a congenial home in the counterworld—the otherworldliness—of the Church. It is scarcely a surprise that Shakespeare employs quasi-resurrections—the seeming return from the dead—in fourteen of his plays, and that eleven of these take place in the comedies and romances.[65]

The example of Sebastian and Viola's quasi-resurrection points to a world without pain where, as the mystic Julian of Norwich prophesied, all manner of thing shall be well. This is at once the prospective world of the Church and the hoped-for, but as yet unrealized, playworld of *Twelfth Night*. The Epiphany stands as a manifestation of God's love and the inauguration of a kingdom of peace on earth and good will toward men (see Luke 2:14). As yet, however, that kingdom has not fully come, at least not to Illyria. Such a kingdom might be the "what you will" of the subtitle's open-ended framing of the play's action, but for now we will have to content ourselves with Orsino's offer to "entreat [Malvolio] to a peace" (5.1.380), the prospective but as yet unrealized reconciliation of these imperfect human beings. Against the comic and possibly even gracious closure of Viola and Sebastian's reunion, Shakespeare offers us the counterpoint of Feste's more mundane refrain, "the rain it raineth every day" (392), with Malvolio ungraciously shut outside the circle of human grace.

NOTES

1. John Manningham, *Diary of John Manningham*, ed. John Bruce (London: Camden Society, 1963), 18.
2. *The Diary of John Manningham of the Middle Temple, 1602–1603.*, ed. Robert Parker Sorlien (Hanover, NH: University Press of New England, 1976), 218.
3. Karen Greif, "Plays and Playing in Twelfth Night," in *Twelfth Night: Critical Essays*, ed. Stanley Wells (New York: Garland, 1986), 270.
4. David Bevington, ed., *The Complete Works of Shakespeare*, 7th edition (Boston: Pearson, 2014), 336.
5. Garber, *Shakespeare After All* (New York: Anchor, 2005), 530; Harold Bloom, *Shakespeare: The Invention of the Human* (New York: Riverhead, 1998), 238.
6. Hans-Georg Gadamer, *Truth and Method*, trans. Joel Weinsheimer and Donald G. Marshall, 2nd rev. ed. (New York: Continuum, 1999), 164.
7. Bruce, *Diary of John Manningham*, 18.
8. Critics have speculated wildly in their effort to interpret M. O. A. I. For a review of the literature, see Peter J. Smith, "M. O. A. I. 'What Should That Alphabetical Position Portend?': An Answer to the Metamorphic Malvolio," *Renaissance Quarterly* 51, no. 4 (1998): 1199–224.
9. David E. Linge, "Editor's Introduction," in Hans-Georg Gadamer, *Philosophical Hermeneutics*, ed. and trans. David E. Linge (Berkeley: University of California Press, 1977), xii.
10. Keir Elam, ed., *Twelfth Night*, 3rd ed. (London: Arden Shakespeare, 2009), 220n.
11. David Bevington, *The Complete Works of Shakespeare*, Longman, 336; Sean Benson, "'Perverse Fantasies'?: Rehabilitating Malvolio's Reading," *Papers on Language & Literature* 45, no. 3 (Summer 2009): 264–68.
12. Peter Milward, "The Religious Dimension of Shakespeare's Illyria," in *Shakespeare and the Mediterranean*, ed. Thomas Clayton, Susan Brock, and Vicente Forés (Newark: University of Delaware Press, 2004), 382.

13. Maurice Hunt, *Shakespeare's Religious Allusiveness: Its Play and Tolerance* (Burlington, VT: Ashgate, 2003), 80. For a corroborating view, see Stevie Davies's *William Shakespeare*, Twelfth Night (New York: Penguin, 1993), 96–105.

14. The controversy over hermeneutics can hardly be overstated and is well documented. See, for instance, Alan J. Hauser and Duane F. Watson, eds., *A History of Biblical Interpretation* (3 vols. Grand Rapids: W. B. Eerdmans, 2003–) esp. vol. 2; Werner Schwarz's *Principles and Problems of Biblical Translation* (Cambridge: Cambridge University Press, 1955); and Gerald Bray's "The Renaissance and Reformation," *Biblical Interpretation: Past and Present* (Downers Grove, IL: Intervarsity Press, 1996), 165–224.

15. Quoted in James Simpson, *Burning to Read: English Fundamentalism and Its Reformation Opponents* (Cambridge: Belknap Press of Harvard University Press, 2007), 54. The translation is Simpson's. For the Latin text, see *Enchiridion Symbolorum, Definitionum et Declarationum de Rebus Fidei et Morum*, eds. Henricus Denziger and Adolphus Schönmetzer's (Barcelona: Herder, 1967), 366.

16. John Foxe, *The Acts and Monuments*, ed. George Townsend (New York: AMS Press, 1965), 1226.

17. John Milton, *Complete Prose Works of John Milton*, ed. Don M. Wolfe, vol. 1 (New Haven: Yale University Press, 1953), 592.

18. This is not to deny the persistence of English Catholicism, which faced active persecution in Elizabeth's reign. For the history of that perseverance, see especially Eamon Duffy, *The Stripping of the Altars: Traditional Religion in England, c.1400–c.1580* (New Haven: Yale University Press, 1992); and Robert S. Miola's *Early Modern Catholicism: An Anthology of Primary Sources* (Oxford: Oxford, 2007). "Papistry" was a continuing target among evangelical polemicists, but increasingly the derogatory term was directed by Puritans at practices within the Church of England. See also Simpson, *Burning to Read*, 179.

19. T. Edlyn Tomlins, ed., *The Statutes of the Realm*, vol. 3 (London: Dawsons, 1963), 894.

20. Simpson, *Burning to Read*, 30, brackets his. Simpson believes that "Protestant" is the incorrect term to use; he uses "evangelical" instead.

21. Milward, "The Religious Dimension," 382–83, argues that Feste adopts the role of a Puritan curate.

22. Quoted in Gadamer, *Truth and Method*, 185.

23. A. D. Nuttall, *Shakespeare the Thinker* (New Haven: Yale University Press, 2007), 241.

24. Maria would seem to disagree with this ascription of Malvolio's religious affiliation when she says, "The devil a puritan that he is, or anything constantly, but a time-pleaser" (line 146). Her point, however, is not that Malvolio is not a Puritan, but rather that if he is one (and she is the one who had declared it so), it is overshadowed by his inconstancy, his "time-pleasing."

25. Hunt, *Shakespeare's Religious Allusiveness*, 80; Milward, "The Religious Dimension," 380–87; Jeffrey Knapp, *Shakespeare's Tribe: Church, Nation, and Theater in Renaissance England* (Chicago: University of Chicago Press, 2002), 174.

26. Garber, *Shakespeare After All*, 529.

27. Northrop Frye, *A Natural Perspective: The Development of Shakespearean Comedy and Romance* (New York: Columbia University Press, 1965), 65.

28. William Tyndale, *Tyndale's Old Testament: Being the Pentateuch of 1530, Joshua to 2 Chronicles of 1537, and Jonah*, ed. David Daniell (New Haven: Yale University Press, 1992), 8.

29. Lawrence A Sasek, *Images of English Puritanism: A Collection of Contemporary Sources, 1589–1646* (Baton Rouge: Louisiana State University Press, 1989), 218–19.

30. Thomas Hobbes, *Behemoth: The History of the Causes of the Civil Wars of England*, ed. William Molesmith (New York: B. Franklin, 1963), 28.

31. Hunt, *Shakespeare's Religious Allusiveness*, 79.

32. Tomlins, *The Statutes of the Realm*, 3: 895.

33. Simpson, *Burning to Read*, 30.

34. J. L. Simmons, "A Source for Shakespeare's Malvolio: The Elizabethan Controversy with the Puritans," *Huntington Library Quarterly* 36, no. 3 (May 1, 1973): 181.

35. David Willbern, "Malvolio's Fall," *Shakespeare Quarterly* 29, no. 1 (January 1, 1978): 87.

36. Nuttall, *Shakespeare the Thinker*, 246.

37. Aristotle, *Poetics*, in *The Complete Works of Aristotle: The Revised Oxford Translation*, ed. Jonathan Barnes, trans. I. Bywater, vol. 2, Bollingen Series 71:2 (Princeton: Princeton University Press, 1995), 1460a1.

38. On evangelicals' resistance to "private interpretation," see Simpson, *Burning to Read*, 134–37.

39. *Oxford English Dictionary (OED)*, s.v. "affect."

40. In 2.2 Malvolio "returns" the ring that Olivia is actually giving to Viola as a cryptic token of affection. Viola figures this out, Malvolio does not, and thus it could be argued that the scene demonstrates how Viola is a more astute reader than Malvolio. Yet Malvolio was *not* present during Olivia and Viola's conversation, has no knowledge that Viola gave no ring to Olivia on Orsino's behalf, and is subsequently told that the ring should be returned by way of the servant (1.5.301–02). Malvolio is simply—understandably—ignorant of what happened between Olivia and Viola. Viola picks up on the subtext (she knows she gave Olivia no ring), but there is no reason that Malvolio should. The scene shows how carefully Malvolio follows Olivia's instructions, and he has no reason (much less inclination) to see the returning of the ring as anything other than another refusal of Orsino's importuning.

41. *OED*, s.v. "complexion."

42. When he later appears before Olivia cross-gartered (3.4), he quotes from the letter, yet makes no mention of the anagram. The absence of his mentioning it cannot constitute dispositive evidence of his wariness to recite it to her, but the absence is striking because M. O. A. I. is the closest Maria ever comes to using his name in the letter.

43. The Catholic Church, for instance, insists that the Bible must be construed alongside the traditions of oral teachings from the time of the apostles on. The teaching authority of the Church, the Magisterium, informs Roman Catholicism's understanding of scripture.

44. Patrick Collinson, "Antipuritanism," in *The Cambridge Companion to Puritanism*, eds. John Coffey and Paul Chang-Ha Lim (Cambridge: Cambridge University Press, 2008), 30.

45. Peter Lake, "'A Charitable Christian Hatred': The Godly and Their Enemies in the 1630s," in *The Culture of English Puritanism: 1560–1700*, eds. Christopher Durston and Jacqueline Eales (New York: St. Martin's Press, 1996), 148.

46. Garber, *Shakespeare After All*, 517.

47. This reference has never been historically identified, but there are ample examples of such marriages. John Webster's *The Duchess of Malfi* (1614) is another literary example based on historical precedents.

48. Stephen Booth, *Precious Nonsense: The Gettysburg Address, Ben Jonson's Epitaphs on His Children, and* Twelfth Night (Berkeley: University of California Press, 1998), 147.

49. Nuttall flatly denies this point, arguing that Shakespeare "writes as if the Reformation hasn't even happened—and we are all friends" (20). He further adds that "his plays are eloquent of nothing so much as a rosy unconsciousness of division. Neither the Reformation nor the shock waves it produced in the counter-Reformation of Catholicism—the Council of Trent—make any palpable impression on the plays" (17). While I respect Nuttall's fine criticism, the weight of critical opinion is against him here.

50. Catechetical instruction was pervasive during Elizabeth's reign: Margaret Spufford, "'I Bought Me a Primer,' or, 'How Godly Were the Multitude?': The Basic Religious Concepts of Those Who Could Read in the Seventeenth Century," in *The World of Rural Dissenters, 1520–1725*, ed. Margaret Spufford (Cambridge: Cambridge University Press, 1995), 73, estimates that by the time the play was written, over one million catechisms were in circulation among an English population of approximately four million. See also Beatrice Groves, *Texts and Traditions: Religion in Shakespeare, 1592–1604* (Oxford: Oxford University Press, 2007), 13–14.

51. By way of contrast, Lady Capulet had told Juliet it would be an easy task: "Read o'er the volume of young Paris' face, / And find delight writ there with beauty's pen" (*RJ*, 1.3.82–3).

52. Gadamer would have no problem with the textualizing of persons, as he emphasizes the intersubjective, dialectical nature of understanding. A text can be one of the subjects that must

Chapter 2

interact with another subject, a reader, but so too can readers be counterpoised against one another as objects of interpretation (as we shall see with Viola and Sebastian) with no literal text present. Roger Ebertz, in "Beyond Worldview Analysis: Insights from Hans-Georg Gadamer on Christian Scholarship," *Christian Scholar's Review* 36, no. 1 (Fall 2006): 14, also notes, "In the full course of his works, Gadamer extends the same model beyond texts to all objects of study or interpretation. In seeking to understand a text, or another person."

53. Gadamer, *Truth and Method*, 269.

54. Ibid.

55. Lloyd E. Berry and William Whittingham, eds., *The Geneva Bible: A Facsimile of the 1560 Edition* (Madison: University of Wisconsin Press, 1969), John 20:17; Lewis, "Soft Touch"; Cynthia Lewis, "Viola's 'Do Not Embrace Me' as Icon," *Notes and Queries* 35 (233), no. 4 (December 1988): 473–474. See, too, Sean Benson, *Shakespearean Resurrection: The Art of Almost Raising the Dead* (Pittsburgh: Duquesne University Press, 2009), 55–58.

56. For an alternative view in which this scene "contains no promise of transcendent fulfillment," see Ko, "The Comic Close of Twelfth Night and Viola's Noli Me Tangere," 398. The play evokes the language of the Resurrection, substituting in its place the romance convention of a recognition scene (Aristotle's *anagnorisis*) between the twins. Such may not be, strictly speaking, transcendent fulfillment, but the quasi-resurrection—Shakespeare's evocation of the sacred in the midst of the mundane—succeeds well enough in most stage and film productions I have seen.

57. Hans Urs von Balthasar, *Theo-Drama: Theological Dramatic Theory*, volume 1: *Prolegomena*, trans. Graham Harrison (San Francisco: Ignatius Press, 1988), 1:384.

58. Aristotle, *Poetics*, 1460a1.

59. Nuttall, *Shakespeare the Thinker*, 243.

60. Bevington for one glosses "conceived against him" as "seen and resented in him," which would indicate that they are merely observing Malvolio's character flaws, not "devising" them, as Evans glosses the word in the Riverside edition. *OED* notes that "conceive" can mean "observe," but this is a rare usage. Much more common is the connotation "imagined," which is figuratively connected with the literal sense of giving birth to, the primary meaning of the word. Shakespeare's use of the word here suggests that Malvolio's detractors may be exaggerating any faults they do observe.

61. Peter L. Berger, *Redeeming Laughter: The Comic Dimension of Human Experience* (New York: Walter de Gruyter, 1997), 210.

62. Ibid., 210–11, italics his.

63. Ibid., 214.

64. Ibid., 215.

65. Benson, *Shakespearean Resurrection*, 2.

Chapter Three

"Monsters of the Deep"

King Lear *and the Problem of Evil*

If the first two chapters demonstrate Shakespeare's concern for religious toleration, as well as the natural affinity between church and theater, chapters 3 and 4 examine his interest in more radical challenges to traditional religious belief. A number of critics have argued that the tragedies in particular present a movement (perhaps even a personal one on Shakespeare's part) toward religious or philosophical nihilism. George Santayana put the point bluntly:

> But for Shakespeare, in the matter of religion, the choice lay between Christianity and nothing. He chose nothing; he chose to leave his heroes and himself in the presence of life and of death with no other philosophy than that which the profane world can suggest and understand. [1]

King Lear is the usual linchpin in this argument, and chapter 3 examines the critical view that the play depicts a hostile or godless universe. Chapter 4, in turn, examines the theological possibility of corpses reviving and coming back to harm the living. This is, as we shall see, an impossibility in Reformed theology, but it has a distinct presence in English folklore and in the beliefs of pre-Christian cultures, and Shakespeare is not averse to exploring the possibility of the living dead walking the streets of ancient Rome, as well as the ramparts of *Hamlet*'s Elsinore. Together, these two chapters examine how Shakespeare engages religious skepticism and heterodoxy. The Church has its own systematic theologies and apologias, some of which Shakespeare draws upon in elegant ways, but he also casts an imaginative eye to the challenges heterodoxy represents to traditional belief, as well as to our under-standing of who we are and our place in a providential or godless universe.

The problem of evil in *King Lear* is particularly acute, so serious that many critics believe the play offers Shakespeare's bleakest vision of the world, one that purportedly subverts belief in divine providence and moves in the direc-tion of nihilism.[2] William Elton thought that the play depicts the "annihila-tion of faith in poetic justice" and offers as its *mise-en-scène* a "grimly dark and God-forsaken world."[3] Indeed, the play world in *Lear* has so often been construed as a place *without* God that literary critics increasingly regard the issue as having been decisively settled.[4] "On this ultimate stage of fools," writes Marvin Rosenberg, "no one—except possibly Lear dying in illusion—is so foolish as to see any evidence of divinity at work."[5] Joseph Wittreich, too, suggests that what renders any and all theistically tinged perspectives "inadequate to the play is the realization, finally, that while *not* being denied a place in the cosmos God *is* being written out of the world of *King Lear*." Moreover, he adds, "If this is a Christian tragedy it is one that decimates the Christian myth."[6]

Reacting against such views, Maynard Mack demurred to what he called this "fashionable existentialist *nausée*" that sees in the play the idea

> that "we inhabit an imbecile universe." Perhaps we do—but Shakespeare's *King Lear* provides no evidence of it that till now we lacked. . . . Shakespeare can hardly have imagined that in *King Lear*'s last scene he was telling his audiences something they had never known, or was casting his solemn vote on one side or other of the vexing philosophical and theological questions in-volved in the suffering of the innocent and good. The scene has, besides, his characteristic ambiguity and balance. No world beyond this one in which "all manner of things will be well" is asserted; but neither is it denied.[7]

While Mack steers a middle course of what we might call interpretive agnos-ticism, it scarcely seems adequate in light of the tremendous suffering that occurs in the play. Surely critics such as Elton are not amiss to see in state-ments such as Gloucester's "As flies to wanton boys are we to th' gods; / They kill us for their sport" (4.1.36–37) some sort of deep reflection on the benevolence or, as is more routinely asserted, the lack thereof in the cosmos.

Drawing upon the work of Alvin Plantinga, I will offer a free will defense of the problem of evil in *King Lear*. In so doing, I am neither attempting a proof of God's existence nor proposing a Miltonian theodicy or justification of "the ways of God to men."[8] I argue instead merely for the logical possibil-ity of his existence within the *Lear* frame, and in doing so, I offer a rebuttal to the implicit warrant in much of the scholarship relating to the cosmology in *King Lear*; namely, that the play is structured in such a way as to demon-strate the logical impossibility of God's existence in a world containing moral evil. My task is to show that it is not only logically possible, but also that Shakespeare's characters (imitating human beings, their models) would make at least one morally evil choice in any world that Shakespeare (or God) could have actualized. If the moral choices Shakespeare's characters make are intended to be seen as being significantly free, as I believe they are, then it was not in Shakespeare's mimetic power as an artist "to create a world containing moral good but no moral evil."[9]

"Of all Shakespeare's plays," as Alison Shell remarks, "*King Lear* has most often lent itself to an atheistical reading,"[10] and I want to focus on the logic of these arguments. Let us begin, then, with David Loewenstein's statement of the problem of evil in *King Lear*. He has cogently argued "that Shakespeare was capable of taking great risks when it came to dramatizing religious beliefs (or their absence) and daring enough to write a drama that imagines a dark, pitiless world without God or gods in an age in which providential thinking dominated religious culture."[11] Indeed, Shakespeare's thought was heterodox enough to explore precisely this daring possibility. Yet Loewenstein goes further, arguing not for the mere possibility of a godless world in *Lear*, but for its dramatic embodiment: "Shakespeare wrote a radical play flaunting the very idea of providentialism and the belief in an interventionist deity who responds to human misery, chaos, injustice, and savagery."[12] For Loewenstein, as for other critics, *Lear* depicts human viciousness and suffering—Gloucester's blinding, for instance—and while Shakespeare could have, like many pious writers of the day, provided a theistic framework to mitigate or explain such evil, *King Lear* instead "offers no sense of any kind of providential order to explain its harsh dramatization of human suffering."[13]

Likewise, in response to Lear's late and momentary hope, "This feather stirs; she lives! If it be so, / It is a chance which does redeem all sorrows / That ever I have felt" (5.3.270–72), Greenblatt asks

> What would it mean to "redeem" Lear's sorrows? To buy them back from the chaos and brute meaninglessness they now seem to signify? To reward the king with a gift so great that it outweighs the sum of misery in his entire life? To reinterpret his pain as the necessary preparation—the price to be paid—for a consummate bliss? In the theater such reinterpretation would be represented by a spectacular turn in the plot—a surprise unmasking, a sudden reversal of fortunes, a resurrection—and this dramatic redemption, however secularized, would almost invariably recall the consummation devoutly wished by centuries of Christian believers. . . . *If it be so*: Lear's sorrows are not redeemed; nothing can turn them into joy, but the forlorn hope of an impossible redemption persists, drained of its institutional and doctrinal significance, empty and vain, cut off even from a theatrical realization.[14]

In Greenblatt's typically powerful reading, only the prospect of a resurrection could compensate for such horrific suffering that has rendered Lear's life one of "brute meaninglessness."

The warrant in both Greenblatt's and Loewenstein's arguments is that in order to show God exists and is just, Shakespeare would have to evoke a miracle play—a staged theodicy—in the midst of *King Lear*'s pre-Christian setting: "a truly Christian play would have to dramatize the miraculous intervention of the gods or otherwise catch them red-handed as they intrude into the affairs of men."[15] At Gloucester's blinding, a servant calls out, "Now, heaven help him!" (3.7.111), and Loewenstein is surely correct to comment here that the play "raises the possibility that providence, or an equivalent supernatural power, might intervene on the behalf of the miserable Gloucester."[16] What the play offers instead is silence, a disturbing divine aporia: "no kind of religious order or assurance of justice operates; in this tragedy there is no evidence that divine vengeance is ever executed, despite the language characters use to invoke it."[17] R. A. Foakes concurs: "Characters invoke the gods when it suits them, but there is no sign that the gods listen, or are even there."[18] For such critics, absence of evidence of divine participation in human affairs constitutes evidence of absence: God is most likely nonexistent. Although I would agree that this possibility is firmly embedded in the framework of the play—part of Shakespeare's wonderful heterodoxy—godlessness is hardly the only contingency we are offered.

Jonathan Dollimore, too, objects to the use of metaphysical language both in the play (e.g., Gloucester's "Grace go with you, sir!" [5.2.4]) and from "redemptionist" critics who attempt to invest characters with a divine essence or soul.[19] When Cordelia and Lear die, Albany voices what Dollimore considers the utterly unpersuasive view of a god who redeems:

> when [Albany] cries "The Gods defend her!"—i.e., Cordelia—instead of the process being firmly consolidated we witness, even before he has finished speaking, Lear re-entering with Cordelia dead in his arms. Albany has one last desperate bid for recuperation, still within the old punitive / poetic terms:
>
> All friends shall taste
>
> The wages of their virtue, and all foes
>
> The cup of their deservings. (5.3.308–10)
>
>   Seconds later, Lear dies. The timing of these two deaths *must surely* be seen as cruelly, precisely subversive.[20]

In Dollimore's cultural materialist reading, the very idea of divine justice is untenable, absurd even, in the face of such suffering. On one level, Dollimore offers a hermeneutic: Albany speaks of heavenly justice, but Lear and

Cordelia both die, and thus we "must surely" interpret their deaths as an ironic critique of Albany's position. Loewenstein likewise regards all such "appeals to supernatural powers" as "bitterly ironic."[21] But is this how Shakespeare works; does he debunk ideas so heavy-handedly? Is he thus disabusing us of belief in divine justice? This is plausible, I suppose, but it seems unlikely; Greer suggests that those who would embrace an atheistic reading have missed the point:

> It would be a mistake to interpret the futility of Lear's appeals to his gods as evidence of atheism on Shakespeare's part. Rather, like Montaigne, he denies man's right to scan the ways of God or to assume that God's will coincides at any point with his own. This Christian skepticism is neither pessimistic nor cynical, for it is based in acceptance of the benighted human condition.[22]

Lear's seemingly futile appeals to the gods, along with his death soon after Albany's profession of divine justice, tantalize us: they raise hermeneutic problems that ask us whether we ought to regard such moments as endorsing atheism or, on the other hand, Job-like patience. As Hannibal Hamlin has shown, the language of Job suffuses the play,[23] and a theological reading based on an acceptance of the benighted human condition is as plausible as an atheological reading; together, these contradictory interpretations reflect an ambivalence and religious exploration at the heart of the play. Shakespeare is thus portraying orthodox and heterodox (or even, from a pious perspective, blasphemous) understandings of the world. I would like to elaborate on this case for a religiously orthodox interpretation of the play, but to do so, I need first to examine in detail the philosophical argument for God's nonexistence in the playworld of *King Lear*.

Let us first recast the atheistic reading of *King Lear* so as to see its participation in a long history, one dating to Epicurus, of engagement with the philosophical problem of evil. Consider, for instance, David Hume's justly famous formulation of the problem: "Is [God] willing to prevent evil, but not able? Then is he impotent. Is he able, but not willing? Then is he malevolent. Is he both able and willing? Whence then is evil?"[24] John Mackie offers a contemporary form of the argument that renders explicit the premises that are implicit in almost all iterations of the atheistic reading of *King Lear*: "In its simplest form the problem [of evil] is this: God is omnipotent; God is wholly good; yet evil exists."[25] As a set of propositions:

1. God is omnipotent
2. God is wholly good
3. Evil exists.[26]

Most theists accept the truth of all three propositions. For Hume and Mackie, these three propositions—irrespective of their truth value as independent statements—constitute an inconsistent set; that is, there is a logical contradiction between the conjunction of the first two propositions and the third. Those who propound an atheistic reading of *Lear* clearly accept the truth of (3) as self-evident within the play, and they also seem to accept for the sake of the argument the perfect being theology that assigns to God both omnipotence and absolute goodness. They further assume that God's omnipotence affords him the power to let the good "taste / The wages of their virtue" and the wicked the "cup of their deservings." The atheological reading also stipulates that a good god *ought* to orchestrate matters so that people get their fair share in this life. Notably—tellingly—absent from their analysis is any consideration *sub specie aeternitatis*, of a life hereafter.[27] If God, in this view, were all-powerful and wholly good, then as a consequence of these qualities he both could and would overcome all evil in this life, or simply remove it. Instead, when Albany declares that everyone will receive their just desserts, Lear dies, and thus the timing of his and Cordelia's deaths "must surely"— note the logical necessity in Dollimore's phrasing—be "subversive." What is subverted in his view is any traditional notion of a powerful and benevolent god who loves and cares for his creation. Since evil exists so palpably in *King Lear*, God most likely does not exist or, if he does, he does so not in the "old punitive / poetic" terms represented most notably in the Bible. Either way, the idea of a personal God concerned with the wellbeing of his creatures is largely and perhaps entirely null and void.

As a way of beginning to address the atheistic reading of *King Lear*, one could argue that many of the characters do get the cup of their deservings, especially Goneril, Regan, Cornwall, and Edmund. Moreover, "with Albany, Edgar, and Kent now in power, it is by no means clear that divine justice, long delayed as it is (and at a cost), is simply frustrated."[28] Yet one has to grant that evil and suffering exist in the play and cannot simply be discounted: Gloucester is blinded, Cordelia is hanged just before the "token of reprieve" arrives to spare her life (5.3.254), and Lear also succumbs to death. Samuel Johnson's response was one of all-but-professional avoidance: "I was many years ago so shocked by Cordelia's death that I know not whether I ever endured to read again the last scenes of the play till I undertook to revise them as an editor."[29] Whatever one might wish to say about *King Lear*, one cannot deny the problem of moral evil that it presents. Indeed, so prominent is the problem in *King Lear* that Dollimore feels no need to belabor his claim that the play indicts theistic belief: "I do not mean to argue again the case against the Christian view since, even though it is still sometimes advanced, it has been effectively discredited."[30] The opposite, though, is true: the deductive problem of evil as it has been articulated since the time of Epicurus has been thoroughly disproven and discredited by Plantinga's free will defense.

With the problem now in mind, let us turn to a couple of propositions implicit in almost all atheolocial readings of the play, beginning with the idea that "a good thing always eliminates evil as far as it can."[31] There may be exceptions to this, as when a good state of affairs (*G*) outweighs some evil state of affairs (*E*), as in the simple algebraic equation $G > E$. Plantinga offers the following example: "there are people who display a sort of creative moral heroism in the face of suffering and adversity—a heroism that inspires others and creates a good situation out of a bad one."[32] One could argue this of Lear, of Cordelia, perhaps of Edgar and Gloucester as well. After their loss in battle, for instance, Edgar tells Gloucester, "Men must endure / Their going hence, even as their coming hither; / Ripeness is all" (5.2.9–11). Cordelia displays the same heroic equanimity in defeat: "We are not the first / Who with best meaning have incurred the worst. / For thee, oppressèd King, I am cast down; / Myself could else outfrown false Fortune's frown" (5.3.3–6). But as those who have advanced an atheistic reading point out, the suffering these characters undergo seems to outweigh any good state of affairs: $E > G$. Thus, the events of the play render dubious an optimistic—one might even say wishful—accounting of the problem of evil in *King Lear*. For the sake of the argument, then, I will concede that whatever heroic good these characters display does not outweigh or even balance the evil they suffer in the play.

Second, atheological interpretations almost always imply that there are absolutely no limits to what an omnipotent being can do. This is a crucial error. There are, to be sure, no *nonlogical* limits to what an omnipotent being can do, but there are a number of logical limitations. No one can create married bachelors or square circles; doing so renders logic incoherent. Here then is the key question: would God's eliminating evil also be nonlogical? In other words, if God is a good and all-powerful being, would he not eliminate evil in this life? If Shakespeare wanted to weigh in on the side of a theistic reading of *King Lear*, then he—so goes the atheistic argument—would wipe the play's slate of evil clean. Since evil exists in *King Lear*, and is arguably overwhelming, many critics persist in thinking that Shakespeare presents us with the inescapable conclusion of God's nonexistence. In a free will defense, however, God's elimination of evil would indeed be nonlogical, impossible. Were Shakespeare to use some *deus ex machina*, as he does with the "fire from heaven" that destroys the wicked in *Pericles* (2.4.9); or to revise *King Lear* as Nahum Tate did in 1681 so as to save Lear and Cordelia, he would violate the tragic realism of his play. More important, he would also violate his characters' freedom of action.

To understand this, we first need to note that Mackie (along with many of those who argue for *Lear* as an atheist play) is a philosophical compatibilist—he believes that divine determinism and human free will are compatible:

"If God has made men such that in their free choices they sometimes prefer what is good and sometimes what is evil, why could he not have made men such that they always freely choose the good?"[33] Mackie is drawing upon Leibniz's notion (*Théodicée*, 1710) of *possible worlds*:[34] the actual world we inhabit appears to be quite contingent—it could have been otherwise—and thus there are many possible worlds, some of which, such as our own, are actualized or come into being, while others do not. Writers have this quasi-divine power in the fictions they create:

> The poet's eye, in a fine frenzy rolling,
>
> Doth glance from heaven to earth, from earth to heaven;
>
> And as imagination bodies forth
>
> The forms of things unknown, the poet's pen
>
> Turns them to shapes and gives to airy nothing
>
> A local habitation and a name. (*MND* 5.1.12–17)

Shakespeare is quite familiar with possible worlds. In *The Winter's Tale*, for instance, a gentleman describes the reaction of Leontes and Camillo when the old shepherd reveals to them how he found Perdita, whom they had presumed to be dead: "They looked as they had heard of a world ransomed, or one destroyed. A notable passion of wonder appeared in them." (5.2.15–17). As part of his rich artistic syncretism, not to mention his heterodox thinking, Shakespeare mixes the pre-Christian setting of the play, complete with its Delphic oracle, with this subtle allusion to Christ's ransoming of souls: "the Sonne of man came not to be served, but to serve, and to give his life for the ransome of manie."[35] It is a possible world envisioned at the margins of the pagan world the characters inhabit.

Shakespeare not only actualizes possible worlds, but he also conceives of other contingent worlds that may or may not come into being on his stage. The Celtic Lear legend is itself clearly contingent: it exists first in the fictive world of Geoffrey of Monmouth's *Historia regum Britanniae* (ca. 1135) and then in later redactions, the most important of which for Shakespeare—the one on which he based his play—was the anonymous *The True Chronicle History of King Leir* (pub. 1605). Even within the framework of Shakespeare's *King Lear*, various characters contest the world as they find it. The bastard Edmund, for instance, regards the law of primogeniture as both unjust and contingent: "Wherefore should I / Stand in the plague of custom and permit / The curiosity of nations to deprive me, / For that I am some twelve or fourteen moonshines / Lag of a brother?" (1.2.2–6). Edmund would replace such arbitrary social conventions with the Darwinian "goddess" "Nature" who has created him with "more composition and fierce quality" than she has bestowed on his legitimate brother Edgar (lines 1, 12).

To give Mackie his due, it is possible that there are worlds where human beings choose only the good. If God exists, he could have made human beings in such a way that they always choose the good, but the problem is that if they are made in such a way (i.e., determined) always to choose good over evil, does this not render the notion of their *freely* doing so suspect, if not absurd? As Milton suggests concerning the prospect of angels being compelled, willy-nilly, to serve God, "Can hearts, not free, be tried whether they serve / Willing or no, who will but what they must / By destiny and can no other choose?"[36] In other words, how can a human being determined always to act in one way freely act in another? Shakespeare could have exercised similar control in the worlds of his plays, but they would then certainly lose their verisimilitude. One could argue that Shakespeare already exercises such control because he determines how his characters react, but Stanley Cavell rebuts the assertion by appealing to Shakespeare's remarkable ability to create lifelike characters: "The actors are determined—not because their words and actions are dictated and their future sealed, but because, if the dramatist has really peopled a world, the characters are exercising all the freedom at their command. . . . They are, in a word, men and women."[37]

Hegel famously claimed that in creating characters who act like real human beings, Shakespeare "makes them free artists of their own selves,"[38] a view Cavell corroborates specifically in relation to the characters in *King Lear*: "these figures are radically and continuously *free*, operating under their own power, at every moment choosing their destruction."[39] Their freedom to choose has every appearance of being an attempt on Shakespeare's part to mimic human freedom of action. This is natural: plays are fundamentally, as Aristotle observed, imitations of human actions performed by characters who are recognizably similar to real human beings.[40] "The purpose of playing," as Hamlet instructs the actors come to Elsinore, "is to hold as 'twere the mirror up to nature" (*Ham.* 3.2.20–22), and the natural world, with its complement of human beings, contains both moral good and evil. Let us assume, then, that Shakespeare's characters are free to act, and that this freedom corresponds (by way of mimesis) to the creaturely freedom of action that humans exercise in the moral decisions they make.[41] One might quibble about what precisely is evil in the play, but if one defines moral good as that which leads to human flourishing, and moral evil as that which leads to human suffering, then it is easy to regard Gloucester's blinding or Cordelia's hanging as evil. But we need even not argue the point, since those who advance an atheistic reading of the play stipulate as a fundamental basis of their position the overwhelming presence of moral evil in *King Lear*.

Unlike Mackie, however, Plantinga is a philosophical incompatibilist: he believes that determinism and human freedom of action are logically irreconcilable. The free will defense is, in essence, "the idea of *being free with respect to an action*."[42] Philosophers refer to this kind of freedom as *significant freedom*, or as the *freedom of indifference*, which means that one is both free to perform an action and equally free to refrain from performing it. If God determines that people will always choose what is good, then in an incompatibilist understanding they are not significantly free. But if people have significant freedom, that very freedom creates or allows for an unfortunate contingency:

> some of the free creatures God created went wrong in the exercise of their freedom; this is the source of moral evil. The fact that free creatures sometimes go wrong, however, counts neither against God's omnipotence nor against His goodness; for He could have forestalled the occurrence of moral evil only by removing the possibility of moral good.[43]

The question arises as to why God would not create beings who never go wrong in their moral choices; why give them the creaturely freedom to go wrong? Although this is philosophically vexing beyond the real purview of this chapter, John Hick offers one intriguing possibility:

> virtues which have been formed within the agent as a hard-won deposit of her own right decisions in situations of challenge and temptation, are intrinsically more valuable than virtues created within her readymade and without any effort on her own part.[44]

In traditional theology, both Catholic and Reformed churches, though circumscribed and influenced in part by various circumstances, are fundamentally free. Milton's God makes the point emphatically, noting that human beings are

authors to themselves in all

Both what they judge and what they choose, for so

I formed them free and free they must remain

Till they enthrall themselves. I else must change

Their nature and revoke the high decree,

Unchangeable, eternal, which ordained

Their freedom.[45]

To be sure, there are possible worlds where people always go right in their decisions, but those worlds correspond neither to the world of Shakespeare's plays nor to their usual (mimetic) model—the actual world. How is it, then, that in our world, as well as in Shakespeare's plays, God (or Shakespeare) could only do away with moral evil by also doing away with moral good?

For an answer, let us turn to the blinding of Gloucester. While he betrays an express and lawful command not to aid Lear—"Wast thou not charged at peril," Regan asks him (3.7.55)—it is nonetheless hard to argue that the punishment he faces—blinding—does not constitute a moral evil. The punishment goes well beyond "the form of justice" and is thus extra-judicial; it employs excessive violence; and its stated purpose is that of "revenge" (lines 7, 25–26). Cornwall acknowledges the moral evil of his blinding of Gloucester, "which men / May blame but not control" (27–28). Even John Calvin, who in some cases limits the freedom of the human will, nonetheless remarks that people understand the difference between right and wrong: "there are some general reflections about what is honorable . . . imprinted in the understanding of all people."[46] The servants, too, certainly see the action as morally blameworthy; the first servant even gives up his life in an attempt to defend Gloucester. But he is killed, after which Cornwall then has the freedom of indifference to remove Gloucester's eyes. We know the decision he makes—"Out, vile jelly!" (86)—but what is remarkable about this moment is its extraneousness to the sources.[47] None of the legends that contain the Lear story has a blinding scene; to include one, Shakespeare drags in the story of the blind Paphlagonian king from Philip Sidney's *Arcadia* (1590). In Sidney's telling, the old king was "by the hard-harted ungratefulness of a sonne of his, deprived, not onely of his kingdome . . . but of his sight, the riches which Nature graunts to the poorest creatures."[48] Shakespeare not only incorporates the scene, transferring the blinding to a daughter and son-in-law, but he also greatly expands upon it, exchanging Sidney's brief narrative account for a shockingly graphic staging of the deed—perhaps the single most horrific moment in Shakespeare's *oeuvre*. While the inclusion of the Sidney material allows Shakespeare to literalize Gloucester's symbolic blindness to his two sons' respective merits, it also, and more crucially, allows Shakespeare to present this act of torture for what it is.

Consider the moment before the decision is actually reached, either by Cornwall or, ultimately, by Shakespeare. Let us stipulate a state of affairs (*S*) in which Gloucester receives the conspiratorial letters and, as a consequence, sends Lear to Dover. Here are the two possibilities (represented as counterfactuals of freedom)[49] for what comes next:

> (1) If the state of affairs (*S*) had been obtained, Cornwall would have blinded Gloucester.

(2) If the state of affairs (*S*) had been obtained, Cornwall would not have blinded Gloucester.

There is no compulsion from the sources that either (1) or (2) takes place: Sidney's blinding of the Paphlagonian king has no ties to any of the Lear legends. Shakespeare pulls it in for its symbolic value, to be sure, but it is necessary neither to the plot nor to any exigencies of war. Adventitious as it is, the blinding is gratuitous, and as such it reflects Shakespeare's depiction of a grave moral evil.

Moreover, we know that in both versions of Shakespeare's play, a quarto of 1608 and the apparently revised folio version of 1623, (1) is true, and let us further assume that Cornwall is a free artist of himself (i.e., that he acts with significant freedom). With this in mind, then, if (1) is actual, then (2) is not possible for Shakespeare or—and here is the real point of Plantinga's argument—for God. (One can easily transpose this occurrence to the real world, for similar acts of horrific violence do in fact occur on a daily basis.) Now, (1) and (2) can't both be true by the law of noncontradiction. When a choice is made, other choices are foreclosed, and in this case if (1) is true, then (2) becomes logically impossible. But atheistic readings of the play insist that God, if he exists, ought to override creaturely freedom and thus to restrict either Cornwall's significant freedom, or to ride in and save the day with a miracle. Loewenstein suggests that this moment in *Lear* frustrates a theistic interpretation because neither "divine justice . . . nor evidence of God's 'wrath & revenging hand'" appears.[50] Yet as René Fortin observes, "it is not at all presumed in the mainstream of Christian orthodoxy that God will intervene on call for his faithful; nowhere is a god of sweetness and light promised to man on this earth."[51] "These," as Wittreich notes, "are the presumptions of Shakespeare's critic, not of his play, and certainly not of the play's scriptural counterpart."[52]

Another possibility exists than that of a *deus ex machina*; Plantinga explains it by way of an example in which a character Maurice, like Cornwall, has to make a choice. For the sake of illustrating the identical possibility within the world of *King Lear*, I will replace Maurice's name with that of Cornwall:

> whether or not it is within God's power to actualize it [i.e., a possible world] depends upon what [Cornwall] would do if he were free in a certain situation. Accordingly, there are any number of possible worlds such that it is partly up to [Cornwall] whether or not God can actualize them. It is, of course, up to God whether or not to create [Cornwall] and also up to God whether or not to make him free with respect to the action of [blinding Gloucester]. . . . But if He creates [Cornwall] and creates him free with respect to this action, then whether or not he actually performs the action is up to [Cornwall]—not God.[53]

In Plantinga's thinking, God weakly actualizes our world, which is in part brought to completion—strongly actualized—by the choices human beings make in the exercise of their significant freedom. In *King Lear*'s world, as well as our own, the exercise of significant freedom has consequences, even for God.

The various redactions of the Lear legend offer Shakespeare possible worlds he could have used to create his own version, and he considers multiple contingencies in the very midst of the scene: Goneril exhorts Cornwall to "pluck out his eyes" (3.7.5); Regan recommends that he "hang him instantly" (4); and the first servant demands that Cornwall cease and desist altogether. Cornwall's choice of blinding Gloucester appears to be freely made, and the moral evil of the choice is brought home by his servant: "Hold your hand, my lord! / I have served you ever since I was a child; / But better service have I never done you / Than now to bid you hold" (75–78). Once Cornwall's choice is made, however, it is impossible to effect proposition (2). This, along with other examples of moral evil in the play, so bothered Nahum Tate that he decided to revise *King Lear* to make it fit his idea of a world where good always triumphs over evil in this life. Although Tate retains Gloucester's blinding in his redaction of *King Lear*, he leaves him alive at the end of the play. To Gloster's "Now, gentle gods, give Gloster his discharge," Lear replies, "No, Gloster, thou hast business yet for life."[54] A world where good always and at every moment triumphs over evil is a possible world, but neither the one in which we live nor the one Shakespeare invokes in the play. Such miraculous events occur in *Pericles*, but that is a different kind of play altogether, and *The Tragedy of King Lear* need not follow its generic imprint.

It is also striking that at the close of *The True Chronicle History of King Leir*, Cordelia and the eponymous king win the war and survive for a few years afterward—they are robust enough to enjoy a continental sojourn. Leir tells his daughter and son-in-law, "Come, sonne and daughter, who did me advaunce, / Repose with me awhile, and then for Fraunce."[55] Yet *Leir* is something of an outlier among the sources on this point. In other sources upon which Shakespeare may have relied, Lear dies and she succeeds him— only to be overthrown and jailed by her nephews. Geoffrey of Monmouth, Raphael Holinshed, John Higgins, and Spenser all uniformly record Cordelia's imprisonment, despair, and suicide by hanging.[56] In the 1596 edition of *The Faerie Queene*, for instance, Cordelia rules peaceably for a time

Till that her sisters children, woxen strong

Through proud ambition, against her rebeld,

And overcommen kept in prison long,

Till wearie of that wretched life, her selfe she hong. (2.10.32.6–9)

Thus departing from Leir's triumphant account, but in a way consistent with
the other sources he knew, Shakespeare deepens the moral evil: Cordelia is
not only defeated, but is the victim, as the sources would have it, of suicide,
or, as *King Lear* has it, of homicide. Edmund gave the order for her death,
but did so in the service of Cordelia's sisters who, as Goneril's poisoning of
Regan shows (5.3.98–99), are not squeamish about sororicide. *King Lear*
never shies from horrific and even nihilistic violence.

Dollimore and Loewenstein regard such profusion of moral evil in the
play as deductive proof of God's nonexistence. But a deductive proof is
necessarily true—true in every possible world—yet it is possible that even in
the world of *King Lear* with its grave evils, God exists and is good. One can
adopt an atheistic reading of *Lear*, to be sure, but one cannot apply the
deductive problem of evil to it because that proof is, unfortunately, unsound.
As should be evident, I am persuaded by Plantinga's contention that, logically speaking, there are possible worlds God cannot actualize, one of which is a
world where significantly free creatures are capable of moral good but not of
moral evil. Atheistic readings of *King Lear*, following Leibniz and Mackie,
want God to be able to create any world whatsoever, even a world that is
logically impossible. A world where creatures have significant freedom but
cannot choose moral evil is, again, as illogical as the idea of married bachelors or square circles. God cannot ensure a world in which significantly free
creatures never go wrong. If God exists and is omnipotent, and yet it was not
in his power to create a world with moral good but not moral evil, then it
follows that it is possible for both God and evil to exist. Thus, the deductive
problem of evil has effectively been discredited, despite implicit attempts to
revive it in discussing *King Lear*.

But to return for a moment to Mackie's compelling demurral, a world in
which creatures can go wrong in the moral choices they make is not necessarily one in which they do; there are possible worlds where creatures might
only choose the good. For such a world to be obtained and not be illogical,
such creatures would have to enjoy a rationality that invariably overcomes
irrational or base impulses, perhaps even to experience an intrinsic goodness
or moral probity that would lead them always to make the right choice. Such
a scenario is envisioned by philosophical compatibilism and involves no
logical contradiction as a possible world. It is even possible that such beings
could enjoy significant freedom—they would have the freedom to go wrong,
but they would invariably choose the good. As Plantinga argues, however,
such worlds are impossible if creatures suffer from a malady he calls *transworld depravity*. If one has this condition, one goes wrong at least once in
one's moral choices. If creatures do not suffer from transworld depravity,

then a world where creatures only choose the good is possible: a person (P) who is significantly free would only go right with respect to an action (A) in a possible world (W). But if P in another possible world W' suffered from transworld depravity, all else being equal (that is, P is significantly free with respect to A) and W' were actual, then "P would go wrong with respect to A."[57] Such a world is logically possible, and it looks as if it resembles quite closely the world we live in, as well as the world of *King Lear*. The play functions, in this sense, as allegory, using fiction to point or gesture toward a world—our world—of nonfictional ideas and things.

Plantinga further remarks that not only is it possible that there are "persons who suffer from transworld depravity. More generally, it is possible that *everybody* suffers from it."[58] *King Lear* would appear to be a case in point. Lear seems to suffer from transworld depravity in his decision to divide his kingdom and disown Cordelia. She seems to suffer from a mild case of it in her initial refusal to say "nothing" of her love and respect for him (1.1.87). Edmund also suffers from it, as do Regan, Goneril, Cornwall, Oswald, and arguably others as well. There is in fact no shortage of characters who go wrong with respect to their actions. If people do suffer from transworld depravity, then not even an all-powerful god could "create any of the possible worlds containing . . . moral good but no moral evil" because such persons would "go wrong with respect to at least one action in any world God could have actualized."[59] Of course, for the theist the inductive problem of evil remains—how does one explain God's goodness in a world where natural disasters, for instance, cause great human suffering. Lear's senescence and perhaps his death appear to be examples of natural as opposed to moral evil. As vexing as the inductive problem of evil is for theists, it is not our concern here. Atheistic readings of *Lear* invoke reason to demonstrate deductively and conclusively that it is not possible for God to exist in a world where moral evil also exists, yet such a world is indeed logically possible.

Of course, Shakespeare could not have read Plantinga, but he need not have done so in order to engage in *King Lear* the deductive problem of evil. Let me offer two examples. First, consider how *King Lear* invokes the idea of human beings strongly actualizing through their choices a world put in place (i.e., weakly actualized) by the divine. Shakespeare explicitly raises the idea that "the heavens" use the free choices of human beings in order to complete the world. Consider Lear's belated recognition of his duty to the homeless: "Take physic, pomp, / Expose thyself to feel what wretches feel, / That thou mayst shake the superflux to them / And show the heavens more just" (3.4.33–36). Lear's phrasing seems to indicate that humans work to reveal or "show" the justice at the heart of the divine. His request of "pomp" that it "shake the superflux" is an echo of the scriptural mandate to leave the gleanings from the harvest, as the writer of Leviticus has it, "for the poor and for the stranger" (Lev. 19:9–10). It would seem that Lear believes humans can strongly actualize a more just world through virtuous choices. In the same way, Edgar tricks his father into thinking he has fallen off Dover cliff in order to rescue him from his suicidal despair: "Think that the clearest gods, who make them honors / Of men's impossibilities, have preserved thee" (4.6.73–74).[60] Properly pagan in his polytheism, Edgar's line nonetheless resonates with scripture: "With men this is unpossible, but with God all things are possible."[61] As with Lear, Edgar's language and actions suggest that human beings can work in concert with the heavens.

Second, transworld depravity is also cognate with the idea of a fallen humanity, of a perversity so deep that it continually expresses itself even when one is free to choose the good. One could plausibly further describe this as original sin or even as the idea of total depravity, the latter prospect of which Plantinga notes in an aside: "(I leave as homework the problem of comparing transworld depravity with what Calvinists call 'total depravity')."[62] To take up Plantinga's challenge, it might be objected that because the Church of England in Shakespeare's day "was, in effect, a Calvinist church,"[63] he may have considered the human will so "bound" by human sinfulness as to be unfree in all matters. This is a popular though misguided reading of Calvin, who on the one hand believed postlapsarian reason to be so fallen as to make it impossible for anyone freely to know or love God without a "spiritual revelation" that comes from the Holy Spirit.[64] Yet Calvin also cites Paul's remark in Romans that the gentiles, those to whom the Mosaic law had not been given, are nonetheless "a law to themselves and show that the works of the law are written on their hearts" so that they are not "completely blind with regard to the knowledge of how to live" (2:14–15). Given this ethical awareness of good and evil, the sinner nonetheless "knowingly and *willingly* gives himself to evil."[65] Far from denying free will in general ethical (as opposed to spiritual) matters, Calvin repeatedly underscores human free will and, thereby, responsibility:

> We must note this distinction: which is, after having been corrupted by the fall,
> a person sins voluntarily and not in spite of his heart, not by constraint. He
> sins, I say, by a feeling very inclined but not forcibly constrained; he sins by a
> movement of his own passion and not constrained from elsewhere.[66]

If humans have free will in general ethical matters in Shakespeare's plays, a point that Cavell, again, affirms, they nevertheless in their fallenness—Plantinga's transworld depravity—choose perversely with distressing frequency. Lear's "darker purpose" in dividing his land points to a degree of inscrutability and irrationality in human decision-making (1.1.36), as does the rashness of his decision to disown Cordelia. Edmund's adulterous pledge of fidelity to Goneril—"Yours in the ranks of death" (4.2.25)—similarly underscores the dark stirrings of the human heart. People sometimes go wrong in their choices, and in *King Lear* there appears to be no less than a depravity of decision-making. Frustrated by the moral evil he sees, Albany well understands the idea of transworld depravity:

> If that the heavens do not their visible spirits
>
> Send quickly down to tame these vile offenses,
>
> It will come,
>
> Humanity must perforce prey on itself,
>
> Like monsters of the deep. (4.2.47–51)

Criticism of *Lear* has often divided between redemptionist critics and those who see the play as endorsing religious and philosophical nihilism, with "nothing" writ into the cosmos of the play. Yet the play's openness to both of these approaches is palpable. Writing of Shakespeare's famed complementarity, Norman Rabkin suggests, "We find ourselves able at almost any point in the play to read it as godless or divine; these are the terms implicit in the action of *King Lear* and explicit in its language."[67] Indeed, my argument is not that God exists—or must—in the world of *Lear*'s Celtic Britain, but that he could, and logic demonstrates that possibility, even as it cannot establish his existence as a likelihood, much less a necessity. It is possible, as Loewenstein claims, that the gods in *Lear* are mere "projections of the human imagination" "in a godless world stripped of providential moral significance."[68] But this is merely an assertion—plausible, to be sure, but by no means an inescapable truth. The possibility that *Lear* can be read at almost any point as divine often mystifies secular critics, who believe, as Fortin demonstrated in his powerful critique of their position, "that nothing short of poetic justice would validate a religious argument," and "that the universe in which the tragic ordeal takes place would have to be transparently meaningful."[69] No such transparency is forthcoming.

Similarly frustrated by *Lear*'s opacity, Nicholas Brooke writes, "I have never been clear what constitutes a 'Christian play.' I should have supposed that label would involve some effort to justify God's ways to men, to make the mysterious less inscrutable."[70] Providence is resolutely inscrutable in *King Lear*, yet in a way entirely consistent with Calvinist doctrine, as well as scriptural passages from Job to Paul's acknowledgment, "For now we see through a glass darkly; but then shall we see face to face. Now I know in part; but then shall I know even as I am known."[71] The play scarcely presents a theodicy, much less this-worldly justice, but it does open the logical possibility of God's mysterious and abiding presence within its frame. Shakespeare's having understood this doctrine of divine inscrutability in all its complexity, "it would hardly have needed saying," as Shell notes, "that a play illustrating God's providence did not have to end happily for everyone."[72]

Finally, although the dramatic form of Shakespeare's "argument" is quite different from Plantinga's philosophical proof, we should recall Sidney's remark in *The Defence of Poesy* (pub. 1595) that the first poets were philosophers, and vice versa.[73] With the later division of intellectual labor, "whatsoever the philosopher saith should be done, [the poet] giveth a perfect picture of it."[74] Moral philosophers such as Alasdair MacIntyre understand the value of literature in ethical formation.[75] *King Lear* offers a perfect illustration of the vexing problem of moral evil, while at the same time it opens the possibility of God's existence in a world actualized, for good or ill—tragically at times for ill—by the exercise of human freedom. At the same time, while God's existence is possible in the framework of *Lear*, one can hardly dispute the contention of Dollimore, Loewenstein, Greenblatt, and others that it is not a particularly optimistic prospect. Judith Anderson has even remarked that *Lear* may constitute "an allegory of nihilism."[76] *King Lear* is a troubling play for theists, and the view that it presents a radical challenge to orthodox belief seems to me beyond question.

Yet for anyone, believers and skeptics alike, belief or unbelief in relation to cosmological questions is never certain with deductive proof or apodictic certitude—there always remains, for any honest person, the possibility that he or she may be wrong. Nor is this a writ for agnosticism, as people can reason and find evidence in support of their positions, and indeed hold them with conviction, if not absolute certainty. *King Lear* maintains a remarkable equipoise between the possibility of a personal god, on the one hand, and the prospect of divine nonexistence on the other. Lear's final vision—or delusion—of a possibly revivifying Cordelia underscores the critical divide: "Do you see this? Look on her, look, her lips, / Look there, look there" (5.3.310–11). As Anderson remarks, "The question of vision—of what Lear finally sees and grasps—is posed more starkly, more forcefully, and probably less optimistically at the end of this play than in any other Renaissance work I know, and yet it remains a question. Only a fool would resolve its irreducible ambivalence."[77] In light of Shakespeare's interest in accommodating both theistic and atheistic interpretations of the play, we should remind ourselves of the *argumentum in utramque partem* that was taught to Elizabethan schoolboys and became a distinctive feature of his dramatic ambivalence.[78] Shakespeare's redoubtable complementarity renders either reading plausible, and one would be wise to approach the play with the same humility and openness, not to mention intellectual curiosity, with which Shakespeare wrote *King Lear*.

NOTES

1. George Santayana, "The Absence of Religion in Shakespeare," in *Interpretations of Poetry and Religion* (New York: Harper, 1957), 152.

2. George Knight, *The Wheel of Fire: Interpretations of Shakespearean Tragedy* (Cleveland: World Publishing, 1962); D. G. James, *The Dream of Learning: An Essay on the Advancement of Learning, Hamlet and King Lear* (Oxford: Clarendon press, 1951), 80, 92–93; Nicholas Brooke, *Shakespeare: King Lear* (London: Edward Arnold, 1963), 59; R. A. Foakes, *Hamlet Versus Lear: Cultural Politics and Shakespeare's Art* (Cambridge: Cambridge University Press, 2004), 217.

3. William Elton, *King Lear and the Gods* (San Marino, CA: Huntington Library, 1966), 334 and 236.

4. Jonathan Dollimore, *Radical Tragedy*, 3rd ed. (New York: Palgrave Macmillan, 2004), 196.

5. Marvin Rosenberg, *The Masks of King Lear* (Berkeley: University of California Press, 1972), 325.

6. Joseph Anthony Wittreich, *"Image of That Horror": History, Prophecy, and Apocalypse in King Lear* (San Marino CA: Huntington Library, 1984), 45, italics his.

7. Maynard Mack, *King Lear in Our Time* (Berkeley: University of California Press, 1965), 115–16.

8. John Milton, *Paradise Lost*, in *Complete Poems and Major Prose*, ed. Merritt Yerkes Hughes (New York: Macmillan, 1957), 1.26.

9. Alvin Plantinga, "The Free Will Defense," in *Philosophy of Religion: Selected Readings*, ed. Michael L. Peterson, 4th ed. (New York: Oxford University Press, 2010), 313.

10. Alison Shell, *Shakespeare and Religion* (London: Arden Shakespeare, 2010), 186.

11. David Loewenstein, "Agnostic Shakespeare?: The Godless World of King Lear," in *Shakespeare and Early Modern Religion*, ed. David Loewenstein and Michael Witmore (Cambridge & New York: Cambridge University Press, 2015), 155.

12. Ibid., 160.

13. Ibid.

14. Stephen Greenblatt, *Shakespearean Negotiations: The Circulation of Social Energy in Renaissance England* (Berkeley: University of California Press, 1988), 125, italics his.

15. René E. Fortin, "Hermeneutical Circularity and Christian Interpretations of King Lear," *Shakespeare Studies* 12 (January 1979): 115.

16. Ibid., 162.

17. Ibid., 163.

18. Foakes, *Hamlet Versus Lear*, 214; Sean Benson, *Shakespearean Resurrection: The Art of Almost Raising the Dead* (Pittsburgh: Duquesne University Press, 2009), 116–17.

19. Dollimore, *Radical Tragedy*, 195–96.

20. Ibid., 206, italics mine.

21. Loewenstein, "Agnostic Shakespeare?," 165.

22. Germaine Greer, *Shakespeare: A Very Short Introduction* (Oxford: Oxford University Press, 2002), 111–12.

23. Hannibal Hamlin, *The Bible in Shakespeare* (Oxford: Oxford University Press, 2013), chap. 8.

24. David Hume, "Evil Makes a Strong Case Against God's Existence," in *Philosophy of Religion*, 279.

25. J. L. Mackie, "Evil and Omnipotence," in *Philosophy of Religion*, 289.

26. Plantinga, "The Free Will Defense," 298.

27. What distinguishes Loewenstein's atheological reading of the play from those of earlier interpreters is the guardedness of his position: he often qualifies his denials of providentialism in the play and indeed raises in his title the possibility of agnosticism. Yet he, too, does not conceive in his essay of the possibility that the cosmos of *King Lear* is also consistent with traditional religious belief in a benevolent deity.

28. Benson, *Shakespearean Resurrection*, 109.

29. *Samuel Johnson on Shakespeare*, ed. William Kurtz Wimsatt (London: MacGibbon & Kee, 1960), 98.

30. Dollimore, *Radical Tragedy*, 190.

31. Plantinga, "The Free Will Defense," 300.

32. Ibid., 303.

33. Mackie, "Evil and Omnipotence," in *Philosophy of Religion*, 293.

34. Gottfried Leibniz, "Best of All Possible Worlds Theodicy," in *Philosophy of Religion*, 283.

35. Lloyd E. Berry and William Whittingham, eds., *The Geneva Bible: A Facsimile of the 1560 Edition* (Madison: University of Wisconsin Press, 1969), Matt. 20:28; Naseeb Shaheen, *Biblical References in Shakespeare's Plays* (Newark: University of Delaware Press, 1999), 712.

36. John Milton, *Paradise Lost*, 5.532–34.

37. Stanley Cavell, *Disowning Knowledge in Six Plays of Shakespeare* (Cambridge: Cambridge University Press, 1987), 89.

38. G. W. F. Hegel, "Dramatic Poetry," in *Philosophers on Shakespeare*, ed. Paul Kottman, trans. T. M. Knox (Palo Alto: Stanford University Press, 2009), 77.

39. Cavell, *Disowning Knowledge*, 88, italics his.

40. Aristotle, *Poetics*, in *The Complete Works of Aristotle: The Revised Oxford Translation*, ed. Jonathan Barnes, trans. I. Bywater, vol. 2, Bollingen Series 71:2 (Princeton: Princeton University Press, 1995), 1449b1.

41. In *Renaissance Self-Fashioning: From More to Shakespeare* (Chicago: University of Chicago Press, 1984), 255–57, Greenblatt considers human freedom of action and identity to be circumscribed by various social forces. Indeed, one can argue the point, as we will see in regard to Gloucester's blinding, but there remains, under any circumstances, an irreducible element of human freedom as well.

42. Plantinga, "The Free Will Defense," 306, italics his.

43. Ibid.

44. John Hick, "Soul-Making Theodicy," in *Philosophy of Religion*, 320.

45. Milton, *Paradise Lost*, 2005, 3.122–28.

46. John Calvin, *Institutes of the Christian Religion: The First English Version of the 1541 French Edition*, trans. Elsie Anne McKee (Grand Rapids: Wm. B. Eerdmans Publishing, 2009), 68.

47. Johnson noted the same alteration of Shakespeare's sources in regard to Cordelia's death: "Shakespeare has suffered the virtue of Cordelia to perish in a just cause, contrary to the natural ideas of justice, to the hope of the reader, and what is yet more strange, to the faith of the chronicles" in *Samuel Johnson on Shakespeare*, 97.

48. Geoffrey Bullough, ed., *Narrative and Dramatic Sources of Shakespeare*, vol. 2 (New York: Columbia University Press, 1958), 2:403.

49. Also known as *counterfactual conditionals* , these are propositions "pertaining to, or expressing, what has not in fact happened, but might, could, or would, in different conditions" (*Oxford English Dictionary*, s.v. "counterfactual").

50. Loewenstein, "Agnostic Shakespeare?," 163.

51. Fortin, "Hermeneutical Circularity and Christian Interpretations of King Lear," 118.

52. Wittreich, *Image of That Horror*, 118.

53. Plantinga, "The Free Will Defense," 312–13.

54. Nahum Tate, *The History of King Lear*, ed. James Black, Regents Restoration Drama Series (Lincoln: University of Nebraska Press, 1975), 5.6.145–46.

55. Bullough, *Narrative and Dramatic Sources of Shakespeare*, 1958, 2: 402.

56. The works in question are *Historia Anglicana*, Holinshed's *Chronicles*, *The Mirror for Magistrates*, and *The Faerie Queene*, the relevant excerpts of which can be found in Bullough, *Narrative and Dramatic Sources of Shakespeare*, 1958, 7: 311–19, 323–34.

57. Plantinga, "The Free Will Defense," 314.

58. Ibid., 315, italics his.

59. Ibid.

60. See F. W. Brownlow, *Shakespeare, Harsnett, and the Devils of Denham* (Lanham: University of Delaware Press, 1993), 126. For an opposing view of the scene in which Edgar's actions are depicted as being duplicitous, see Greenblatt, *Shakespearean Negotiations*, 118.

61. Berry and Whittingham, *The Geneva Bible*, Matthew 19:26; Shaheen, *Biblical References in Shakespeare's Plays*, 616.

62. Plantinga, "The Free Will Defense," 314.

63. Shell, *Shakespeare and Religion*, 10, 181.

64. Calvin, *Institutes of the Christian Religion*, 71–72.

65. Ibid., 73–74, italics mine.

66. Ibid., 83.

67. Norman Rabkin, *Shakespeare and the Common Understanding.* (New York: Free Press, 1967), 10–11.

68. Ibid., 166, 170.

69. Fortin, "Hermeneutical Circularity and Christian Interpretations of *King Lear*," 115.

70. Nicholas Brooke, "The Ending of *King Lear*," in *Shakespeare, 1564–1964: A Collection of Modern Essays by Various Hands*, ed. Edward Alan Bloom (Providence: Brown University Press, 1964), 74.

71. Berry and Whittingham, *The Geneva Bible*, 1 Cor. 13:12.

72. Shell, *Shakespeare and Religion*, 195.

73. Philip Sidney, *The Defence of Poesy*, in *Sir Philip Sidney: A Selection of His Finest Poems*, ed. Katherine Duncan-Jones (Oxford: Oxford University Press, 1994), 102.

74. Ibid., 111.

75. Alasdair MacIntyre, *After Virtue: A Study in Moral Theory*, 3rd ed. (Notre Dame: University of Notre Dame, 2007) 121.

76. Judith H. Anderson, *Reading the Allegorical Intertext: Chaucer, Spenser, Shakespeare, Milton* (New York: Fordham University Press, 2010), 190.

77. Ibid., 200.

78. Neil Rhodes, *Shakespeare and the Origins of English* (Oxford and New York: Oxford University Press, 2004), 89–90.

Chapter Four

Hamlet's Walking Dead

"the great, ever-living dead man."
—Coleridge, *Biographia Literaria*, 1817

In the next two chapters, I offer diametrically opposed—sacred and profane—readings of *Hamlet* in order to see (as in *King Lear*) how Shakespeare
explores contradictory and competing beliefs within the same play. Chapter 4
grounds the play in the material world of corpses rising from their interment,
while chapter 5 examines Hamlet's wrestling with and response to the divine
call on his life. We will begin with Shakespeare's invitation to a materialist
reading of the play, and to an extreme interpretation now enjoying a certain
vogue in popular culture. Adaptations of *Hamlet* as a work of zombie fiction
are already underway, and I wish to examine them, first, to show the historical invalidity of such interpretations—they go too far and end up as mere
camp. Yet Shakespeare's interest in the afterlife and ghosts does lead him
also to consider the possibility of physical revenants rising from their graves.
Although these neither are nor could be zombies *per se* as we now understand the concept, folk and pagan (and even, to a minor extent, Catholic)
belief certainly envisioned subhuman (e.g., soulless) creatures returning from
the dead to harry the living. The existence of the walking dead contravenes
orthodox Christian belief, but *Hamlet* repeatedly tantalizes us with that very
prospect, including the possibility of Old Hamlet as a physical revenant.

The past decade has seen the appropriation of Shakespeare's plays into the
popular subculture of the undead, right along with other literary and political
luminaries—witness the recent slate of book and film titles: *Pride and Prejudice and Zombies*; *Little Vampire Women*; *Alice in Zombieland*; *Abraham
Lincoln: Vampire Hunter*; *Abraham Lincoln vs. Zombies*; and even *Jane

Slayre.[1] If Shakespeare was "not of an age, but for all time,"[2] as Ben Jonson eulogized him, perhaps we should not be surprised, given the groundswell of interest in zombie literature and film,[3] to see his assimilation into the subgenre. In Lori Handeland's *Shakespeare Undead* (2010), he is a zombie-hunting vampire who joins forces with an unhappily married transvestite, Katherine Dymond (the Dark Lady of the sonnets, no less) to overcome a zombie horde that Shakespeare had raised from the dead. When the zombies run amok, Hamlet grows belatedly—bathetically—penitent: "He was sorry for the raising now."[4] In Chris Stiles's stage adaptation, *Hamlet, Zombie Killer of Denmark* (2010), Rosencrantz and Guildenstern are undead (also the film title of a recent zombie mashup of Tom Stoppard's play[5]), along with Old Hamlet, Claudius, Laertes, Yorick, Bernardo, Francisco, and a host of others. In scene 13, Hamlet asks the gravedigger whose grave it is he is digging:

GRAVEDIGGER: It be no one's grave at the moment. Its owner has

vacated.

HAMLET: Vacated? What do you mean?

GRAVEDIGGER: I mean, good sir, I bury the dead, but they don't stay

dead, they become undead, rising from the earth.

HAMLET: You're speaking of Zombies?

GRAVEDIGGER: I'm surely not speaking to zombies. Terrible

conversationalists, they are. Lots of groaning.[6]

As if this weren't enough, Ryan Denmark's campy filmic treatment, *Romeo and Juliet vs. The Living Dead* (2009), portrays Romeo as a zombie with whom our eponymous heroine falls in love.[7]

Clearly, liberties are being taken. One might say that such adaptations would make Shakespeare turn over in his grave, but that phrase has also become a zombie trope, the very kind of language one finds in these appropriations. Unfortunately, to date such adaptations are excessive and constitute mere risible parodies of the plays he actually wrote. What is worth note, however, is Shakespeare's abiding interest in radical religious belief, which finds one avenue of expression in the longstanding fascination with the walking dead; that is, with the prospect of soulless corpses somehow reanimating. In particular, Shakespeare repeatedly and deeply problematizes the figure of Old Hamlet, suggesting an ambivalence in his ontological status between that of a ghost and of a revivified corpse. He does this, in part, by referencing other corpselike figures in *Hamlet* and elsewhere.

In yet another adaptation, a mash-up of a Facebook newsfeed with *Hamlet*, Sarah Schmelling has already suggested that even though "Horatio thinks he saw a ghost," he was mistaken: "Hamlet's father is now a zombie."[8] The question, however, is whether Shakespeare's *Hamlet* is malleable enough to allow for such a heterodox reading. Although Schmelling's reading goes too far and is, in generic terms, a clever travesty, the current fascination with zombieism can nonetheless offer a window into Shakespeare's own preoccupation with the living dead, and in particular the possibility of representing Old Hamlet as a physical revenant rather than as a traditional ghost figure. He is not a zombie as we understand the term, but he can nonetheless be portrayed, and legitimately so, as a corpselike figure. Shakespeare would have found precedent for such a representation in English folklore and old wives' tales of corpses coming back to harrow the living, which is precisely what Old Hamlet does. No doubt there will continue to be zombie adaptations of *Hamlet*, but I want to obviate the excesses of such approaches and point to what our current fascination with zombies can teach us about Shakespeare's own abiding interest in physical revenants.

Shakespeare's plays need not be forced into a postmodern mold they cannot possibly fit. The word *zombie* first appears in English only in the nineteenth century in the West Indies and southern United States.[9] Shakespeare simply could not have known the term, and thus to speak of zombies in light of his work is to be hopelessly prochronistic. Yet the idea of the dead emerging from their graves neither begins with nor is unique to zombieism. Consider one variant: the resurrection motif in the plays. Hans Urs von Balthasar's comments on the return of those presumed dead in the recognition scenes of the romances: "[Shakespeare] takes the risk of portraying the return from the realm of the dead as a pure gift to those in mourning," as a "metaphor for the grace of existence."[10] Yet Shakespeare also tantalizes us with a much darker strain that is no gift, but a nightmare in which the dead stalk the living, "making night hideous, and . . . horridly to shake our disposition" (*Ham.* 1.4.54–55). Freud locates one expression of *das Unheimliche*, the uncanny, precisely in this context: "Many people experience the feeling in the highest degree in relation to death and dead bodies, to the return of the dead."[11] Paulina, for one, considers the idea as "monstrous" that her dead husband, Antigonus, should "break his grave / And come again to me." (*Winter's Tale* 5.1.41–43). She does not claim that the idea is impossible, only grotesque.

Although Catherine Belsey and Adam Cohen have recently touched upon the phenomenon of revivified corpses in the Shakespearean corpus, no sustained attention has been given to the living dead.[12] Much work, by way of contrast, has been done on the undead, particularly the representation of ghosts on the early modern stage. [13] Elizabeth Prosser has calculated that over fifty ghosts appeared on stage between 1560 and 1610; Greenblatt has further argued that "Shakespeare's celebrated ghost scenes—easily the greatest in all of English drama—are signs of a deep interest that continues through virtually his entire career." [14] I want to extend the analysis of Shakespeare's fascination with the undead to his interest in the more aberrant case of the living dead. Indeed, the accommodating plasticity of Shakespeare's language—the subterranean latency that "bodes some strange eruption to our state" (*Ham.* 1.1.73)—allows directors, for instance, to stage the figure of Old Hamlet as a revivified corpse. Even more remarkably, he is only one of several physical revenants who dot the Shakespearean landscape. Shakespeare's heterodox interest in the religious implications of the soulless dead returning to harry the living also, as we shall see, anticipates the religious nihilism *Lear* explores.

A zombie is "a soulless corpse," originally "said to have been revived by witchcraft," and this usage, as we shall see, is not incompatible with Shakespeare's depiction of physical revenants, particularly in *The Tempest*. [15] Yet zombies are not, strictly speaking, reanimated, at least not in the etymological sense of their soul or spirit—what Aristotle in *De Anima* calls the "the principle of life" [16] —being reactivated or somehow made functional in the body. In early Greek, as well as Judeo-Christian thought, upon death the "dust returne to the earth as it was, and the spirit returne to God" or to some other ideal realm. [17] *The Winter's Tale* reflects this mind-body split. Leontes declares that he shall remain a widower unless Paulina chooses a wife like Hermione for him, but he insists there are

No more such wives, therefore no wife. One worse,

And better used, would make her sainted spirit

Again possess her corpse, and on this stage,

Where we're offenders now, appear soul-vexed,

And begin, "Why to me?" (5.1.56–60)

If her spirit were to repossess her corpse, he tells us, then Hermione might appear once again before Leontes, but otherwise it would be impossible. While Shakespeare never pronounces on the precise ontological status of these revenants, he does explore the possibility of their existence. As Hamlet says, ostensibly of Claudius but perhaps glancingly and suggestively of his father, whose ghost keeps reappearing to him, "The body is with the King, but the King is not with the body. The King is a thing—" (4.2.28–29). We'll return to Old Hamlet's thingness shortly.

A revenant may be 1) a bodiless ghost; or 2) a fully reanimated being with a physical body and immaterial soul or mind, as in the New Testament's understanding of resurrection; or 3) a walking dead corpse, presumably with impaired (possibly demonically possessed) mental functioning. *Hamlet* oscillates between the first and third of these choices, presenting to us both a Roman horde roaming the streets and the even more ambivalent figure of Old Hamlet. Yet in the early modern period, any apparent reanimation of the dead was already suspect in the eyes of the Reformers: a sign that the devil "hath power" either to "assume a pleasing shape" (*Ham.* 2.2.600–01) or to ventriloquize the dead: "Hell can put life into a senseles body / and raise it from the grave, and make it speake, / Use all the faculties alive it did, / To worke the Devill's hellish stratagems!"[18] As Peter Marshall remarks, Reformed belief insisted that "a body cannot walk without a soul."[19] Much of this was of course a reaction to belief in and sightings of purgatorial spirits, which were anathema to the Reformers. As the physician Thomas Browne noted, "ghosts of departed persons are not the wandring soules of men, but the unquiet walkes of Devils."[20] The authorized Reformation discourse was directed against ghostly revenants as mere Catholic superstition. Bodily resurrection could and would take place only at the Apocalypse: "certain it is," John Foxe inveighed, "that no dead man materially can ever rise againe, or appear, before the judgement day."[21] The walking dead were not only not true; they were not even, to use Foucault's expression, *"dans le vrai"*— within the framework of that which *could* be true[22] —and thus outside the discursive and theological realms of Reformed thought.

Yet both folk beliefs and Catholic tales (interrelated as they were) concerning the living dead persisted despite official animadversions. The exempla of medieval sermons, for instance, "often included stories of ghosts and walking corpses in order to suitably impress the audience."[23] Among various old legends are two series of accounts of physical revenants, those who, as Jacqueline Simpson remarks, "are not ghosts in the usual sense of that word but 'walking dead,' corpses that have literally emerged from their graves."[24] In the earlier series, the Augustinian canon William of Newburgh relates four tales of the walking dead in his *Historia Rerum Anglicarum* (ca. 1198), all the while attesting to their authenticity:

> It would not be easy to believe that the corpses of the dead should sally (I know not by what agency) from their graves, and should wander about to the terror or destruction of the living, and again return to the tomb, which of its own accord spontaneously opened to receive them, did not frequent examples, occurring in our own times, suffice to establish this fact, to the truth of which there is abundant testimony.[25]

Two centuries later, but just a few miles down the road, an anonymous author (presumably a monk) added some paranormal stories to an early fifteenth-century manuscript in the Cistercian abbey at Byland.[26] One of his stories concerns three living kings who are "confronted," as Belsey notes, "by three emaciated corpses,"[27] the latter three serving as *memento mori* for the kings. Although she calls these figures "the walking dead," Belsey regards them as ghosts.[28] Yet she is distinctly aware of the problem their corporeity raises: "What *were* they, these living dead who defied the categories by which people reduced the world to knowledge? Although they are named as 'spirits' . . . [they] are nonetheless substantial."[29] What is a substantial ghost if not a physical revenant? Even more intriguing is Belsey's juxtaposition of these "living dead" with Old Hamlet:

> These figures are material, corporeal, and decomposing; they have come from their graves to confront the Living. When Hamlet calls the Ghost a dead corpse that has burst its cerements, cast up by the sepulcher to revisit the night (1.4.47–53), he invests the phantom with a physicality quite remote from the ethereal wraiths of Victorian imagining.[30]

One need not regard Old Hamlet as a zombie in order to regard him as a corpselike figure. Likewise, the very corporeity of the figures who confront the three kings allows us to interpret them as physical revenants. Old Hamlet's corporeality renders him a figure of the uncanny, of "what arouses dread and horror," in Freud's formulation,[31] which is precisely what Horatio confesses upon seeing the dead king: "It harrows me with fear and wonder" (1.1.48).

Old Hamlet can certainly be interpreted as a spirit—all three versions of Shakespeare's play, as well as what little is known of the *Ur-Hamlet*, refer to him as a ghost or spirit. Indeed, Marcellus's attempts to strike it prove futile: "For it is as the air invulnerable" (1.1.151). Old Hamlet flits in and out— ghostlike—from time to time, and is at one point apparently visible only to Hamlet (3.4). Shall we say, then, that the ontological status of Old Hamlet is settled for us in the twentieth century, or was settled for Shakespeare and his contemporaries in the sixteenth? Shakespeare's play scripts, especially the second quarto of 1604/05, trouble and challenge such a univocal reading, as they contain little to prevent, and much to encourage, the use of a more subversive hermeneutic.

Just before Old Hamlet makes his second entrance in the play, Horatio recounts for his own wonder-wounded hearers a bizarre episode from Roman history:

In the most high and palmy state of Rome,

A little ere the mightiest Julius fell,

The graves stood tenantless, and the sheeted dead

Did squeak and gibber in the Roman streets. (1.1.117–20)

The speech, which goes on for some length, is present in quarto 2 (Q2) but absent from both quarto 1 (Q1) and the First Folio, and derives from Thomas North's translation of Plutarch's *Lives*. Plutarch, however, has no reference to open graves, but only to "spirits running up and down in the night."[32] Shakespeare's "sheeted dead" would almost seem to conjure an image of ghosts, but these are quite clearly corpses in their burial shrouds, what we would call the walking or living dead. Shakespeare's immediate source here, an instance of his "imitating himself,"[33] is Calpurnia's speech from *Julius Caesar* (ca. 1599): "A lioness hath whelped in the streets / And graves have yawned and yielded up their dead" (2.2.17–18).[34] As George Walton Williams comments, Shakespeare's classical sources—Plutarch in particular—"all mention the presence of spirits or ghosts in the city, [yet] none specifically says they come from 'open graves', as they do in *Julius Caesar*."[35] That particular locution is exclusive to scripture: "And the graves did open themselves, and many bodies of the Saints which slept, arose, and came out of the graves,"[36] presumably as resurrected—fully human—persons.[37] But in syncretizing his classical and New Testament sources, Shakespeare *embodies* the ghosts of Roman lore, changing them from the undead—ghosts—into what appear to be physical revenants.

Moreover, Shakespeare has these corpses squeak and gibber in the streets, which Ann Thompson and Neil Taylor in the Arden 3 *Hamlet* gloss as having "made inarticulate noises (perhaps evoking those made by bats)."[38] A more apt and appropriately eerie comparison is to the inarticulate and subhuman moaning that is a staple of zombie lore. Thus, even though *Hamlet* is not a zombie play, it does partake of the zombiesque, but its evocation of the living dead lies not in modern zombie tales but in older folk belief. William of Newburgh's third tale of the walking dead, for instance, concerns an "excessively secular" chaplain at Melrose who, after he died, kept "issuing from the grave at night-time" "with loud groans and horrible murmurs, round the bedchamber of his former mistress." At her request, a friar kept vigil over the cemetery: "Midnight had now passed by" when the dead chaplain appeared, "rushing upon him with a terrible noise, and [the friar] struck the axe which he wielded in his hand deep into his body. On receiving this wound, the monster groaned aloud, and, turning his back, fled."[39] Why is it the living dead make such "terrible noise" and groan, or, as in Horatio's equivalent, squeak and gibber? It is never explained in either case, but clearly something has gone horribly awry: they could lack a soul, as is the case with traditional voodoo zombies of cinema culture; or be possessed by the devil, as William fears; or simply lack the necessary consciousness—brain functioning—to speak. Whether brain-dead or sans an animating spirit, their speech pathologies are understandable. Whatever the precise etiology, Horatio's image of Roman revivification is certainly not the joyous reunion of the saints, as in scripture, but something sinister and unnatural.

The reference to the Roman horde coming out of their graves ought to remind us of Old Hamlet as well. Hamlet tells him: "Thou com'st in such a questionable shape. . ." (1.4.43)—questionable indeed. Writing of the day-to-day demands of early modern dramaturgy, Marshall remarks, "Most dramatists who placed ghosts on the stage did not unduly agonize over their precise ontological status," which makes Hamlet's statement all the more unusual.[40] The characters continually refer to Old Hamlet as an indeterminate being— *it*:[41] "Speak to it, Horatio" (1.1.49); "Is it not like the King ?" (62); "If it assume my noble father's person, / I'll speak to it" (1.2.249–50); and so on.[42] *It* is also used as an indefinite pronoun to refer to a skull—" This might be the pate of a politician . . . might it not?" (5.1.77–80)—as well as to the corpse of Polonius: "Tell us where 'tis, that we may take it thence / And bear it to the chapel" (4.2.7–8). When discussion of Old Hamlet first occurs in the play, Horatio's first question (in Q2), "What, has this thing appeared tonight?" (1.1.26), anticipates Hamlet's "The King is a thing—" (4.2.29). What exactly is he? A few lines after Horatio's reference to the Roman "sheeted dead" who have risen from their now-tentantless graves, his ruminations are interrupted by the entrance of Old Hamlet. On one level, this would appear to return us from the material world of physical revenants to the immaterial realm of ghosts. Yet the apposition is close and therefore unsettling: one wonders if the figure of Old Hamlet offers less of a contrast to the Roman horde roaming the streets than an uncanny resemblance to them, perhaps as one of their kind.

Notice, too, how at the moment of Old Hamlet's first entrance in the play, Horatio's evocation of the walking dead moves seamlessly from classical Rome to current events:

And even the like precurse of feared events,

As harbingers preceding still the fates

And prologue to the omen coming on,

Have heaven and earth together demonstrated

Unto our climatures and countrymen.

Enter Ghost. (1.1.125–29)

What "like precurse of feared events"? Horatio has just spoken of the terrible signs in the sky—"stars with trains of fire and dews of blood, / Disasters in the sun" (122–23). Is he then referring only to the apocalyptic skies, or is he suggesting that the raising of Roman dead also serves as a harbinger and "prologue to the omen coming on" stage in the form of Old Hamlet? The possibility cannot be denied, and he confirms that not just the skies, but "heaven and earth together demonstrated" these disturbing events (128). Moreover, having conjured what he thought was Old Hamlet's ghost to "Speak, speak!" (55) during their first encounter, Horatio suggests in his Q2 speech that an apparition of the king would be a mere "mote . . . to trouble the mind's eye" (116) in comparison to the antique Roman (and possibly current Danish) dead whose rising he then recounts. His biblical allusion— "And why seest thou the mote, that is in thy brothers eye, and perceivest not the beame that is in thine own eye?"[43] —is telling: it subtly casts a corpselike Old Hamlet as a mote compared with what happened in Rome; compared, that is, with the far worse beam of multiple physical revenants wandering about. Although they note the biblical allusion, Taylor and Thompson read against the evidence of Horatio's reference: "Horatio presumably doesn't mean to underestimate the significance of the Ghost but to see it as a serious concern."[44] Old Hamlet is indeed a serious problem—but less so, a mere mote, in comparison to a Roman horde of walking dead.

Hamlet later asks whether Old Hamlet is "a spirit of health or goblin damned" (1.4.40), as if these are the only two possibilities. His reply, "I am thy father's spirit" (10), seems to place himself, ontologically speaking, in the spirit realm as a ghost. To be sure, the history of performance, as well as interpretation, regards Old Hamlet as an immaterial spirit—a point rein-forced in the diaphanous ghost of recent filmic adaptations such as Michael Almereyda's Manhattan biopic of the play.[45] Perhaps, however, we need not "take," as Hamlet later does, "the ghost's word for a thousand pound" (3.2.284–85). I would like to extend my reading of Old Hamlet's "question-able shape" as tantalizing us with the prospect of his corpse emerging from the margins, both in the deconstructive sense of a marginal reading as well as in the literal sense of *margin*: "the ground immediately adjacent to a . . . body of water"[46] —in this case the graves in which "your water is a sore decayer of your whoreson dead body" (5.1.171–72).

Could Old Hamlet be played as a walking corpse? Shakespeare lays the groundwork for such a staging by emphasizing Old Hamlet's physicality. When Hamlet first sees the figure of his dead father, he addresses him as a person:

King, father, royal Dane. Oh, answer me!

Let me not burst in ignorance, but tell

Why thy canonized bones, hearsèd in death,

Have burst their cerements; why the sepulcher

Wherein we saw thee quietly inurned

Hath oped his ponderous and marble jaws

To cast thee up again. (1.4.45–51)

Like the antique Roman horde, Old Hamlet has come out of his cerements, or winding sheets. This, again, implies physical revivification, and the suggestion is made explicit when he tells us that the tomb has cast him up again. Hamlet says nothing about Old Hamlet's being immaterial. The body of Old Hamlet, not his spirit, has been cast up from the maw of death. Still perplexed by this seeming reality, Hamlet asks, "What may this mean, / That thou, dead corpse, again in complete steel / Revisits thus the glimpses of the moon" (1.4.51–53). For those who wish to read Old Hamlet unambiguously as an immaterial ghost, they have to explain away the explicitness of this language.

Not only does Old Hamlet not sound like a traditional ghost, but "from a more pragmatic standpoint," as Cohen remarks, his physicality

> may even be a function of theatrical necessity. Shakespeare had to use a flesh and blood actor in order to portray the ghost of King Hamlet. . . . Instead of attempting to obscure or gloss over this fact, he may be attempting to take advantage of it. . . . While it is astounding to see ghosts on the stage, it is even more astounding to see apparitions that are materially indistinguishable from actual corpses, ghosts that literally matter.[47]

Old Hamlet is repeatedly said to be dressed in "the very armor he had on / When he the ambitious Norway combated" (1.1.64–65; 3.4.141). Perhaps Old Hamlet does not look so much like the dead king as actually to be him in the flesh, which is quite in keeping with the actual limitations of staging practice. In Shakespeare's day to all but the most technically advanced stagings in our own, Old Hamlet would be played by a flesh-and-blood actor.

Furthermore, instead of simply disappearing instantaneously as a diaphanous ghost might be able to, Old Hamlet exits in plodding fashion—"See, it stalks away" (1.1.54)—and is again said to walk "with martial stalk" (70), which suggests predation,[48] and this is precisely the fear Old Hamlet's initial appearances occasion. The first Old Hamlet would have made some of his entrances and exits via the trapdoor,[49] thus suggesting the infernal, as in *Dr.*

Faustus.[50] But emerging or, rather, erupting from the ground resonates equally well with the Byland Abbey and Newburgh accounts of physical revenants. Hamlet even speaks of his physical presence underground: "Well said, old mole. Canst work i'th'earth so fast?" (1.5.171). Animal-like burrowing is hardly ghostlike behavior. "If," as Arthur McGee suggests, "the Ghost merely walked on from the wings how could the sentries have regarded it as a ghost?"[51] Hamlet notes at one point, "Look where he goes even now out at the portal!" (3.4.142). Without trapdoors, as in some modern productions, staging Old Hamlet presents technical problems that are easily solved by having him walk on and off stage, thus inviting ontological questions for sentries and audiences alike—"Who's there?" (1.1.1). Even if he comes through the trapdoor, it functions as a signifier whose signified points ambivalently to Old Hamlet either as a ghost or as a physical revenant.

How might one realistically stage Old Hamlet as a revivified corpse? We routinely read Marcellus's famous line, "Something is rotten in the state of Denmark" (1.4.90), as a metaphor, but if we allow, as contemporary productions can, for a representation of Old Hamlet as a rotting corpse—he has been decomposing anywhere from two to four months (3.2.126)[52] —we can read the line literally. That Old Hamlet was buried in late fall or early winter, when Danish temperatures would have been near or below freezing, means that his body could have been preserved by the frost, with much, if not all, of his body's soft—fleshy—tissue still intact.[53] If this seems too gruesome, the play pointedly takes up such considerations: the first clown (or gravedigger) informs us that most corpses "will last you some eight year or nine year. A tanner will last you nine year" (5.1.166–67). His informal and gruesome musings on taphonomy—the decomposition rate of the human body[54] —are anecdotally well-informed, if comically exaggerated. The tanner's hide is virtually embalmed, he informs us, "so tanned with his trade that 'a will keep out water a great while" (169–70). Any form of water, as the gravedigger tells us in Q1, is a "parlous devourer of your dead body, a great soaker."[55] A director could, therefore, depict Old Hamlet in a state of advanced putrescence, with the visible head wound (typical also of cinematic zombies) from the "leprous distillment" poured in his ear (1.5.64–65); or as seemingly hale as he was in life; or somewhere in between. Old Hamlet can be staged with textual impunity as a rotting corpse.

Even Old Hamlet's declaration that he is a (purgatorial) spirit, "Doomed for a certain term to walk the night" (1.5.11), scarcely settles his ontological status.[56] Unlike the numerous references to Old Hamlet as a *thing*, as a *dead corpse*, and as *it*, there are only five references to him as a ghost, which we have always interpreted to mean bodiless spirit. But the word *ghost* was itself highly variable—the *Oxford English Dictionary* (*OED*) records thirteen distinct valences, the ninth of which, now obsolete, defines a ghost as "a corpse."[57] This usage was operative from at least 1567, and the *OED* cites

Shakespeare as having used it in this sense as early as *Henry VI, part 2.*[58] None of *Hamlet*'s uses of *ghost* necessitates that we interpret its signification in only one way. Consider Hamlet's warning to his friends that they had best let him follow Old Hamlet: "Unhand me gentlemen. / By heaven, I'll make a ghost of him that lets me!" (1.4.84–85). He could be referring to a spirit or to a corpse or to both. "Today," as Cohen remarks, "we draw clear distinctions between a spirit or ghost on one hand and a revivified dead body on another, but Shakespeare seems to intentionally cloud this distinction."[59] If one reads Old Hamlet as a physical revenant who, as in Q1, prosaically enters Gertrude's chamber "*in his night-gown*,"[60] then the references to him as a *ghost* become as unstable in our day as they were in Shakespeare's. We have always interpreted Old Hamlet as a bodiless spirit, but Shakespeare's text also and alternatively accommodates understanding him as a corpselike figure.

My reading takes seriously the play's ambivalence between a ghostly and corporeal Old Hamlet. Old Hamlet is not entirely ghostly in the text's depiction of his being, yet one has to concede that neither is he unequivocally a corpse; the play's oscillation between these two poles allows a director to employ and perhaps never quite to resolve this ambivalence. Old Hamlet has enough corpselike traits for us to regard him as one. Even seemingly intransigent problems such as his selective manifestation to Hamlet and not to Gertrude in 3.4 can readily be accounted for by placing Old Hamlet behind the arras near the corpse of Polonius: Hamlet is privy to Old Hamlet's speech— poured whisperingly, perhaps, as asides into the ear of his son—while Gertrude sees no one except Hamlet and believes he madly speaks either to the dead body of Polonius or to "th'incorporal air" behind the arras (3.4.122). Such blocking on stage would explain why Hamlet, Horatio, Marcellus, and Barnardo are able to see him in act 1 while Gertrude cannot in act 3.

Consider, too, a number of other allusions to revivified corpses in Shakespeare's *oeuvre*, beginning with *The Tempest*. While "neglecting worldly ends" back in Milan (1.2.89), Prospero had instead begun to acquire skills as a sorcerer: "I have bedimmed / The noontide sun," he tells us. His powers culminate in his realization of the Faustian dream of resurrecting the dead:[61] "graves at my command / Have waked their sleepers, oped, and let 'em forth / By my so potent art" (5.1.41–42, 48–50).[62] As with the earlier references to the Roman "sheeted dead," Prospero's claim pushes beyond the raising of mere spirits. These are *sleepers*, which is a frequent metaphor for the dead in scripture and elsewhere.[63] Naseeb Shaheen detects yet another echo of St. Matthew's "And the graves did open themselves."[64] While we never learn the precise status of Prospero's revivified corpses, it is reasonable to interpret them as physical revenants rather than as fully human. Prospero recoils from what he has done as something unnatural: "But this rough magic / I here abjure" (5.1.50–51).[65] It is unlikely, given Prospero's use of black magic, that these revivified corpses have been restored to their status quo ante; they instead recall Horatio's Roman horde.

If we recall Paulina's fear that the dead Antigonus should "break his grave / And come again to me" (*WT* 5.1.42–43), she envisions the same nightmarish scenario realized in Prospero's macabre sorcery."[66] As I have written elsewhere of Shakespeare's pagan characters, the mere idea of the dead revivifying horrifies them, and Shakespeare counterpoises this pagan imaginary against the beatific reunion promised in the Christian resurrection of the dead.[67] What would Antigonus's return to life mean; what, in other words, would be the ontological status of his body? "At the sound of the Last Trumpet," according to Reformed thought, the resurrected saints "would be perfect, agile, and luminous (like the transfigured body of Christ)."[68] In Paulina's eyes, however, a revivified corpse would not be luminous, but ominous, sinister, as in Horatio's Roman horde squeaking and gibbering in the streets, or as in Prospero's equally horrified recollection of the dead whom he has raised. We never learn the precise status of these potential or actual revenants, but they are envisioned as disturbingly subhuman revenants.

The emaciated corpses visiting the three kings serve to prefigure our own death, our coming decay made visibly manifest,[69] glimpses of which Shakespeare also gives us in the revivified Roman horde; in the potentially resurrected Antigonus; in Prospero's reanimated corpses; and of course in Old Hamlet. Crucially, though, with the exception of Old Hamlet, Shakespeare's physical revenants are merely imagined as such, conjured for us by second-hand narrative description. They do not appear on stage, perhaps making them more imaginatively horrific, yet along with Old Hamlet they could be represented on the contemporary stage and screen. Given the physical presence of the stage actor playing Old Hamlet, a staging of him as corpselike seems plausible, prepared as it is by Shakespeare's ambivalent representation of him. Shakespeare need not have had our knowledge of zombieism in order to share our fascination with the possible reanimation of lifeless corpses. Thus, we hardly need to do violence to the Shakespearean text, as in Stiles's *Hamlet, Zombie Killer of Denmark* or Handeland's *Shakespeare Undead*, in order to envision the walking dead in his plays.

Why might Shakespeare have permitted in the language of the text, and even encourage in performance, a representation of Old Hamlet as a corpse? Historically, theirs was an age where the theaters were closed repeatedly for fear of unnatural death via infectious plague,[70] and *Hamlet* is rife with offhand allusions to "contagion" (3.2.389); "plague" (4.7.14); "pestilence" (5.1.178); and the rampant "infected" (3.2.256) and "diseased" (20–21). In 1603 alone, as William Camden recorded, "there died in London 38,244; of which number there were 30,578 of the Plague."[71] Eric Mallin has argued that "The

second quarto of *Hamlet*, contemporaneous with a deadly epidemic," is rid-
dled with plague references in response to it.[72] The grave digger tells Hamlet,
"we have many pocky corpses nowadays" (5.1.165), and Old Hamlet would
seem to fit right in. Moreover, the atmospheric conditions in Elsinore—"a
foul and pestilent congregation of vapors" (2.2.303–04)—also play into the
longstanding association of the walking dead with pestilence.

Consider the leitmotif of contagion in William of Newburgh's second
account of the living dead, which retells the story of a wealthy "rogue" who
"after his death sallied forth (by the contrivance, as it is believed, of Satan)
out of his grave by night."[73] The "wiser" sort among the townsfolk felt the
need to act immediately against it for fear that "the atmosphere, infected and
corrupted by the constant whirlings through it of the pestiferous corpse,
would engender disease and death to a great extent."[74] Similarly, William's
fourth and final tale concerns "a certain man of evil conduct" who had, like
Old Hamlet (1.5.78–80), died unshriven—"destitute of Christian grace." He
subsequently emerged "from his grave at night-time" and, again like Old
Hamlet, "wandered through the courts and around the houses." The towns-
people feared encountering him "and being beaten black and blue by this
vagrant monster. But these precautions were of no avail: for the atmosphere,
poisoned by the vagaries of this foul carcase, filled every house with disease
and death by its pestiferous breath."[75] At the very least, Old Hamlet is a
figurative "transmitter of destruction," as Mallin remarks, "pour[ing] another
venom, the virulent narrative of his death, into Hamlet's ears."[76] At worst, he
could serve as a living reminder, as well as a walking carrier, of the plague.

Aside from the historical associations with plague and infected bodies,
Shakespeare also seems to be exploring the heterodoxy of staging Old Hamlet as a physical revenant. In light of modern science, which eschews the
immaterial (e.g., spirit, mind) as empirically unverifiable and possibly nonexistent, Old Hamlet can be understood as a walking corpse, as in William of
Newburgh's description of the living dead. Surely this is part of the modern
fascination with zombies, and a similarly heterodox belief was present in the
early modern period. In 1661 Thomas Ady, an English physician and human-
ist, objected to "Old Wives Fables, who sit talking, and chatting of many
false old Stories of Witches, and . . . walking Spirits, and the Dead walking
again; all which lying fancies people are more naturally inclined to listen
after than to the Scriptures."[77] Old Hamlet as a physical revenant is clearly
heterodox in Reformist thought, yet not quite so removed from the penumbra
of Roman Catholic orthodoxy.

Ghosts were a subject of serious Reformation controversy, and it is telling
that both the Byland Abbey and Newburgh accounts are medieval, Catholic,
and closely tied to tales of the wanderings of purgatorial spirits. The concept
of Purgatory became a lightning rod among the Reformers: although not all
of them immediately gravitated to Tyndale's view of Purgatory as a "poet's

fable"[78] (the young Luther, for instance, took a soft line on the possibility of its existence), by the time of Donne and Milton Purgatory was pure superstition in need of no refutation.[79] *Hamlet* occupies a liminal space at the turn of the century when there was Catholic as well as widespread popular belief—popular, no doubt, even among lay Protestants—that ghosts often did return, as Old Hamlet does, to "disclose hidden wrongs, or urge the restitution of ill-gotten gains."[80] Medieval religious culture was steeped in thought and images that made Purgatory an orthodox and daily part of Catholic life. At vespers, the office of the dead was recited, and chantries were endowed to pray for the dead to pass quickly through the "sulf'rous and tormenting flames" of Purgatory (*Ham*. 1.5.3). To be sure, purgatorial spirits are not corporeal, but they, along with the physical revenants in the Newburgh and Byland Abbey accounts, are what we might call the walking dead. In the pious and popular imagination, Catholic and otherwise, precise ontological distinctions were probably not made, and old Hamlet would to some extent be unremarkable, even as a corporeal figure. To put it another way, although the Newburgh and Byland Abbey accounts resemble tales of wandering purgatorial spirits, they nonetheless concern walking corpses, not spirits, and thus their subjects bear a resemblance to zombies, even if they are more rightly understood as physical revenants.

On the one hand, a ghostly Old Hamlet points toward the religious, to a metaphysics of the numinous, whether one wants finds him an "honest ghost" (1.5.44) of Catholic orthodoxy or something, in Reformist eyes, distinctly heterodox that "abuses [Hamlet] to damn [him]" (2.2.604). Interestingly enough, it is Hamlet himself who holds these competing orthodoxies up to his view, as well as to our own, without settling the question definitively. On the other hand, if we understand Old Hamlet as a walking corpse, this points to a metaphysics of the phenomenal or material, which, again, is quite close to the understanding of the living dead in modern zombieism. The play, not surprisingly, allows both readings: the one admits the possibility of the immaterial real (ghosts, demons, God); the other admits to the view that only the material is real or existent, and thus one can understand the current interest in portraying *Hamlet* as a zombie play, complete with apocalyptic cosmology.

In zombie literature and film, human beings inhabit a godforsaken or godless universe. Humans struggle, alone, against a zombie onslaught that promises only to overrun them. The idea of a personal God who creates human beings in his image and cares for the entirety of creation is absent. In films such as *Zombie Apocalypse* (2011)[81] and novels such Max Brooks's *World War Z* and Colson Whitehead's *Zone One*, the particular mechanisms by which physical revenants function are left unclear and remain physiologically dubious, but they are clearly material in nature: "The plague stopped the heart, one's essence sloughed off the pathetic human meat and dogpaddled through the ectoplasm or whatever, and then the plague restarted the heart."[82] There is mention neither of a nonphysical mind nor of an immaterial soul; the human body is revivified by purely physical means, in the same way that one would restart a lawn mower or other machine. The soulless dead do not *reanimate*—the idea is contradicted in the very etymology of the word.

In a similar vein, Paulina envisions Antigonus's (soulless) revivification from the dead as being utterly "monstrous." *Hamlet*'s Roman horde risen from their graves conjures the same horrific image, as does Prospero's remembrance of his ability to call forth the soulless dead from their graves. These are the subhuman living dead, and as such, they represent a heterodox departure from Reformed and, to a lesser extent, Catholic theology. What prevents them from becoming truly radical is that they are unstaged—merely imagined—and thus they remain only in the speculative framework of the plays. The physical presence of Old Hamlet, by way of contrast, teases audiences. He tests our understanding of the heterodox: he is possibly a ghost, or a demon—"the devil hath power / T'assume a pleasing shape" (2.2.600–01)—or even a physical revenant. Shakespeare never resolves his ontological status, nor perhaps should we. It is part of Shakespeare's vaunted negative capability, his seemingly limitless capacity to hold varying possibilities up to view for us, even radical religious and folk beliefs.

Shakespeare need not have read the legend of the three kings or the Newburgh and Byland Abbey accounts of the walking dead. Belief in the dead revivifying to harry the living stretches to time immemorial and was well understood in Shakespeare's day, as is evident in the corpselike figures he envisions in *The Tempest*, *The Winter's Tale*, and *Hamlet*. Hobgoblins (Puck), sprites (Ariel), ghosts (Old Hamlet, Banquo), fairies (Queen Mab, Oberon, Titania), leprechauns, and other such creatures all belong to traditional folklore. Shakespeare need not have believed in their existence, either, in order to represent them, which is what he did over and again. Thus, it is no stretch of the imagination to suggest that his ambivalent treatment of Old Hamlet both hints at and ties into longstanding folk legends of the walking dead. As the least propagandistic of authors, Shakespeare is comfortable representing heterodox and even radical religious beliefs: he freely explores such imaginative possibilities, testing them against more standard Catholic and Reformed beliefs that Old Hamlet is either a ghost or a demon, respectively. A revivified Old Hamlet harrying the dead would indeed be a radical challenge to traditional theological beliefs, but Shakespeare seems interested in staging the possibility, not simply in denying it.

There is no question, too, that from the frozen, murky castle walls of Elsinore in the play's opening scene, *Hamlet* is intended to be unsettling. Lacan helps us recall its eeriness:

For those who read the text, it is something that knocks you over backwards, makes you bite the carpet and roll on the ground, it is something unimaginable. There is not a verse of Hamlet, nor one of his replies, which does not have in English a percussive power, a violence of language which makes of it something which one is at every moment absolutely stupefied. You could believe that it was written yesterday, that one could not write things like that three centuries ago.[83]

Hamlet's seemingly endless contemporaneity allows us, four centuries later, to reexamine his depiction of Old Hamlet in light of our ongoing fascination with the living dead. So familiar have we become with the play that we run the risk, as Lacan remarks, of domesticating it and its uncanny figure of Old Hamlet—he who confronts his son and us at every turn, continually disturbing and frustrating our attempts to categorize the otherness he represents.

Finally, as I was writing this essay, director Jonathan Levine's *Warm Bodies*, another *Romeo and Juliet* zombie mash-up, was wending its way through the cineplex.[84] Its zombie Romeo, known simply as R, begins to revivify: he dreams and slowly begins to reacquire the ability to speak, in the end living happily ever after with his Julie. For his part, too, Chris Stiles has given us a zombie Hamlet in a very loose adaptation of the play, but the time cannot be far away—perhaps should not be if Shakespeare is to remain our contemporary[85]—when productions faithful to Shakespeare's language offer us a corpselike Old Hamlet fully in keeping with the play's wonderful ambivalence. Foucault declared that the "only role" of critical commentary "is to say *finally*, what has silently been articulated *deep down*."[86] My reading of Old Hamlet as a physical revenant relies on a close reading of Shakespeare's ambivalent treatment of him. Shakespeare was clearly interested in both ghosts and the walking dead of popular religious and folk belief; his plays adumbrate this latter possibility in ways modern staging can circumspectly employ.

NOTES

1. Seth Grahame-Smith, *Pride and Prejudice and Zombies* (Philadelphia: Quirk Books, 2009); Nickolas Cook, *Alice in Zombieland* (Naperville, IL: Sourcebooks, 2011); Seth Grahame-Smith, *Abraham Lincoln: Vampire Hunter* (New York: Grand Central Publishing, 2011); Richard Schenkman, director, *Abraham Lincoln vs. Zombies* (2012); Lynn Messina, *Little Vampire Women* (New York: HarperTeen, 2010); and Sherri Browning Erwin, *Jane Slayre* (New York: Gallery, 2010).

2. Ben Jonson, "To the Memory of My Beloved, the Author," in *The First Folio of Shakespeare*, ed. Charlton Hinman, 2nd ed. (New York: W. W. Norton, 1996), 10.

3. "Zombies are back," declared Warren St. John, "Market for Zombies? It's Undead (Aaahhh!)," *New York Times*, March 26, 2006, print edition, sec. 9, 2. Recent films include Edgar Wright, dir., *Shaun of the Dead*, 2004; Danny Boyle, dir., *28 Days Later*, 2003; Ruben Fleischer, dir., *Zombieland*, 2009; Yannick Dahan and Benjamin Rocher, dirs., *La Horde*, 2010. Novels include Stephen King, *Cell: A Novel* (New York: Scribner, 2006); Colson Whitehead, *Zone One: A Novel* (New York: Doubleday, 2011); Max Brooks, *The Zombie Survival*

Guide: Complete Protection from the Living Dead (New York: Three Rivers Press, 2003); Max Brooks, *World War Z: An Oral History of the Zombie War* (New York: Three Rivers Press, 2007).

4. Lori Handeland, *Shakespeare Undead* (New York: St. Martin's Griffin, 2010), 13; she also wrote a sequel, *Zombie Island: A Shakespeare Undead Novel* (New York: St. Martin's Griffin, 2012).

5. Jordan Galland, dir. *Rosencrantz & Guildenstern Are Undead* (Indican, 2010).

6. *Hamlet, Zombie Killer of Denmark: A Comedy in One Act* (Crystal Beach, Ontario: Theatrefolk, 2010), 26–27.

7. Ryan Denmark, dir., *Romeo and Juliet vs. The Living Dead*, 2009.

8. Sarah Schmelling, "Hamlet (Facebook NewsFeed Edition)," in *The Best of McSweeney's Internet Tendency*, eds. Chris Monks and John Warner (San Francisco: McSweeney's, 2014), 79.

9. *OED*, s.v. "zombie."

10. Hans Urs von Balthasar, *Theo-Drama: Theological Dramatic Theory*, volume 1: *Prolegomena*, trans. Graham Harrison (San Francisco: Ignatius Press, 1988), 384; Cynthia Marshall, *Last Things and Last Plays: Shakespearean Eschatology* (Carbondale, IL: Southern Illinois University Press, 1991), xiv.

11. Sigmund Freud, "The 'Uncanny'," in *The Standard Edition of the Complete Psychological Works of Sigmund Freud*, ed. and trans. James Strachey, vol. 17 (London: Hogarth Press, 1953), 241.

12. Catherine Belsey, "Shakespeare's Sad Tale for Winter: Hamlet and the Tradition of Fireside Ghost Stories," *Shakespeare Quarterly* 61, no. 1 (2010): 1–27; Adam Max Cohen, *Wonder in Shakespeare* (London: Palgrave Macmillan, 2012), esp. 43–52.

13. Robert West, *The Invisible World: A Study of Pneumatology in Elizabethan Drama* (New York: Octagon Books, 1969); Katharine Briggs, *The Anatomy of Puck* (New York: Arno Press, 1977); Belsey, "Shakespeare's Sad Tale for Winter"; Stephen Greenblatt, *Hamlet in Purgatory* (Princeton: Princeton University Press, 2002). On the distinction between the living dead—zombies—and the undead—ghosts and vampires—see Kyle Bishop, "Dead Man Still Walking," *Journal of Popular Film & Television* 37, no. 1 (Spring 2009): 16–25, esp. 20.

14. Eleanor Prosser, *Hamlet and Revenge* (Stanford: Stanford University Press, 1967), 255; Greenblatt, *Hamlet in Purgatory*, 156–57.

15. *OED*, s.v. "zombie." A zombie was originally "the name of a snake-deity in voodoo cults of . . . West Africa and Haiti," and this seems entirely consistent with the exotic paganism and sorcery associated with Shakespeare's Bermudan isle.

16. Aristotle, *On the Soul*, in *The Complete Works of Aristotle: The Revised Oxford Translation*, ed. Jonathan Barnes, trans. J. A. Smith, vol. 1, Bollingen Series 71:2 (Princeton: Princeton University Press, 1995), 402a1.

17. Lloyd E. Berry and William Whittingham, eds., *The Geneva Bible: A Facsimile of the 1560 Edition* (Madison: University of Wisconsin Press, 1969), Eccles. 12: 7; Thomas Aquinas, "The Summa Contra Gentiles," in *Introduction To Saint Thomas Aquinas*, ed. and trans. Anton C. Pegis (New York: Modern Library, 1965), esp. 282, 289; St. Gregory of Nyssa, *The Soul and the Resurrection*, trans. Catharine P. Roth (Crestwood, NY: St. Vladimir's Seminary Press, 1993), esp. 37; Plato, "Phaedo," in *Plato*, trans. H. N. Fowler, The Loeb Classical Library [Greek Authors] (Cambridge: Harvard University Press, 1943), sec. 80c–81c.

18. William Sampson, *The Vow Breaker or, The Faire Maide of Clifton*, ed. Hans Wallrath (1636; rpr. Vaduz: Kraus Reprint Ltd., 1963), 3.1.110–13.

19. Peter Marshall, *Beliefs and the Dead in Reformation England* (Oxford: Oxford University Press, 2002), 248. See also Anthony Anderson, *The Shield of Our Safetie* (London, 1581), sig. H1v; John Preston, *A Sermon Preached at the Funeral of Mr. Arthur Upton* (London, 1619), 33; and Henry Smith, *The Sermons of Master H. Smith Gathered into One Volume* (London, 1592), 540, all of which are cited in Marshall.

20. Thomas Browne, *Religio Medici*, in *The Major Works*, ed. C. A. Patrides (New York: Penguin Books, 1977), 108.

21. John Foxe, *Actes and Monuments* (London, 1570), 409–10.

22. Michel Foucault, "The Discourse on Language," in *The Archaeology of Knowledge*, trans. Rupert Sawyer (New York: Pantheon Books, 1972), 224.

23. Jean Delumeau, *Sin and Fear: The Emergence of a Western Guilt Culture, 13th–18th Centuries*, trans. Eric Nicholson (New York: St. Martin's Press, 1990), 68.

24. Jacqueline Simpson, "Repentant Soul or Walking Corpse? Debatable Apparitions in Medieval England," *Folklore* 114, no. 3 (December 1, 2003): 390.

25. William of Newburgh, *The History of William of Newburgh* (ca. 1198), trans. Joseph Stevenson (1896; rpr. Lampeter, Wales: Llanerch Publishers, 1996), 658.

26. The manuscript is transcribed in M. R. James, "Twelve Medieval Ghost-Stories," *The English Historical Review* 37, no. 147 (July 1, 1922): 413–422. See also Marshall, *Beliefs and the Dead in Reformation England*, 16, 256; and Simpson, "Repentant Soul or Walking Corpse?," 389.

27. Belsey, "Shakespeare's Sad Tale for Winter," 11.

28. Ibid., 10, 16.

29. Ibid., 20, her italics.

30. Ibid., 12.

31. Freud, "The 'Uncanny'," 219.

32. Geoffrey Bullough, ed., *Narrative and Dramatic Sources of Shakespeare*, vol. 2 (New York: Columbia University Press, 1958), 83.

33. Peter Ackroyd, *Shakespeare: The Biography* (New York: Anchor, 2006), 238.

34. Consider, too, the minor character Balthasar's singing a song to Diana in which he asks, "Graves, yawn and yield your dead, / Till death be utterèd, / Heavily, heavily" (*Ado* 5.3.19–21).

35. George Walton Williams, "Antique Romans and Modern Danes in Julius Caesar and Hamlet," in *Literature and Nationalism*, eds. Vincent Newey and Ann Thompson (Savage, MD: Barnes & Noble, 1991), 43–44.

36. Berry and Whittingham, *The Geneva Bible*, Matthew 27:52–53; Naseeb Shaheen, *Biblical References in Shakespeare's Plays* (Newark: University of Delaware Press, 1999), 526, 537.

37. In *Matthew Henry's Commentary: Matthew to John*, vol. 5 (New York: Fleming H. Revell Company, n.d.), 432, Henry comments, "Death to the saints is but the sleep of the body, and the grave the bed it sleeps in; they awoke by the power of the Lord Jesus. . . . We may raise many enquiries concerning it, which we cannot resolve."

38. Ann Thompson and Neil Taylor, eds., *Hamlet*, 3rd ed. (Arden Shakespeare, 2006), 159n; David Bevington, ed., *The Complete Works of Shakespeare*, 7th edition (Boston: Pearson, 2014), 1099n.

39. William of Newburgh, *The History of William of Newburgh*, 658–59. Old Hamlet has a similar penchant for appearing "at this dead hour," "in the dead waste and middle of the night" (1.1.69; 1.2.199).

40. Marshall, *Beliefs and the Dead in Reformation England*, 257–58.

41. See Marjorie B. Garber, *Shakespeare's Ghost Writers: Literature as Uncanny Causality* (New York: Methuen, 1987), 144; David Scott Kastan, *A Will to Believe: Shakespeare and Religion* (Oxford: Oxford University Press, 2014), 121.

42. See also 1.1.44–54, 143–54, 1.2.215–20, 248; 1.4.38, 58, 61–63, 66–69, 79; 1.5.174; and 3.4.140.

43. Berry and Whittingham, *The Geneva Bible*, Matt. 7:3 and Luke 6:42; Shaheen, *Biblical References in Shakespeare's Plays*, 537.

44. Thompson and Taylor, eds., *Hamlet*, 159n.

45. Michael Almereyda, dir., *Hamlet*, 2000.

46. *OED*, s.v. "margin."

47. Cohen, *Wonder in Shakespeare*, 46.

48. *OED*, s.v. "stalk."

49. Arthur McGee, *The Elizabethan Hamlet* (New Haven: Yale University Press, 1987), 49.

50. Christopher Marlowe, *Dr. Faustus: Based on the A Text*, ed. Roma Gill, 2nd ed. (W. W. Norton, 1990), 13.108–15.

51. McGee, *The Elizabethan Hamlet*, 49.

52. There is some discrepancy in the stated time since interment: Hamlet insists that his father has been dead for two months (3.2.128–29), or possibly even less (1.2.138), while Ophelia puts the date four months ago.

53. Marc S. Micozzi, "Frozen Environments and Soft Tissue Preservation," in *Forensic Taphonomy: The Postmortem Fate of Human Remains*, eds. William D. Haglund and Marcella H. Sorg (Boca Raton: CRC Press, 1997), 171-80, esp. 171–72.

54. *OED*, s.v. "taphonomy."

55. William Shakespeare, *The First Quarto of Hamlet*, ed. Kathleen O. Irace (New York: Cambridge University Press, 1998), 16.65; R. W. Mann, W. M. Bass, and L. W. Meadows, "Time Since Death and Decomposition of the Human Body: Variables and Observations in Case and Experimental Field Studies," *Journal of Forensic Sciences* 35, no. 1 (January 1990): 103–111, esp. 105, 108–110; William D. Haglund and Marcella H. Sorg, "Human Remains in Water Environments," in *Advances in Forensic Taphonomy*, 201–19.

56. Alison Shell, *Shakespeare and Religion* (London: Arden Shakespeare, 2010), 113.

57. *OED*, s.v. "ghost." An apparition can also be material. *OED*, s.v. "apparition."

58. Warwick comments upon seeing the dead body of Humphrey, the Duke of Gloucester, "Oft have I seen a timely-parted ghost, / Of ashy semblance, meager, pale, and bloodless" (3.2.161–62). Gloucester's ghost is merely his corpse.

59. Cohen, *Wonder in Shakespeare*, 45.

60. Shakespeare, *The First Quarto of Hamlet*, 11.56 sd.

61. Marlowe, *Dr. Faustus*, 1.24–26.

62. Prospero's reference derives most directly from Medea's claim, "I call up dead men from their graves" in Golding's 1567 translation of Ovid's *Metamorphoses*. See Geoffrey Bullough, ed., *Narrative and Dramatic Sources of Shakespeare*, 8: 314–15.

63. See also Berry and Whittingham, *The Geneva Bible*, 1 Cor. 15.18; and Philippe Ariès, *The Hour of Our Death*, trans. Helen Weaver (New York: Knopf, 1981), esp. 24.

64. Shaheen, *Biblical References in Shakespeare's Plays*, 749.

65. Sean Benson, *Shakespearean Resurrection: The Art of Almost Raising the Dead* (Pittsburgh: Duquesne University Press, 2009), 173–75.

66. Ibid., 154.

67. Ibid., 29.

68. Marshall, *Beliefs and the Dead in Reformation England*, 226. See also Berry and Whittingham, *The Geneva Bible*, 1 Cor. 15:51–54; and the priest's statement that Ophelia "should in ground unsanctified [be] lodged / Till the last trumpet" (5.1.229–30).

69. Simon Pegg, "Afterword," in Robert Kirkman, *Miles Behind Us*, vol. 2, *The Walking Dead* (Berkeley: Image Comics, 2009), 133.

70. On plague and the closing of the theaters, see Ackroyd, *Shakespeare*, 419; Jonathan Bate, *Soul of the Age: A Biography of the Mind of William Shakespeare* (New York: Random House, 2009), 335; and Gary Taylor, "Shakespeare Plays on Renaissance Stages," in *The Cambridge Companion to Shakespeare on Stage*, eds. Stanley Wells and Sarah Stanton (Cambridge: Cambridge University Press, 2002): 1–20, esp. 18–19.

71. William Camden, *Annals of the Reign of Queen Elizabeth*, quoted in John Nichols, ed., *The Progresses and Public Processions of King James the First*, 4 vols. (London, 1828; rpt. New York: AMS P, 1980), 1:228n.

72. Eric S. Mallin, *Inscribing the Time: Shakespeare and the End of Elizabethan England* (Berkeley: University of California Press, 1995), 104–05. See also Paul A. Slack, "Mortality and Epidemic Crisis, 1485–1610," in *Health, Medicine, and Mortality in the Sixteenth Century*, ed. Charles Webster (Cambridge: Cambridge University Press, 1979), 9–60, esp. 22; and F. P. Wilson, *The Plague in Shakespeare's London* (Oxford: Oxford University Press, 1999).

73. William of Newburgh, *The History of William of Newburgh*, 657.

74. Ibid., 658.

75. Ibid., 660. The idea has proven equally appealing on the modern stage: John Heimbuch's play, *William Shakespeare's Land of the Dead* (2012), sets *Henry V* amidst a plague.

76. Mallin, *Inscribing the Time*, 67.

77. Thomas Ady, *A Perfect Discovery of Witches* (London, 1661), 169.

78. William Tyndale, *An Answer to Sir Thomas More's Dialogue* (Cambridge: Parker Society, 1850), 143. Quoted in Greenblatt, *Hamlet in Purgatory*, 35.

79. Greenblatt, *Hamlet in Purgatory*, 33, 38–41. On the solidification of the Reformers' opposition to Purgatory, see also 10-13, 23–37.

80. Ibid., 41.

81. Nick Lyon, dir., *Zombie Apocalypse*, 2011.

82. Whitehead, *Zone One*, 226–27.

83. Jacques Lacan, *The Seminar of Jacques Lacan*, ed. Jacques-Alain Miller, trans. Cormac Gallagher, vol. 6 (New York: Norton, 2002), 177.

84. Jonathan Levine, dir. *Warm Bodies*, 2013.

85. See Jan Kott, *Shakespeare Our Contemporary* (London: Methuen, 1967).

86. Foucault, "The Discourse on Language," 221, italics his.

Chapter Five

Hamlet as Meta(physical)theater

If *Hamlet* teeters on the brink of an apocalyptic world with revivified corpses and thus anticipates the possibility of religious nihilism that *King Lear* so trenchantly explores, the play also offers opportunities to understand its stance vis-à-vis the Church in a more traditional light. As noted in the introduction, the religious ideas within Shakespeare's plays can typically be located somewhere within the orbit of the Church's teachings, but they often arrive at a more orthodox stance only after—or alongside—a serious probing of the heterodox. *Hamlet* is perhaps the quintessential example of this phenomenon, as it encapsulates within its pages an almost constant tension between the orthodox and the unorthodox. The last chapter explored a distinctly heterodox reading of Old Hamlet as a corpselike figure, yet this position joins the myriad of interpretations of Hamlet and his eponymous play as being religiously heterodox, and perhaps even openly secular and materialist. The prevailing modern view is that Hamlet, a professed believer, belongs more properly to a line of bloody revengers that stretches from Seneca's Thyestes to Thomas Kyd's Hieronimo in *The Spanish Tragedy*. *Hamlet* itself clearly belongs to the genre of revenge tragedy, which is also at odds with orthodox Christian teaching. The apostle Paul, for instance, places revenge beyond the jurisdiction of human action: "Dearly beloved, avenge not yourselves, but rather give place unto wrath: for it is written, Vengeance is mine; I will repay, saith the Lord" (Romans 12:19). Yet the play underscores in no uncertain terms Hamlet's natural desire for revenge:

Does it not, think thee, stand me now upon—

He that hath killed my king and whored my mother,

Popped in between th'election and my hopes,

Thrown out his angle for my proper life,

And with such coz'nage—is't not perfect conscience

To quit him with this arm? (5.2.63–68)

Hamlet's conscience, as we shall see, is where the real struggle between revenge and forbearance plays out. Lest we miss the point of his heterodoxy, he suggests that forgiveness in this case would constitute a mortal sin—not against God, but against his own sense of honor: "And is't not to be damned / To let this canker of our nature come / In further evil?" (68–70). As either a revenger or a misguided and self-appointed scourge, Hamlet wants to, and very nearly does, embrace heterodoxy. The opposition between the sacred and the profane is felt nowhere more keenly than in *Hamlet*. Chapter 4 offered a heterodox, perhaps even godless reading of *Hamlet*, and I would like to counterpoise this and other secular readings of the play against a modern theistic reading grounded in the religious aesthetics of Hans Urs von Balthasar.

The nineteenth and twentieth centuries saw a shift from theological to psychological criticism; the contrast between the two is perhaps most clearly seen in Freud's treatment of religious faith:

> These [religious beliefs], which are given out as teachings, are not precipitates of experience or end-results of thinking: they are illusions, fulfillments of the oldest, strongest and most urgent wishes of mankind. The secret of their strength lies in the strength of those wishes. As we already know, the terrifying impression of helplessness in childhood aroused the need for protection—for protection through love—which was provided by the father; and the recognition that this helplessness lasts throughout life made it necessary to cling to the existence of a father, but this time a more powerful one. Thus the benevolent rule of a divine Providence allays our fear of the dangers of life. [1]

In Freud's reading, religious belief is mere wish-fulfilment, Hamlet's religious longing illusion. People are afraid of uncertainty, the unknown, and thus faith is a mere bugbear, "a lost cause" "comparable to a childhood neurosis." [2] But as Plantinga has argued, religious belief is an illusion for Freud because he merely *assumes*, but does not appear to present an argument for, atheism: "he simply takes it for granted that there is no God and theistic belief is false; he then casts about for some kind of explanation of this widespread phenomenon of mistaken belief." [3]

Likewise for Balthasar, applying psychoanalysis of this sort to Shakespearean drama "is necessarily to misinterpret the core of the action." Instead, he suggests that we can glimpse in certain of them "a genuine, Christian dramatic genre."[4] Secular critics often find themselves uncomfortable discussing the religious and its alleged naïveté, yet Shell points out how the term *secular* itself is largely anachronistic when it is applied by modern scholars to the early modern period.[5] Indeed, as Debora Shuger remarks, the English Renaissance constituted not merely "a culture whose members generally were religious," but a culture so suffused with religion that it became the "cultural matrix for explorations of virtually every topic: kingship, selfhood, rationality, language, marriage, ethics, and so forth."[6] Hamlet's own exploration of these topics, especially selfhood, is at the center of the play. He wishes devoutly—sacrilegiously even—"that the Everlasting had not fixed / His canon 'gainst self-slaughter" (1.2.131–32) or, for that matter, revenge killings. As Hamlet knows, in a theological approach to life—the life of faith—nothing escapes sacred order.[7] Identity is always understood in relation to God as creator: one can raise oneself along what Rieff calls the divine "vertical in authority" in "obedience to the commandments of sacred order," or lower oneself.[8] Either way, "to be human is to be always somewhere in that vertical,"[9] and in that relationship, each person is responsible to God for her actions.[10] For Rieff, this means action:

> In the traditions out of which I come, the truth was that life's path, however the mischance may occur that was earlier called fate, depended upon an understanding that whatever is done would be done in such a way that men would feel the presiding presence. . . . The presence presiding would see that truth, which, in your knowledge, you would share with the presence, an awesome knowledge that nevertheless demanded action.[11]

Hamlet gives every indication that he, too, feels the presiding presence—what Calvin called the *sensus divinitatis*—and the need to act in response.

Balthasar sheds light on this dialectic, as his theological aesthetics can help us to understand *Hamlet* not as metatheater, but as Metatheater—or, to be even more precise, as metaphysical theater. In the first of his five-volume *Theo-Drama*, Balthasar argues for a deep affinity between the Church and theater because each is fundamentally dramatic. For Balthasar, the Bible is not so much narrative as divine and human "theo-drama" unfolding before our eyes. Aidan Nichols, one of Balthasar's commentators, explains: "The Church has sometimes used drama to express the action-filled content of revelation, but her theologians have not in any all-embracing way (till Balthasar!) presented revelation as itself divine theatre."[12] God's revelation in the world is not an object or a thing, but an *event* culminating in "decisive action—Good Friday turns into Easter," with Christ as "God's act" in response to human fallenness: "This revelation, however, in its total shape . . . is dramatic. It is the history of an initiative on God's part for his world. . . . and the acceptance of it is the 'event' of transformation that takes place in man, in which man is crucified to the world and raised up by God and to

God."[13] Harold Fisch has similarly argued that the Old Testament covenant "and the response to it by the human partners to the covenant are not merely high drama, but high drama bracketed so as to draw our attention to its dramatic character. Nor is this surprising. Indeed, it would have been surprising if Shakespeare had overlooked so powerful a dramatic model."[14] Shakespeare almost certainly knew the model, including its notion of God as the dramatist of human life.[15]

It is this idea upon which Balthasar builds his dramatic criticism. "God, as Creator, is always 'involved' in the world, and this means that there is always a divine-human dramatic tension. . . . a play is always going on 'in front of the curtain.'"[16] Theo-drama takes place on the world stage; the stage drama is metatheater, set in motion before those already in the existential play of life. Balthasar suggests that in the profoundest human theater, the existential search for meaning by characters on stage corresponds to the theo-drama of real persons in relation to God. Theater thus offers not merely an imitation of an action but something even deeper than that which is suggested in Aristotle's analysis: "an illumination of existence," "a mirror in which existence can directly behold itself."[17] How is this accomplished?

An astute psychologist of the theatrical experience, Balthasar posits a twofold pleasure that theatergoers experience. First, in what he calls "self-projection," the experience on stage "spills over" to the audience: "the seriousness of what is being enacted can be so overpowering that the spectator is seized by it and recalled to the 'authenticity' of his own existence,"[18] to what Fisch calls "the play-without-the-play."[19] Second, plays offer the pleasure of a solution. As in the "drama of existence," plays "awaken in the spectator a tense expectation that he will learn something revealing about the mystery of life."[20] We want to know what the play is about, what it means and what, specifically, it means for us in the unfolding drama of our own lives. Boundaries between theater and life, and indeed between theater and theology, blur.[21] Theater attunes us to look to the reality of our own lives, to what lies behind or hidden in the quotidian in order to understand each person's "drama of existence." For a believer such as Hamlet, "in and through the temporal 'play' [of life] as such we can glimpse (but not seize hold of) an eternal meaning."[22] Church and theater thus share common aims and even heuristic practices: the Church not only uses (in the mass, Eucharist, and other rituals) but is theater. As one of novelist Peter De Vries's characters remarks of scripture, "it's great drama. Sheer theater—God's word."[23]

The best plays can open what Balthasar calls a "metaphysico-religious" window into our existence:

> for as long as theatre has existed, in all its high periods—which were clearly characterized by something over and above the business side of things—people have asked more of drama than [mere diversion]. *People have sought*

insight into the nature and meaning of existence, things that cannot simply be read off from its immanent course but radiate from a background that explodes the beautiful and gripping play on the stage—which suddenly becomes inwardly relevant to the spectator—and that relates it to something that transcends it.[24]

Transcendence begins with the immanence of the stage performance, but then, as Balthasar comments, "the 'I' of the stage [actor] blends with the 'I' of the spectator, merging with the latter's living finitude. In this way, it points in the opposite direction too, beyond itself. That is, it points toward the intention of the author, and beyond him to the horizon of all meaning whatsoever."[25] This is Metatheater, the play outside the play. Rieff has argued that one role of the Renaissance artist was to remind one's audience of the great truths, with Shakespeare as one of the "older symbolists who saw in what there is that which is."[26] The stage can point not merely to itself but to the divine-human stage, and thus to the ultimate mystery of life.

Hamlet is a prime example of what Balthasar describes as a play "written from within a particular horizon of faith and consciousness."[27] Even Claudius, the fratricide, lives and breathes within that horizon: he recognizes that his offense "smells to heaven" and "hath the primal eldest curse upon't" (3.3.36–37). For Balthasar, when an author, human or divine, creates a dramatic event, "the important thing is that a horizon is opened up for 'some solution or another,' that is, the aspect of epiphany as such."[28] Hamlet's situation is that of a Christian believer who finds himself in a role, the contours and demands of which he does not understand until the end of the play, and perhaps even then not fully. Although Balthasar scarcely mentions *Hamlet* in his general discussion of Shakespeare or of theater, some mystery of the theo-drama, of the inscrutability of God's will, remains in this life beyond Hamlet's grasp, though he is clearly reaching toward it. In the end, *Hamlet*'s conscience opens into an epiphany that asks him to act within both the horizontal plane of human existence as well as the vertical plane of the divine.

It is important to remind ourselves that despite the elusiveness of Hamlet's character, he is, as Bevington has recently commented, "devoutly Christian."[29] Contemplating suicide, he wishes in vain "that the Everlasting had not fixed / His canon 'gainst self-slaughter! (1.2.131–32). He later enjoins Ophelia, "Nymph, in thy orisons / Be all my sins remembered" (3.1.90–91). His vocabulary—his mental apparatus—is steeped in the language of Christendom, even veering into a *Lear*-like vision of a dark apocalypse. Told by Rosencrantz that "the world's grown honest," his only reply is "Then is doomsday near" (2.2.237–39), a radical response echoing popular millenarianism. Likewise, when he comes upon Claudius praying, he would kill him but relents when he concludes that doing so now would send Claudius's soul "to heaven": "And am I then revenged, / To take him in the purging of his soul, / When he is fit and seasoned for his passage? / No!" (3.3.84–87).

Although an avowed believer, Hamlet is not the most saintly of persons, as he freely confesses to Ophelia: "I am very proud, revengeful, ambitious, with more offenses at my beck than I have thoughts to put them in, imagination to give them shape, or time to act them in. What should such fellows as I do crawling between earth and heaven?" (3.1.126–29). That last image is a creaturely one, with dark overtones of bestial crawling. Unlike *The Winter's Tale*'s Leontes and Polixenes, who "knew not / The doctrine of ill-doing, nor dreamed / That any did" (1.2.69–71), Hamlet is almost preternaturally—morbidly—aware of his own transgressions, as well as of original sin, and advises Ophelia accordingly: "We are arrant knaves all; believe none of us. Go thy ways to a nunnery" (3.1.130–31). He is indeed revengeful, misogynistic (if not a misanthrope as well), and, one could argue, a murderer several times over by play's end.[30] Hamlet should never be confused with a Christ figure, but at the same time it is important not to forget, as readers occasionally do, that the play is written from the horizon of Christendom, nominally Catholic, though with infusions of Reformation thought, including Hamlet's curious choice of university in Wittenberg. Imperfect and wayward believer that he is, Hamlet still sees the world in light of this framework.

His problem is how to live in the corrupt currents of his world, and to know what to do in light of Old Hamlet's allegation of his brother's fratricide. For Nietzsche—no friend of the Gospel—"Christianity is a *praxis*, not a doctrine of faith."[31] This is perhaps especially true in a Catholic framework; it is what one does, how one lives, rather than simply what one believes. Yet Nietzsche, perhaps the exemplar of the modern unbeliever, reduced Christianity to orthopraxy, to a mere code of conduct. Doing so, according to Balthasar, "fails to preserve the distance between God's praxis which operates on man and man's praxis which takes its direction from God's. 'God shows his love toward us in that, while we were yet sinners, Christ died for us' (Rom. 5:8)."[32] But for the Christian to understand the divine praxis requires a correct doctrine of faith.[33] Getting the doctrine right in a given situation is no simple task:

> for Nietzsche, and anyone else who is not entirely naïve, philanthropy is only *one* role, *one* way of acting on the world stage. There are many other, opposed ways, and they are unfortunately indispensable: the struggle for survival in which the strongest or the greatest talent prevails; self-defense—both social and individual—against unjust attack now or in the future; the administration of justice with its sanctions; and so forth.[34]

Benighted and confused as he is, Hamlet is trying to figure out what to do, with no real guides other than the specter of his father and the calling of his faith, neither of which is a certain guide to the course of action he should take. He could turn the other cheek (Matthew 5:39) and go to his death, as Claudius no doubt hopes, but Hamlet, as presumptive heir to the throne and stepson to his would-be murderer, has an equal and powerful right to self-defense and to the defense of his kingdom: "The great characters are not simply individuals, they carry the burden of the common good; kings, heroes, generals, statesmen, rebels either represent a suprapersonal order or else they question it."[35] Hamlet's position is uniquely ambivalent, as he represents the suprapersonal order of the state through his lineage and status as heir to the throne, but with Claudius having "popped in between th'election and [his] hopes" (5.2.65), he questions that order: "The king is a thing—" "Of nothing" (4.2.29, 31). He would just as soon overthrow the suprapersonal order Claudius also represents, even if doing so means his own demise. Hamlet has to balance the sometimes competing goods of his personal life as son to Old Hamlet and of his political life as Prince of Denmark—not to mention his life as a child of God. Unfortunately, he has no clear course of action, especially since he, unlike the audience, has not overheard Claudius's confession and must instead rely on dubious circumstantial evidence such as Claudius's reaction to *The Mousetrap.*

A course of action implies a role; what role, if any, is Hamlet to play? The Senecan revenger; the madcap Amleth of the sources; the passive dolt of Claudius' machinations; the dutiful son who moves on after his father's death; or the Christian pacifist? For Erasmus, "the whole life of mortal men, what is it but a sort of play, in which various persons make their entrances in various costumes, and each one plays his own part until the director gives him his cue to leave the stage?"[36] Such is Hamlet's confusing situation, as he himself notes of Claudius's directing a "play" to kill him: "Being thus benetted round with villainies— / Ere I could make a prologue to my brains, They had begun the play" (5.2.29–31). Hamlet's metatheatrical awareness surfaces here and in *The Mousetrap*, but Shakespeare firmly embeds it in the widely held idea of life as a stage on which all people play various, often changing, roles. Like Balthasar, Alasdair MacIntyre suggests that this is the play-like feature of life: "We enter upon a stage which we did not design and we find ourselves part of an action that was not of our making. Each of us being a main character in his own drama plays subordinate parts in the dramas of others, and each drama constrains the others. In my drama, perhaps, I am Hamlet."[37] Hamlet is called to different roles by Old Hamlet, by Gertrude, by Ophelia, by his duties as prince, by his own conscience, and so on.

In ancient Greek drama, the tragic actor used a mask because he was not allowed to present his own subjectivity.[38] Hamlet is likewise supremely self-conscious of the masks he wears and from which he is called to step forth: "Good Hamlet," Gertrude tells him, "cast thy nighted color off, / And let thine eye look like a friend on Denmark" (1.2.68–69). Harold Bloom has remarked that "Hamlet can seem an actual person who somehow has been caught inside a play, so that he has to perform even though he doesn't want to."[39] His adopting various roles while resisting others gives him verisimilitude. Asked by his mother why his grief for his dead father seems to bear such an emphasis, Hamlet responds, "Seems, madam? Nay, it is. I know not 'seems'" (1.2.76). He then goes on to explain that none of the various masks of his appearance—mourning clothes, tears, sighing, and other bodily signs of grieving—"can denote me truly. These indeed seem, / For they are actions that a man might play. / But I have that within which passes show; / These but the trappings and the suits of woe" (83–86). His use of hendiadys in the final line neatly reflects the bifurcation he continually points to between the outward, seeming mask he wears and the inner man he claims to be. That inner subjectivity or consciousness passes show because it cannot be seen but is, he claims, irreducibly there.

Hamlet's quandary is an existential one shared by believers and nonbelievers alike: "Not only has the individual in the world theatre to perform the particular function allotted to him (by whom or what?—circumstance?—God?—himself?), he also, if he is to be really himself, has to identify himself with the role he plays, in spite of the fact that at some mysterious point he is *not* identical with it."[40] Hamlet seldom if ever feels identical with the roles he plays. He declares, for instance, that he can hardly play the revenger because Claudius is "no more like my father / Than I to Hercules" (1.2.152–53). He has been tragically miscast and is thus the wrong man for the job: "The time is out of joint. Oh, cursèd spite / That ever I was born to set it right!" (1.5.197–98). To further exacerbate matters, he is pulled in different directions by those who would impose a role on him: Claudius wants him to be the defenseless fledgling killed in the nest—his going back to university in Wittenberg "is most retrograde to our desire" (1.2.114). Likewise, Old Hamlet implores him, over and again, to "revenge his foul and most unnatural murder" (1.5.26). These are would-be roles allotted to Hamlet by other persons and circumstances, and he has to negotiate among these competing demands to find a response that accords both with his inner sense of what is right and of who he is. In postmodernism, as MacIntyre has noted, "The self is now thought of as lacking any necessary social identity."[41] Yet in traditional premodern societies, it is only through membership in a variety of social roles that a person acquires his or her identity: "For according to that tradition to be a man is to fill a set of roles each of which has its own point and purpose: member of a family, citizen, soldier, philosopher, servant of God."[42]

This last role is hardly incidental to the action of the play. Hamlet laments that in the face of his continuing inaction, "Thus conscience does make cowards of us all" (3.1.84), but at the same time we have a recurrent sense of his conscience working in him. Conscience has traditionally been understood by the Roman Catholic Church as "the interior voice of a human being, within whose heart the inner law of God is inscribed. Moral conscience is a judgment of practical reason about the moral quality of a human action. It moves a person at the appropriate moment to do good and to avoid evil."[43] Hamlet's problem is an existential one that, given the play-like nature of life as Balthasar understands it, he must answer for himself:

> Man is placed on the world stage without having been consulted. . . . No one can respond to a question—a cue—without having identified himself, at least implicitly, with a role, a "prosopon," a "person." It is not the sphinx's "What is man?," but the question "Who am I?" that the actor must answer, whether he wishes to or not, either before the play begins or as it unfolds.[44]

The question is presciently framed for us in the play's opening exchange: Bernard's "Who's there?" is directed back at him by Francisco's, "Nay, answer me. Stand and unfold yourself" (1.1.1–2). Hamlet must unfold himself in the course of the play, and the audience is indirectly confronted by the same question because theater "still has the power to place man in acute, inescapable situations that strip him naked and confront him with the unavoidable question: Who is he, this being who exists in terrible finitude?"[45] Hamlet faces just such a crisis with the murder of his father and what he believes to be the whoring of his mother by his uncle. At one point he is "set naked" on his native shore (4.7.44–45), almost like a newborn babe, and at nearly every point he is confronted with the question of who he is. This is what makes theater so compelling: "Existence has a need to see itself mirrored, and this makes the theatre a 'legitimate instrument' in the elucidation of being."[46] Hamlet has to elucidate his own being in light of his beloved father's death and also, as he becomes increasingly aware, of his own imminent demise at the hands of Claudius.

His initial response appears to be one of moribund passivity: "How weary, stale, flat, and unprofitable / Seem to me all the uses of this world!" (1.2.133–34). He is unsteady, uncertain of who he is and what he should do, even after being prompted to his revenge by the ghost of Old Hamlet. Hamlet is keenly aware that others, including his dead father and perhaps even the devil "would play upon [him]" (3.2.363) for their own ends, and prompt him to do their bidding. He decides to be wary of Old Hamlet's advice, and to set out on his own—Horatio as sidekick—to discern the truth. Theater lover that he is, Hamlet uses *The Mousetrap*, the play-within-the play; it would be a laughable ruse were it not for the fact that it convinces Hamlet of his step-father's guilt. He spends much of the rest of his time thinking about killing Claudius. His lone foray into revenge ends disastrously when he stabs Polonius behind the arras; taking matters into his own hands seems as futile as allowing others to direct him. The first four acts show Hamlet in all his confused glory, stymied at every point, overthinking things, outsmarting others, veering toward madness, and ending in self-loathing stasis.

Yet Balthasar argues, again, that one of the distinctive pleasures of the theater is its ability to open a horizon into "some solution or another," what he also calls an "epiphany" or an "embracing revelation of meaning."[47] What epiphany of meaning does *Hamlet* offer? Despair? Hopelessness? A glimpse into the abyss of our "terrible finitude"? The futility of human existence where, as Horatio posits, not providence but mere "accidental judgments [and] casual slaughters" shape human life (5.2.384)? Such a possibility cannot be denied, as readers of this play, or of *King Lear*, know all too well. Shakespeare's remarkable candor as a playwright lies in his unwillingness to flinch from the abyss of existential or religious nihilism, and Hamlet struggles mightily with the meaning of his life and whether it is even worth continuing his existence.

Hamlet is Shakespeare's most religious, and religiously fraught, play, both in its voluminous references to scripture, ecclesiastical and liturgical practice, and in its artistic representation of the believer's response to what Balthasar terms "the history of an initiative on God's part for his world."[48] At the end of 5.1, Hamlet's death is approaching: Claudius and Laertes have worked out their plan, and Hamlet, having discovered on his abortive English voyage the king's attempt to kill him, is well aware that they mean him no good. He is, however, at his wit's end, having been played upon by almost everyone he knows and having also taken matters catastrophically into his own hands. Critics have long noted the sea change that takes place, almost inexplicably, between 5.1 and 5.2 in regard to Hamlet's state of mind. The indecisive, angst-laden prince of much of the play has suddenly come to a resolve, and seems both calm and resigned to what is to follow. What accounts for that change? It is one of the great gaps in English literature, an enigma within the mystery of this most elusive play. For one thing, it takes place offstage, in the interim between the two scenes. Moreover, it happens within Hamlet, but he does not soliloquize the change—we only see its aftermath as 5.2 opens. The change appears to lie in Hamlet's conscience as a believer who, despite his uncertainties, has come to an inner resolve as to how he should conduct himself hereafter. His position has some affinities with stoicism, to be sure, but the play directs our attention pointedly to the inner promptings of his conscience.

Act 5 scene 2 is notable in part because it begins retrospectively, providing a glimpse into that inwardness or subjectivity Hamlet otherwise occludes. He tells Horatio, "in my heart there was a kind of fighting / That would not let me sleep. Methought I lay / Worse than the mutines in the bilboes" (5.2.4–6). He then recounts his attempt to rewrite Rosencrantz and Guildenstern's commission. Having earlier added "some sixteen lines" to *The*

Mousetrap and now, he tells us, being late to the "play" against his life that Claudius had put in motion, he revised the royal orders to the English: "I sat me down, / Devised a new commission, wrote it fair" (31–32). Hamlet had redacted *The Mousetrap* to dubious effect, and it is not clear that his rewriting of the commission is any better, as it results in the immediate deaths of his countrymen and erstwhile friends. Hamlet even describes it as the reckless act it was:

Rashly,

And praised be rashness for it—let us know

Our indiscretion sometime serves us well

When our deep plots do pall, and that should learn us

There's a divinity that shapes our ends,

Rough-hew them how we will— (6–11)

The image of the divine dramatist, of Metatheater, surfaces. Notice, too, that Hamlet initially praises rashness for its own sake, but he then quickly and rightly calls his action an "indiscretion" that only sometimes "serves us well"—and even then through no mere human agency or ingenuity. This is a far cry from Senecan rant or those of the early modern stage revengers who were so popular when Shakespeare's *Hamlet* was first performed around 1600. The deep plotting he has been doing for four-and-a-half acts has *palled*, which the *OED* defines (citing this usage as an example) as "to grow weak or faint; to lose strength, courage, vitality, etc.; to fail, fall away." All of the above seem to apply to Hamlet's deep plots, and yet he immediately ascribes the success of his rashness not to blind chance or luck—the Horatian reading—but to providence: "There's a divinity that shapes our ends." The metaphor is a workaday one, drawn from logging practice: first hewn down, logs then have their ends shaped for future or even their final purpose. Hamlet does not dismiss concerted action between God and human beings, but the finishing work, and by implication the initiative as well, rests with the divine. What Hamlet asserts, in effect, is that God can and sometimes does take human rough edges—error and fallibility included—and refine them, directing them toward an end that humans do not see but that accords, as Paul has it, with God's good and perfect will (Romans 8:28). Playing both sides, or perhaps just placating the prince, Horatio here affirms Hamlet's orthodoxy: "That is most certain" (line 11).

Everyone had wanted to direct Hamlet according to the role they would have him play and by which they would define him. Fitfully compliant, he increasingly resists, directing himself from sullenness to an indiscriminate rashness that even the figure of Old Hamlet has warned him against (1.5.86–89). Here now, at last, he completes the shift in his horizon from others and self to servant of God, who becomes the ultimate director at work in the inner stirrings of Hamlet's conscience. Hamlet has grappled with the problem for some time, noting of his inaction, "Sure he that made us with such large discourse, / Looking before and after, gave us not / That capability and godlike reason / To fust in us unused" (4.4.37–40). Hamlet had always thought of a distinction between his real self and the roles he played. Yet identity, as Balthasar remarks, comes through action, and is missional—even teleological—rather than haphazard in nature. Identity is not merely a "role" that one can take on and off arbitrarily, but an irreplaceable "I" that "could be enabled to take on a genuinely dramatic role in the realm, not of the theatre, but of life."[49] This is the Metatheater to which Hamlet responds, and this understanding of the self as determined in relation to God's leading is heterodox in modern scholarship on the play today, but so widely understood and believed in Shakespeare's day as almost to go without mentioning.

Clement of Alexandria stipulated that a wise person "faultlessly plays the role God has given him in the drama of life; for he knows what he has to do and to suffer."[50] Hamlet is hardly faultless, but he comes to understand what he believes he is called upon to do and suffer. To an unbeliever, Hamlet might just be a madman, psychotic even, but he is no terrorist, indiscriminately killing the innocent: he tells Horatio of his now deceased "friends" Rosencrantz and Guildenstern, "Why, man they did make love to this employment. / They are not near my conscience" (5.2.57–58). Rosencrantz and Guildenstern are the pair of naïfs of Stoppard's play, and they had also been duly warned by Hamlet not to "play upon" him. He could, of course, adopt the role of martyr here, but there is nothing that requires him to do so: Hamlet has a right, political and moral, to self-preservation, and that includes sending his former school friends to the death to which they were willingly escorting him. Hamlet even goes so far as to suggest that "heaven" was "ordinant" in having his signet in his purse for the purpose of convincing the English to carry out the redacted commission. Neither we nor he knows the truth of this claim, but Hamlet believes he is not in the midst of a stage play but in a real-life action going on in front of the curtain—directed by God, even to the detail of signet rings.

It is no surprise Hamlet thinks of his life in dramatic terms, given his love for the theater, but the theological turn his thinking takes is remarkable. Hamlet is troubled throughout the play by the efficacy of action, it being "but the slave to memory" (3.2.186). Human actions, as he repeatedly muses, are variously misguided, benighted, vicious, ignorant, and potentially meaningless. Hamlet comes to realize that apart from the horizon of meaning that God's decisive action in the world opens, human actions, if not nugatory, continually fall prey to any number of the preceding errors. He had even thought that if he could take over the play and rewrite a few key scenes, he could alter his destiny. But he begins to reach an almost mystical position for which words, even for one as loquacious as he, scarcely suffice to account for his vision of life *sub specie aeternitatis*. Not having been consulted either by his parents or by God about his coming onto the stage, he realizes he is not the sole author of his end: "'the play' as he calls it," writes Fisch, "being written in a kind of spontaneous collaboration between himself and the divinity that shapes our ends."[51]

Act 5, scene 2 is the unfolding of this vision, of Hamlet's understanding of his ontologically real being, his "I." Osric enters to explain the terms of the fencing duel with Laertes, and after much ado finally gets to the point: "The King, sir hath laid, sir, that in a dozen passes between yourself and him, he shall not exceed you three hits. He hath laid on twelve for nine, and it would come to immediate trial, if your Lordship would vouchsafe the answer" (163–67). Hamlet knows the game is up. He may not know the precise means of his death, but he knows without question that this is no mere fencing match. His response to Osric is tellingly succinct: "How if I answer no?" (168). Osric does not understand Hamlet's implication here and responds as if he has to restate the obvious: "I mean, my lord, the opposition of your person in trial" (169–70). Hamlet, however, is well beyond Osric; he is speculating to himself what will happen not if he declines to accept the terms that have been offered but, rather, if he declines the match altogether. Will it delay his death? Will it stop the net from closing around him? Can he, in effect, rewrite the play one more time, wresting control from Claudius, or— and here is the real crux—from a mysterious God who has allowed Claudius in his creaturely freedom to kill his father and now intends to kill him as well? Hamlet's question to Osric is ultimately rhetorical, as he knows that the real odds are not twelve for nine, but a virtual certainty that his life is about to come to an end.

Lacan reads Hamlet's acceptance to the terms of the fencing match as mere resignation to the will not of his own desires, but to that of others: "he seems just to lie down and roll over, one more time, as if there were nothing in him to stand in the way of his being constantly and fundamentally at somebody else's beck and call: 'Sir, I will walk here in the hall.'"[52] On the surface, Hamlet offers a seemingly dog-like acquiescence to the King's will. But just as Hamlet speaks past Osric, he, too, speaks past his mighty and fell opposites in Claudius and Laertes. Lacan is right that "Hamlet is always at the hour of the Other,"[53] at somebody else's beck and call. Lacan's *grand autre*, or big Other, is a symbol of an imaginative order or authority figure, but for Hamlet that order points to a real *grand autre*; that is, to God. For MacIntyre, as for Balthasar, the life of Christian virtue "finds purpose and points outside itself; to live well is to live the divine life, to live well is to serve not one's private purposes, but the cosmic order."[54]

Hamlet tells Horatio, "But thou wouldst not think how ill all's here about my heart; but it is no matter" (210–11). Horatio demurs and tells him to forestall the match if he has any misgivings; Hamlet adamantly refuses: "Not a whit, we defy augury. There is special providence in the fall of a sparrow" (217–18). Shakespeare mixes avian allusions here: Hamlet dismisses pagan augury as mere superstition—he need not look to birds in the sky, as the Greeks did. Instead, he shifts in biblical counterpoint from the practice of augury to divine dispensation inspired by scripture: "Are not two sparrows sold for a farthing, and one of them shall not fall on the ground without your Father? Yea, and all the hairs of your head are numbered. Fear ye not therefore, ye are of more value than many sparrows" (Matt. 10:29–31). Hamlet need not divine the gods' will by looking for signs in the sky; he can, rather, trust that whatever vicissitudes he faces, providence is aware of his plight, even to knowing the last detail of his life. Hamlet's final movements could be seen as a death wish, as some secular critics have contended, but it can also be read as a recognition of his own terrible finitude, with the hour now at hand: "If it be now, 'tis not to come; if it be not to come, it will be now; if it be not now; yet it will come. The readiness is all. Since no man of aught he leaves knows, what is't to leave betimes? Let be" (218–22).

Fisch comments:

> Readiness in this context signifies a tense expectancy and also a readiness for action when the moment presents itself. . . . Readiness here is the stance recommended by the psalmist when he speaks of those who "wait on the Lord" (Psalm 37:14). . . . Providence and its workings are very much in Hamlet's mind during this final act of the play. . . . He is now acutely conscious of being guided, challenged, and admonished from moment to moment. In short he is in a dialogue situation and providence is his partner in this dialogue.[55]

One could also call it stoic resignation, even indifference in the face of a hostile universe where God, as in *King Lear*, never speaks directly, if at all. Secular understandings of the play, as I noted in the introduction and argued in chapter 4, are perfectly legitimate. At the same time, Hamlet resolutely believes to have heard the voice of God. As Karol Wojtyła—later John Paul II—noted, a person is intricately involved with the external world precisely because the human subject's "inwardness, its interior life," is constantly aware of and interacting with the world. Such inwardness is the hallmark of Hamlet's existence. "It must be added," Wojtyła remarks, "that [the person] communicates thus not only with the visible, but also with the invisible world, and most importantly, with God."[56] Although we never see this dialogue with the divine because it occurs both offstage and in the interior life of Hamlet's consciousness (which passes show), there is evidence that the conversation has taken place and materially alters Hamlet's action at the end of the play. In part, he recognizes that human beings are not the sole authors of their ends—in the player king's rendering, "Our wills and fates do so contrary run / That our devices still are overthrown; / Our thoughts are ours, their ends none of our own" (3.2.209–11). Here again is the idea of providentially directed drama, of theo-drama. We are also invoked because Hamlet and Claudius and the others watch this play-within-the-play and serve as its audience, as we do theirs. One could even read Hamlet's line fatalistically, but he explicitly repudiates the idea of (pagan) fate, even in a matter as small as the fall of a sparrow.

Since he believes that God attends to matters large and small, Hamlet almost certainly believes that providence will be with him at the moment of his death. How this could happen is unclear—part of the play's liminal "undiscovered country from whose bourn / No traveler returns" (3.1.80–81)—but the philosopher Marilyn McCord Adams suggests one intriguing possibility: a direct encounter with God in the face of what she calls horrendous evils that threaten to overwhelm the goodness of one's life. She suggests temporal evils cannot compare with Anselm's notion of God as the transcendent good:

> From a Christian point of view, God is a being a greater than which cannot be conceived, a good incommensurate with both created goods and temporal evils. Likewise, the good of beatific, face-to-face intimacy with God is simply incommensurate with any merely non-transcendent goods or evils a person might experience. Thus, the good of beatific face-to-face intimacy with God would *engulf* . . . even the horrendous evils humans in this present life here below, and overcome any prima facie reasons the individual had to doubt whether his/her life would or could be worth living. [57]

This is speculation, as it must be, but it is consistent with the biblical promise of life as a good gift from God; it is equally consistent with "the grace of existence" and "the miracles of earthly love" that Balthasar locates in Shakespeare's plays. [58]

If "God is love," as St. John the Evangelist declares, and "we love, because he first loved us," [59] there is no reason to suggest that divine love does not perdure even—perhaps especially—in the face of evil, which is clearly how Hamlet perceives the murder of his father and the repeated attempts on his life. Secular critics have read it in more fatalistic, less providential ways. Consider, for instance, Simon Critchley and Jamieson Webster's arresting recent take on Hamlet's plight: "Hamlet's suicidal nihilistic apprehension of the meaninglessness of life and everyone's faults, while true, is nonetheless the linchpin of his melancholia." [60] It is not clear whether they are asserting merely that Hamlet perceives life as meaningless, or whether they accept his apprehension of the meaninglessness of life when they say that it is "true." A few pages later they note the alleged reality that Hamlet must face: "The truth that Hamlet is exposed to is a hopeless truth, a truth without redemption."[61] One might ask how they know that the truth he finds is both hopeless and without redemption. Their argument focuses on Hamlet's struggle over initial questions of faith and his relation to the divine rather than on his final resolution of such questions. The rich biblical language in 5.2 marks Hamlet's final stance here not as nihilistic fatalism but as opening himself to his part in the theo-drama in response to the divine kenosis (see Philippians 2:5–7): "following Christ," as Balthasar remarks, "which has become possible through his self-surrender, will not consist in doing *some right thing* but in fundamentally surrendering everything, and surrendering it to the God who has totally emptied himself, so that he can use it for the world, according to his own purposes."[62]

His purposes may at times be mysterious to human eyes, but for one who believes, as Hamlet does, in a "special providence in the fall of a sparrow"— they are *ipso facto* legitimate. Hamlet recognizes that his cleverness in rewriting the commission or in redacting *The Mousetrap* has not been enough; neither has outwitting Polonius, Osric, and others; nor has taking matters into his own hands through his antic disposition; nor has the reckless slaying of Polonius. Nothing he could do solely on his own could solve his problems. It is not that he recognizes human action as meaningless, but divorced from a *telos* located in the source of ultimate meaning, it palls or goes astray in one way or another. Hamlet had thought he could rewrite this drama he finds himself thrown into, and Shakespeare, while glancing at Hamlet's attempts to rewrite Claudius's play, points to a higher plane where theo-drama, of divine-human interaction, is at work. And in that *theatrum mundi* where God "does not withdraw deistically from the play he has begun but is always involved with his world,"[63] he is the author and finisher, as Hamlet belatedly but repeatedly acknowledges.

Hamlet's eyes, in other words, have been lifted to that horizon of faith, and he comes to accept not only his death, but providential care in it. Since the death of his father he had felt both unloving and unloved by those closest to him, and now he comes to embrace divine love, even as his worldly isolation increases. Hamlet realizes that any attempt to bring Claudius to justice will almost inevitably result in his own death. He is nonetheless at peace in his spirit because he gives every appearance in 5.2 of having after great struggle surrendered himself to God, to the theo-drama in which he has played a part. As Fisch notes, "World and Word have joined; he feels himself to be acting in concert with providence."[64] Hamlet does not know the precise means of his death, and it is similarly clear that he goes into the match neither with animosity for Laertes nor revengefulness toward Claudius. He knows that both will be brought to him by his adversaries, and he is willing to defend himself with his life. He knows not what precisely is coming his way, nor is the choice of options his to make, but he prepares himself to defend himself—"the readiness is all"—even as he recognizes he will lose his life.

Freud's oedipal reading of Hamlet, enshrined in Olivier's and Gibson's film versions of the play, offers a sexually repressed Hamlet who sublimates his desire for his mother. Lacan, who offered his own take on sublimation, nonetheless believed that "one must never give way on one's desire"[65] ; to do so can only, in his view, lead to various neuroses.[66] For Lacan, Hamlet "has lost the way of his desire"; he "just doesn't know what he wants."[67] Lacan posits the presence of an *objet petit a*, which is "the constant sense we have, as subjects, that something is lacking or missing from our lives";[68] Augustine concedes the reality of the lack but ascribes it to the one perdurable desire of the human heart: "The thought of you [Lord] stirs him so deeply that he cannot be content unless he praises you, because you made us for yourself and our heart find no peace they rest in you. "[69] In a theological reading of the play, what Hamlet really sublimates until 5.2 is the sublime. In place of allowing himself to discern the will of God, he substitutes for much of the play his own desire for revenge and self-willed action, even as he increasingly recognizes their inefficacy. And perhaps this carries into the end by way of his human fallibility: he kills Claudius in an eye-for-an-eye exchange reminiscent of the ghost's promptings, as well as his earlier rash killing of Polonius. Shakespeare allows for a profane reading of Hamlet as Senecan revenger.

Yet in the countervailing reading I have been proposing, he recognizes that inner voice of conscience and its subtle promptings. After he meets the ghost of Old Hamlet in the first act, he tells his mates to go about their daily business as if nothing momentous has happened, while "for mine own poor part / Look you, I'll go pray" (1.5.143–44). This may in part be a rhetorical exercise (Claudius is the only one who openly prays in the play), but can we not also and alternatively take Hamlet's four soliloquies not so much as monologues but as dialogues with a partner who, as in a Bergman film, is always silent but still speaks? Fisch notes that Hamlet's soliloquies, while not technically prayers, nonetheless "display the same rhetorical structure as the religious meditations of his time."[70] In this view, Hamlet can only stop his neurosis-inducing sublimation when he allows his soul's desire for God to rise to the surface and direct him, even as he recognizes his human fallibility in attempting to discern the will of God. This recognition of his own fallenness, which often manifests itself as self-loathing, is one of the reasons he implores Ophelia to pray for him: "Nymph, in thy orisons / Be all my sins remembered" (3.1.90–91). Hamlet never kneels in prayer as Claudius does, but we do learn—moments before he acknowledges "There's a divinity that shapes our ends"—that he has been wrestling in secret with his conscience: "in my heart," he tells Horatio, "there was a kind of fighting / That would not let me sleep" (5.2.4–5). By such internal indirections Hamlet finds directions out. It is, of course, a little maddening that in a play of some 4,000 lines, so little relative attention is given to this true inwardness. But it can hardly be otherwise: *Hamlet* suggests that interaction and interplay between the individual soul and its maker is deeply and profoundly personal, with others looking on but not in. The scarcity of lines devoted to Hamlet's inner conscience does not make it any less real; it attests to the reality of Hamlet's inwardness, which as religious persons attest passes show.

Samuel Beckett had referred to a play's horizon as being "meaningless"—a then-avant-garde sentiment now rendered conventional in much contemporary theater. Balthasar by way of contrast points to a horizon rife with meaning:

> Drama, in presenting us with the right or perverse action of free human beings, will no doubt challenge our personal and social sense of "ought" through its positive or negative models. But in fact, the spectator's expectation is directed, not toward something that awaits creation, but beyond, to an order that freely bestows itself upon us and grants us ultimate meaning. All personal and social projects of self-realization need to be sustained and integrated by a revelation that comes to meet them. Here the given order provided by the author points of itself toward an element of grace that is hoped for, believed, and occasionally almost tangible in the world of concrete reality; ultimately every ethical endeavor and failure is encompassed by this grace.[71]

Hamlet's death can appear meaningless: he challenges the king, kills others, and is ultimately killed himself. But his intention to turn from revenge, as in the biblical prohibition—"Vengeance is mine; I will repay"[72] —stands in stark contrast to the actions of Claudius and Laertes, the latter of whom recognizes only in death the higher law of forgiveness: "Exchange forgiveness with me, noble Hamlet. / Mine and my father's death come not upon thee, / Nor thine on me!" (5.2.331–33).

Hamlet's often overlooked response, "Heaven make thee free of it!" (334) resonates with Balthasar's claim that forgiveness is at the heart of Shakespeare's drama.[73] Claudius never realizes this highest good, Laertes only belatedly, and Hamlet just in time to direct the end of his life accordingly. His rough-hewn efforts having gone astray, he is sustained in the end by his recognition of a providential order that freely bestows itself upon him and grants his life, even in death, meaning. This is not to imply that he is or should be absolved for crimes such as the murder of Polonius. Hamlet's attempts to do good in this world, and even to know what constitutes the good in his particular situation, have vexed him to the utmost. Horatio directs a similarly benighted audience, both those on and off stage, to a horizon they cannot see but where Hamlet's failures are encompassed, he suggests, by a limitless grace: "Now cracks a noble heart. Good night, sweet prince, / And flights of angels sing thee to thy rest!" (5.2.361–62). He intuits the kind of face-to-face encounter with the divine of which Adams wrote.

There are countless ways to interpret *Hamlet*, as the history of literary criticism attests, and I want to suggest, on the one hand, that that wonderful cornucopia allows for a reading of *Hamlet* as Shakespeare's profound theo-drama, with Hamlet as a wayward and erring child of God. That is the epiphany of which Balthasar speaks, and in the silence with which Hamlet heads into eternity, we are left with no more than a glimmer of the revelation that comes to meet him. Piero Boitani describes it as "the appearance of a distant light. The special providence in the fall of a sparrow remains a mystery only glimpsed at: perhaps comprehended by the protagonist, never revealed to the audience. Unless, of course, we identify the fall of the sparrow with that of Hamlet."[74] The point of Jesus's words as reported in Matthew's gospel is precisely to make such an identification: human beings receive more divine solicitude than sparrows, whose falls nonetheless also come within the ambit of providential care. One can acknowledge, as David Scott Kastan does, that "religion obviously matters in this play," and yet also believe the play's central concern is as much with epistemology as with theology. Hamlet wants certainty both in the evidence he gathers and in his attempt to discern the will of God, but both prove elusive: "And in the space of those uncertainties the play transforms theology into tragedy."[75] The language of *Hamlet* forces us into neither a secular nor religious understanding of the play's action, but holds the two in Shakespeare's redoubtable counter-point.

I began this book with a look at the extensive historical record of the theatrical companies' many performances in churches, and *Hamlet* no doubt took on a special resonance when it was performed on church property. Hamlet is a Christian, and thus (even if only in the fiction of the play) he is a member in the mystical body of Christ, the Church universal. His belief that he hears the will of God and that his end has been shaped for him is a leitmotif that speaks to religious people. In this sense, *Hamlet* is, along with *Twelfth Night* and *King Lear*, church drama. This is not to deny the view of any number of modern scholars who view Shakespeare as a supremely secular artist. The sacred and the profane coexist and often compete for our understanding in Shakespeare's plays; his range from orthodoxy to hetero-doxy allows the plays to address secular and religious audiences alike. At the height of his career, in plays as brilliant and as varied as *Hamlet*, *Twelfth Night*, and *King Lear*, Shakespeare at times boldly, at times subtly, turns to the Church that was the subject of fervent belief and fervid controversy among early modern persons, believers and nonbelievers alike. This is at it should be, if the players, whether they performed on secular professional stages or in parish churches, were to live up to their calling as "the abstract and brief chronicles of the time" (*Ham.* 2.2.524). At the heart, too, of Shakespeare's exploration of the heterodox is his intuition or, as I suspect, full recognition of the ways in which theater probes the depths of human experience, including the theater's ability to lay open or suggest both the material finitude of human existence and, at the same time, the horizon of our encounter with the divine.

NOTES

1. Sigmund Freud, *The Future of an Illusion*, ed. James. Strachey, trans. W. D. Robson-Scott (New York: Anchor Books, 1964), 47–48. The work was first published as *Die Zukunft einer Illusion* (Vienna, 1927).

2. Ibid., 87.

3. Alvin Plantinga, *Knowledge and Christian Belief* (Grand Rapids: Eerdmans, 2015), 43, 126.

4. Hans Urs von Balthasar, *Theo-Drama: Theological Dramatic Theory*, volume 1: *Prolegomena*, trans. Graham Harrison (San Francisco: Ignatius Press, 1988), 118.

5. Alison Shell, *Shakespeare and Religion* (London: Arden Shakespeare, 2010), 116, 66.

6. Debora K. Shuger, *Habits of Thought in the English Renaissance: Religion, Politics, and the Dominant Culture* (Toronto: University of Toronto Press, 1997), 6.

7. Philip Rieff, *My Life Among the Deathworks: Illustrations of the Aesthetics of Authority*, ed. Kenneth S. Piver, vol. 1 (Charlottesville and London: University of Virginia Press, 2006), 57.

8. Ibid., 8.

9. Ibid., 50.

10. On this point, see in particular George Wolfgang Forell, *The Protestant Faith* (Englewood Cliffs, NJ: Prentice-Hall, 1960), 155.

11. Rieff, *My Life Among the Deathworks*, 1:36.

12. Aidan Nichols, *No Bloodless Myth: A Guide Through Balthasar's Dramatics* (Washington, DC: Catholic University of America Press, 2000), 21.

13. Balthasar, *Theo-Drama*, 21, 26, 125.

14. Harold Fisch, *The Biblical Presence in Shakespeare, Milton, and Blake: A Comparative Study* (Oxford University Press, 1999), 91.

15. Alasdair C. MacIntyre, *After Virtue: A Study in Moral Theory*, 2nd ed. (Notre Dame: University of Notre Dame Press, 1984), 143–44 and 65.

16. Balthasar, *Theo-Drama*, 129.

17. Ibid., 9, 249.

18. Ibid., 249.

19. Fisch, *The Biblical Presence*, 110.

20. Balthasar, *Theo-Drama*, 260.

21. Ibid., 26.

22. Ibid., 251.

23. Peter De Vries, *The Blood of the Lamb*, Signet Books (New York: New American Library, 1963), 10.

24. Balthasar, 19, 250, and 314, italics mine.

25. Ibid., 314.

26. Rieff, *My Life Among the Deathworks*, 26.

27. Balthasar, *Theo-Drama*, 118.

28. Ibid., 262.

29. David Bevington, "The Debate about Shakespeare and Religion," in *Shakespeare and Early Modern Religion*, eds. David Loewenstein and Michael Witmore (Cambridge & New York: Cambridge University Press, 2015), 34.

30. My view is that Hamlet commits manslaughter in rashly killing Polonius, but, as will become clear in the remainder of this chapter, all of his other killings can be understood as legitimate acts of self-defense.

31. Balthasar, *Theo-Drama*, 32.

32. Ibid., 33.

33. Nichols, *No Bloodless Myth*, 14.

34. Balthasar, *Theo-Drama*, 33, italics his.

35. Ibid., 37.

36. Desiderius Erasmus, *The Praise of Folly*, trans. Clarence H. Miller (New Haven: Yale University Press, 1979), 43–44.

37. MacIntyre, *After Virtue*, 213.

38. Balthasar, *Theo-Drama*, 57.

39. Harold Bloom, *Shakespeare: The Invention of the Human* (New York: Riverhead, 1998), 401.

40. Balthasar, *Theo-Drama*, 46, italics his.

41. MacIntyre, *After Virtue*, 33.

42. Ibid., 59, 33, 129.

43. *Catechism of the Catholic Church* (Vatican City & Washington, DC: Libreria Editrice Vaticana, 2000), 872.

44. Balthasar, *Theo-Drama*, 129.

45. Ibid., 323.

46. Nichols, *No Bloodless Myth*, 19.

47. Balthasar, *Theo-Drama*, 262 and 265.

48. Ibid., 125.

49. Ibid., 645.

50. Nichols, *No Bloodless Myth*, 25.

51. Fisch, *The Biblical Presence*, 111.

52. Jacques Lacan, "Desire and the Interpretation of Desire in Hamlet," ed. Jacques-Alain Miller, trans. James Hulbert, *Yale French Studies* no. 55/56 (January 1, 1977): 30.

53. Ibid., 25.

54. MacIntyre, *After Virtue*, 169.

55. Harold Fisch, *The Biblical Presence*, 109.

56. John Paul II, *Love and Responsibility*, trans. H. T. Willets (San Francisco: Ignatius Press, 1993), 23.

57. Marilyn McCord Adams, "Horrendous Evils and the Goodness of God," in *Philosophy of Religion: Selected Readings*, ed. Michael L. Peterson, 4th ed. (New York: Oxford University Press, 2010), 338, italics hers.

58. Balthasar, *Theo-Drama*, 384.

59. Lloyd E. Berry and William Whittingham, eds., *The Geneva Bible: A Facsimile of the 1560 Edition* (Madison: University of Wisconsin Press, 1969), 1 John 4:8, 19.

60. Simon Critchley and Jamieson Webster, *Stay, Illusion!: The Hamlet Doctrine* (Brooklyn, NY: Verso Books, 2013), 122.

61. Ibid., 133.

62. Balthasar, *Theo-Drama*, 33–34, italics his.

63. Nichols, *No Bloodless Myth*, 28.

64. Fisch, *The Biblical Presence*, 110.

65. Critchley and Webster, *Stay, Illusion!*, 129.

66. Lacan, "Desire and the Interpretation of Desire in Hamlet," 17.

67. Ibid., 12, 26.

68. Sean Homer, *Jacques Lacan* (London: Routledge, 2005), 88.

69. Augustine, *Confessions*, trans. R. S. Pine-Coffin (New York: Penguin, 1961), 21.

70. Fisch, *The Biblical Presence*, 101.

71. Balthasar, *Theo-Drama*, 266.

72. Berry and Whittingham, *The Geneva Bible*, Romans 12:19.

73. Balthasar, *Theo-Drama*, 466.

74. Piero Boitani, *The Gospel according to Shakespeare*, trans. Vittorio Montemaggi and Rachel Jacoff (South Bend: University of Notre Dame Press, 2013), 23.

75. David Scott Kastan, *A Will to Believe: Shakespeare and Religion* (Oxford: Oxford University Press, 2014), 143, 135.

Conclusion

"Test All Things": Shakespearean Heterodoxy

Four hundred years after his death, what does the religious heterodoxy of his plays tell us about Shakespeare's art? Bishop Charles Wordsworth opined in 1864 that none of Shakespeare's Elizabethan contemporaries "has paid homage to Christianity as effectually as Shakespeare."[1] More recently, René Weis suggests, by way of contrast, "Shakespeare does not seem to take his gods too seriously. His is not a drama of faith any more than Marlowe's."[2] There are numerous books that argue for the fundamentally religious nature of Shakespeare's art, and probably by now a greater number that insist on the secularism of his artistry. I have argued that Shakespeare considers possible worlds where God is intimately involved in the lives of persons and—in the same play—a world in which God may not even exist. Such ambivalence is interwoven into the fabric of his plays; to see only one side of that ambivalence is to miss its competing and ultimately incompatible counterpart. Of no other author do such starkly contradictory, and seemingly incompatible, views exist as they do concerning the nature of Shakespeare's art.

That he would juxtapose such contrarieties has occasioned endless speculation concerning Shakespeare's own religious beliefs, or lack thereof. Peter Ackroyd stipulates that he was "a man without beliefs" because he was somehow "above faith"?[3] The idea is Romantic in its sensibilities but implausible—what does it mean, after all, to be above faith? Nonetheless, he does envision Shakespeare as a secular artist, which, as Jeffrey Knapp comments, is the prevailing scholarly view:

> Crediting him with what Keats called "negative capability," modern scholarship has treated the "elusiveness" of Shakespeare's "personality" as the hall-

133

mark of his secularism; yet the ability to tolerate "uncertainties, Mysteries, doubts," as Keats defined negative capability, was a virtue that Erasmus repeatedly claimed for himself as a Christian.[4]

Shakespeare's ability to entertain uncertainties is embodied in the religious heterogeneity of his plays, from the pious affirmations of faith to the doubts and denials of the truth of religious claims. Does he ever resolve these ambivalences? Knapp for one argues that Shakespeare's theater is accommodationist in nature because of "his fears regarding the potential divisiveness of his religious beliefs."[5] Shakespeare wanted at all costs to avoid sectarianism. The plays do evince doctrinal minimalism, even a certain quietism on contentious issues such as baptism and the Eucharist. They are equally receptive to Catholic and various Protestant—Church of England, Calvinist, Lutheran—beliefs and practices. To this extent, the plays are ecumenical, yet they are not only merely exercises in ecumenism, of a religious writer addressing his coreligionists and nonbelievers alike in language that offends few if any sensibilities. Shakespeare is not divisive merely because he fears the effects of his staking doctrinal positions; rather, he stakes such a variety of them—orthodox, heterodox, and radically unorthodox—that readers of all religious persuasions, and of none, can find their own beliefs articulated in the plays.

Shakespeare returns with a reliable consistency to atheistic and other skeptical beliefs embedded alongside their traditional theistic opposites—indeed, that has been the argument of this book. Thus, the plays take pains to accommodate and explore the full implications of various forms of nonbelief. Despite, however, there being multiple and competing ways of construing events, Shakespeare tips the scales in favor of theism by returning again and again to two of the central motifs of Christian belief: Resurrection and forgiveness. In my view, then, Shakespeare's art is subtly and unobtrusively evangelical in its etymological sense: he is a bringer of the "good news" in the midst of a world where other beliefs concerning the ultimate things also compete for our attention. As for his own religious beliefs, it is neither likely on such important questions that he was (or could have been) merely a neutral observer, nor that he was simply indifferent as is *Measure for Measure*'s Barnardine. Modern scholars have been able to interpret Shakespeare's lack of querulousness on religious matters, as well as his avoidance of sermonizing, as a sign of his secularism.[6] Ackroyd, again, asserts that "the safest and most likely conclusion, however, must be that . . . Shakespeare professed no particular faith."[7] Moreover, despite the many fine and nuanced readings one encounters in the turn to religion in Shakespeare studies, the turn itself is a rearguard movement. Charles Taylor notes that "the presumption of unbelief has become dominant . . . in the academic and intellectual life."[8] Alison Shell, too, concedes that even "though it would be wrong to make blanket assumptions about the metaphysical assumptions of Shakespeareans, those writing more or less explicitly from a non-Christian perspective have been in the majority in the recent years."[9]

Harold Bloom, for one, argues that plays such as *Hamlet* and *Lear* will "not yield to Christianization" because they remain recalcitrant to an easy, triumphalist theological reading.[10] If Shakespeare's idea were to christen his plays in such an overt way (as a few critics have indeed argued in the past), then Bloom has a point. Shakespeare, however, is neither John Bale nor John Foxe, nor his plays the mysteries of his medieval forebears; the religious ideas that inform his drama surface in more nuanced and variegated ways. Although we do not know his precise confessional stance, there is evidence—various church and legal records, his epitaph, his family ties and friendships—to conclude with reasonable assurance that Shakespeare was a Christian, which if true would have some consequences for his art, as I think it does. The likelihood of his being a believer is most often denied in modern criticism because of the bleakness of plays such as *King Lear*, yet my position is that it is precisely Shakespeare's faith, not its absence, that permits and even encourages him to explore the heterodox positions he does, including atheism.

To be sure, we cannot know with absolute certainty Shakespeare's religious beliefs, but it does not follow that we cannot draw reasonable inferences based on the evidence we do have. Shell and others make much of Shakespeare's alleged "confessional invisibility," which is true insofar as his precise denominational affiliation is concerned, but on a broader level his faith is not quite so inscrutable. We know neither that he ultimately accepted some form of Protestantism nor that he embraced the old Catholic faith of his family—Richard Davies, Archdeacon of Coventry, claimed that Shakespeare "dyed a papist."[11] Yet with each and every of these denominational variants, the historical record points toward religious belief. His will, for example, records his commending his "soul into the hands of God my Creator, hoping and assuredly believing through the only merits of Jesus Christe my Saviour, to be made partaker of life everlasting."[12] This may be merely formulaic, and thus one has to be cautious about placing much emphasis on it. Fortunately, however, there is other evidence as well. His name appears in the baptismal register of Holy Trinity Church in Stratford-upon-Avon; he married Anne Hathaway there in 1582; their three children, Susanna, Hamnet, and Judith, were also christened there; and he died and was buried in Holy Trinity Church in 1616.[13] This is standard fare, but it is not simply negligible. We do not know if Shakespeare's habitual attendance at his parish church means that he subscribed to the beliefs of the Church of England; any number of recusants attended Anglican services as a matter of conformity; yet they were not unbelievers if they held to a different Christian faith tradition. It is possible that he was a nonbeliever or unbeliever, but the historical evidence we have does not point in that direction. Perhaps it is safest to say that his baptism, as well as those of his children, and his continual presence at divine worship, not to mention his use of Christian discourse and images throughout the plays (more on this in a moment), appeared to form a not inconsequential part of his life.

His epitaph—"Good Frend, for Jesus sake forbeare, / To digg the bones encloased heare! / Bleste be the man that spares thes stones, / And curst be he that moves my bones"— was said in the seventeenth century to be of his own devising,[14] and again appears to be the outward expression of Christian belief. To be sure, it is a plea to leave his bones alone, and carries with it the threat of a curse, but it is posed in the language of Christian belief that is difficult to harmonize with a view of him as a secularist. Shakespeare was an outwardly observant member of the Church of England:[15] no one, not even Robert Greene or Ben Jonson, professional rivals who were not afraid to point out his fallings or shortcomings, ever suggested that he was a nonbeliever. One has to be careful about the evidence here: neither Greene nor Jonson testifies to Shakespeare's religious beliefs one way or the other, and absence of evidence of unbelief does not constitute positive evidence of belief. Yet if Shakespeare were an agnostic or atheist, there might be some indication of this in the biographical or historical record, as with Marlowe, but there is nothing.

If the case for Shakespeare as a Christian is not overwhelming, his alleged secularism rests on even more slender grounds and is akin to the case that the Anti-Stratfordians make for someone other than Shakespeare as the real author of his plays. Despite his rigorous grammar school education, Shakespeare could not possibly, they allege, write with the sophistication he does, and thus there was a conspiracy to hide Edward de Vere's, or Francis Bacon's, or some other candidate's authorship—a conspiracy so good, in fact, that no one in Shakespeare's lifetime, not even his own acting company or his professional rivals, knew the truth or, if they did, were willing to reveal it. The same must be said for the lack of evidence of Shakespeare's nonbelief or unbelief. This does not mean with absolute certainty that he was a Christian, but no reasonable person would make such a claim. Yet to assert that he was a closet atheist or somehow above faith is untenable in light of a historical record that offers little if any evidence to substantiate such a claim.

Moreover, Taylor at the outset of his study poses a simple question: "why was it virtually impossible not to believe in God in, say, 1500 in our Western society, while in 2000 many of us find this not only easy, but even inescapable?"[16] The various answers offered for our own culture's secularity—the invention of the printing press, the gradual rise of Enlightenment thinking, scientific advances, and so on—need not unduly concern us here, as those historical processes bear much of their fruit after Shakespeare's lifetime. Taylor gives three reasons why it would have been unusual for someone in the sixteenth century not to believe in God. First, "the natural world they lived in, which had its place in the cosmos they imagined, testified to divine purpose and action" both in the order and apparent design of creation and in the great natural events that even today are depicted, for insurance purposes, as "acts of God."[17] In his letter to his wife while on tour with the Lord Admiral's Men, in order to avoid the plague in London, Edward Alleyn wrote, "And to my father my mother & my sister Bess hoping in god though the sickness beround about you yet by his mercy it may escape your house which by the grace of god shall."[18] Such expressions, by no means unusual, bespeak a culture of belief.

In addition to the natural world he governed, God was also "implicated in the very existence of society"; the array of institutions that "made up society, parishes, boroughs, guilds, and so on, were interwoven with ritual and worship. . . . One could not but encounter God everywhere."[19] Third, Shakespeare and his contemporaries inhabited a world, as I discussed in chapter 4, that was "enchanted" by spirits, goblins, fairies, demons, and even the walking dead—all the kinds of magical or supernatural entities in response to which modernity has provided the disenchantment of disbelief.[20] "Atheism," Taylor concludes, "comes close to being inconceivable in a world with these three features. It just seems too obvious that God is there, acting in the cosmos, founding and sustaining societies" in a way that no longer obtains in much of the West.[21] If historical criticism has taught us anything, it is that we ought to read Shakespeare in light of his own culture, not of our own.

Was Shakespeare an exception to the thinking of his day that "made the presence of God seemingly undeniable"?[22] It must remain a possibility in the absence of absolute proof to the contrary, yet it is less probable than the case for his belief, for which there is evidence. In addition, he was surrounded largely by believers both in and out of the theater. Not only were laypeople such as the Christian Alleyn involved in the theater, but clergy themselves both acted in plays "as part of their clerical training," and a number of divines—Henry Killigrew, James Shirley, and John Marston, among others—wrote stage plays.[23] Shakespeare associated both in business and pleasure with those such as the Catholic Jonson, while John Heminge and Henry Condell—preservers of his plays and good "fellows" to whom he bequeathed money to buy rings—had become churchwardens at St. Mary Aldermanbury by the time they published the First Folio.[24] In his dedicatory poem to that volume, Leonard Digges calls them "thy pious fellows," thus identifying them as devout and at least hinting that Shakespeare may share their faith.[25] Of course, association with Christians does not make Shakespeare one, but it does suggest that he was not an outsider in such circles, and aroused no public suspicion on their part of his being a covert unbeliever.

Nonetheless, given that Shakespeare's faith was a likelihood rather than a certainty, debate on the matter continues, and takes as another datum the plays themselves. On one side are the nineteenth- and early twentieth-century views of those such as Bishop Wordsworth who read *King Lear* as a drama of Christian redemption. On the other side are those, now in the ascendancy, who argue that *King Lear* reveals, unwittingly or no, Shakespeare's skepticism or even unbelief. Reviewing James Shapiro's *The Year of Lear*, Fintan O'Toole comments on the end of the play and Shakespeare's revisions to it:

> *King Lear* is not apocalyptic, it is far worse. Instead of deserved damnation and merited salvation, there is merely the big fat O, the nothing that haunts the play, the "O, O, O, O!" with which Lear expires. Even Shakespeare seems to have thought twice about this utter annihilation of hope and justice. When he rewrote the play, probably two or three years after its first performance in 1606, he allowed Lear (and the audience) one little moment of merciful illusion. Instead of that terrible "O, O, O, O!," Lear is permitted to lapse with his dying breath into the fantasy that Cordelia's dead lips are moving after all. It is as if even Shakespeare, watching his own play, could not quite bear its unyielding ferocity. [26]

What O'Toole overlooks is that it is merely the *prospect* of nihilism, not its realization, that haunts the play as part of its tantalizing design. R. A. Foakes notes that for a number of critics, Cordelia's lips actually moving would constitute "a blessed release for [Lear] in a moment of imagined reunion"— most likely in an afterlife. [27] O'Toole is correct is that *King Lear* is ferocious, but not unyieldingly so; it is also perfectly legitimate, again, to interpret Lear as a theistic play: "the notion that *King Lear* is utterly nihilistic now looks dated," as Shell comments, "and the fact that a more optimistic reading has also proved sustainable should tell us something." [28] Lear recognizes belatedly that he has taken too little care of the homeless "poor naked wretches" of his kingdom (3.3.28). Those who torture Gloucester by plucking out his eyes are undone, and even Edmund repents and attempts to recall his ordered execution of Lear and Cordelia: "Some good I mean to do" (5.3.248). Edmund thus recognizes a moral order—good versus evil are not merely relativistic, as Albany had remarked to Oswald: "Of Gloucester's treachery / And of the loyal service of his son / When I informed him, then he called me sot / And told me I had turned the wrong side out" (4.2.6–9). This side of *Lear* turns away from nihilism.

What *Twelfth Night*, *Hamlet*, and *King Lear* reveal in their complexity is that Shakespeare entertains both secular and religious readings in his plays. For O'Toole, *King Lear* is worse than a biblical apocalypse because its putative embrace of nihilism displaces Christian theism in a way that frightened even its author: "That such a play is possible at all is one of the great wonders of human creation. That it was written by a liveried servant of a Calvinist king who devoutly believed in salvation and damnation, and performed at his court, seems almost inexplicable." [29] Yet as Roy Battenhouse explained some years ago: "We know that *Pericles*, along with *King Lear*, was on the repertoire of some touring actors who performed these plays in the country house of a Yorkshire Catholic family in 1610. Evidently, neither play in such circles was thought to be, as some moderns suppose, haphazardly episodic or destructive of Christian faith."[30] That *King Lear* or any other play can be read as expression of nihilism does not mean that it must be so read; it is logically possible, as I demonstrated in chapter 3, that a benevolent god exists within the framework of as admittedly dark a play as *King Lear*. Nihilism is also a possibility in this play as in *Hamlet* and in others as well, but Shakespeare never insists on an exclusive reading. What he explores, rather, is the radical contingency of the world we inhabit, as well as visions of other possible worlds, only in some of which God exists.

A number of modern critics nonetheless maintain that such willingness to explore unorthodox religious beliefs in this predominantly Christian culture had to have been the mark of a secularist. Yet as Taylor remarks, early modern religious belief "was the default option, not just for the naïve but also for those who knew, considered, talked about atheism."[31] Descartes, for instance, considered atheism at length in *Meditations on First Philosophy* (1637), the first text of modern philosophy, yet he reasoned his way to belief that God not only exists but is a necessary being: "For what, in and of itself, is more manifest than that a supreme being exists, that is, that God, to whose essence alone existence belongs, exists?"[32] Shakespeare was certainly not naïve, but rather one of the cultural sophisticates who, as I have argued throughout this book, knew, considered, and talked about in the dialectic structure of his plays the possibility, *inter alia*, of atheism. *King Lear* explores this possibility with a vengeance, and the play speaks to us because our disenchanted age is one "in which for more and more people unbelieving construals [of the world] seem at first blush the only plausible ones."[33] Shakespeare's culture, it almost goes without saying, was thoroughly religious; to argue for his secularism on the basis of *King Lear*'s mere contemplation of a godless universe is to assume that only a nonreligious person could consider such a prospect. Not only was atheism a philosophical outlier in the sixteenth century, but those who did conceive of it were usually theists.

While not staking a precise position on this question, Shell suggests in her valedictory comments that even though we can "never know for certain" his religious views, "what we do know is the side he came down upon: that his writing treated all religions, including the Christian doctrine of his time, as subservient to artistic unity and closure."[34] I have argued that the religious undergoes "aesthetic modulation" in the crucible of his art, but his art does not merely subsume the religious.[35] The plays often achieve their unity and closure by means of Shakespeare's extensive religious imagery and tropes. The plays attest, as A. L. Rowse claimed a half century ago, "that his Biblical range is . . . far greater than that of any contemporary dramatist."[36] Indeed, as Richmond Noble and, more recently, Naseeb Shaheen have thoroughly documented, Shakespeare's references and allusions to the *Book of Common Prayer*; the Anglican catechism; daily Morning and Evening Prayer and various other liturgical services (Baptism, Holy Matrimony, Communion, and the like); the Elizabethan *Book of Homilies*; and, especially, the Bible, run well into the several thousands.[37] All of the other sources upon which he relies heavily, including Ovid, Plutarch, and Holinshed, appear to be, in comparison, mere passing acquaintances. Is Shakespeare's imitation of the Bible thus the sincerest form of flattery?

Greenblatt ingeniously attempts to turn this mass of evidence against itself, arguing, for instance, that Bottom's synesthetic rendering of 1 Corinthians 2:9—"The eye of man hath not heard, the ear of man hath not seen, man's hand is not able to taste, his tongue to conceive, nor his heart to report what my dream was" (4.1.209–12)—represents "the joke of a decisively secular dramatist, a writer who deftly turned the dream of the sacred into popular entertainment."[38] Shakespeare has many such comic moments: he turns "They shall also bring forth more fruit in their age: and shall be fat and well-liking" (Psalms 92:14) into Rosaline's description of the men at the court of Navarre: "Well-liking wits they have; gross, gross; fat, fat" (*Love's Labour's Lost* 5.2.269).[39] Yet playfulness is hardly evidence of hollowing out religious discourse; it may occasionally serve this purpose, but not invariably so.

Some characters do subvert religious language, often turning it to profane and even sinister ends. Iago perverts Genesis 3:14 to his own malevolent ends: "I am not what I am" (*Oth.* 1.1.67). Iago's inversion reminds us of God's description of himself as an eternal and non-contingent being. Moreover, characters too numerous to mention also invoke religious discourse quite seriously, as in Isabella's promise of "true prayers / That shall be up at heaven and enter there / Ere sunrise—prayers from preserved souls, / From fasting maids whose minds are dedicate / To nothing temporal" (*Measure for Measure* 2.2.157–61). Taken as a whole—it is a very large body of evidence—biblical, liturgical, catechetical, and homiletic language colored Shakespeare's thought and surfaced in his plays in such multifarious ways that it is more accurate to say that it is integral to—imbricated in the very fabric of rather than merely subservient to—his art. Indeed, if one were to remove the religious language from Shakespeare's plays, they would no longer appear anything like they do; critics have noted, for instance, his use of anachronism to place Christian discourse and imagery even in pagan plays such as *King Lear*, *Julius Caesar*, and *Antony and Cleopatra*.

Shell further argues that none of Shakespeare's plays engages in "the systematic abstract questioning which was to lead to religious heterodoxy and atheism in later generations." She is technically right, though *King Lear*, for one, does appears to engage in sustained questioning of God's existence, even if it is unsystematic. *Lear* is not a *Summa*. Shell has a decidedly conservative take on such theological investigation: "the way in which drama probes areas of [early modern] theological discomfort could be seen not as venturesome heterodoxy, but as a warning to desist one's questioning."[40] This is plausible, but I wish not to pass over the possibility she dismisses; namely, that Shakespeare's was a dramatic experiment in intellectually "venturesome heterodoxy." The plays offer ample evidence to suggest that they explore heterodox possibilities; is this an area into which Christian belief should not go? For Bacon, again, it was the skeptical, unbelieving Pilate who "would not stay for an answer" to his own question about the nature of truth.[41] Bacon ascribes the willingness to engage in such philosophical probing to the believer. Erasmus believed in the freedom of the will given to each person.[42] In his first sermon at St. Paul's Cathedral on Christmas day, 1621, John Donne preached that "Some men by the benefit of this light of reason, have found out things profitable and useful to the whole world . . . and our minds and our inventions, our wits and compositions may trade and have commerce together, and we may participate of one another's understandings."[43] Paul, too, noted that "all things are lawful for me, but not all things are expedient. All things are lawful for me, but all things edify not" (1 Cor. 10:23). He further exhorted the Thessalonians to test or "try all things, and keep that which is good" (1 Thess. 5:21).

Is Shakespeare's testing of heterodox belief unedifying or somehow unwholesome for a Christian? Anthony Munday begrudgingly conceded that if one were to remove playgoers "from the Theater unto the sermon, they will say, By the preacher they may be edified, but by the player both edified and delighted."[44] Even if Shakespeare's testing were thought in certain quarters to be unorthodox, it remains permissible in both Erasmian and Pauline terms, which Milton elaborates on in *Areopagitica*:

> all opinions, yea errors, know, read, and collated, are of main service and assistance toward the speedy attainment of what is truest.
> I conceive, therefore, that when God did enlarge the universal diet of man's body, saving ever the rules of temperance, he then also, as before, left arbitrary the dieting and repasting of our minds.[45]

Shakespeare's exploration of possible worlds constitutes a fearless heterodoxy that is well within this tradition, fearless in part because of his willingness to place Christianity in contest with alternative belief systems. His representation of competing beliefs serves to remind us, not only of error, as Milton notes, but of truth, which is not immediately discernible to the reason, as it is for angels, but must be sought out with effort by mere human beings. Shakespeare adopts a latitudinarian approach to his treatment of ultimate truth, giving us the freedom to choose from the alternatives he presents, though I am inclined to think that he tips the scales in favor of Christianity.

The balance shifts by means of two leitmotifs, forgiveness and resurrection, both of which repeatedly echo and remind us of the gospel even when Shakespeare shows us worlds and ideas where they ought to be absent.

Forgiveness and resurrection are central to the New Testament and to Christianity's understanding of divine action and grace in relation to human beings. An artist committed to a secular understanding of life might draw upon the idea of forgiveness, though it is unlikely she would also couple it with the tropes and images of the Resurrection. These motifs irradiate Shakespeare's work. Let us take forgiveness first because its prominence in Shakespeare's plays has been understood since Robert Grams Hunter's treatment of the subject a half century ago.[46] Forgiveness is especially pronounced in the romances Shakespeare wrote at the end of his career. Prospero offers undeserved mercy to his usurping brother, Antonio: "For you, most wicked sir, whom to call brother / Would even infect my moth, I do forgive / Thy rankest fault—all of them" (5.1.130–32). The play closes, too, with the famous epigram delivered to the audience: "As you from crimes would pardoned be, / Let your indulgence set me free" (Epi. 19–20)—lines closely deriving from the Our Father (Matt. 6:9–12). The matter is not so easily settled, though, in his awkward and unfinished reconciliation with Caliban: "As you look / To have my pardon, trim [my cell] handsomely" (5.1.296–97). His forgiveness is conditional, premised upon a last act of servitude, and there is a further jarring note in Caliban's promise to "be wise hereafter / And seek for grace" (298–99). Prospero remains in the position of God when he should be a supplicant, and thus the whole matter of forgiveness, repeatedly emphasized in this final scene, becomes at best a partially realized hope fraught with the moral failings of human beings.

A less complicated moment occurs in *Cymbeline* when Iachimo is apprehended and his villainy made manifest. His realization of the justice he deserves is immediate; he tells Posthumus, "Take that life, beseech you, / Which I so often owe" (5.5.418–19). Posthumus's response is thoroughly unexpected, especially given the pagan setting of the play: "Kneel not to me. / The power that I have on you is to spare you; / The malice towards you to forgive you. Live, / And deal with others better" (421–24). Forgiveness is not unknown in pagan cultures, yet we ought not to suggest a cultural equivalence or parity here since the biblical teaching on forgiveness clearly distinguishes it from the established and sanctioned practice of vengeance outside the Judeo-Christian world, especially among its pagan precursors. Posthumus's implication that vengeance is not a human prerogative is unequivocally scriptural (Deut. 32:35, Rom. 12:17–19). Shakespeare is not the only dramatic advocate of forgiveness, but the prominence he gives to it, as Balthasar remarked, is unprecedented: "the real dramatist of forgiveness is and remains Shakespeare."[47] Balthasar locates at the heart of these plays the powerful dramatic representation of Christian theology. Shakespearean mercy is almost always accompanied by tropes and imagery that invoke Christian belief, even in those moments, such as Portia's infamous "quality of mercy" speech to Shylock, where mercy is invoked only to be denied. Nonetheless, she recognizes it "as the gentle rain from heaven" and further suggests that mercy "is an attribute to God himself" without which "none of us / Should see salvation" (*Merchant of Venice* 4.1.182–200).

Shakespeare thus sometimes underscores forgiveness by way of its absence: Feste's mocking of Malvolio in the play's final scene is followed, not unexpectedly, by his vow to be revenged on the "whole pack" of his coreligionists who have behaved like wolves toward him. Orsino's command to "entreat him to a peace" (5.1.380) is a form of reconciliation manqué, one deferred beyond the temporal bounds of the play—if it is to occur at all. Yet the hope of forgiveness and reconciliation remains, just as it does in *The Comedy of Errors*, *Much Ado about Nothing*, *The Merry Wives of Windsor*, *As You Like It*, and in the other comedies and romances. Peter Leithart refers to this phenomenon as "deep comedy," which is the mark of those works— the biblical narrative and Shakespeare's plays are his quintessential examples—that are eschatological in nature because they "move toward an end that is greater than the beginning."[48] Deep comedy counterpoints the classical vision of human decline enshrined in the myth of the five metallic ages and the degeneration from the golden to an iron age.[49] Even Shakespeare's tragedies *gesture* toward deep comedy: Hamlet, as we saw in chapter 4, exchanges forgiveness with Laertes before their deaths, even if no reconciliation takes place between Claudius and him, and one can further make the case that Hamlet is merely a Senecan revenger. For his part, Lear implores Cordelia, "You must bear with me. / Pray you now, forget and forgive. / I am old and foolish" (4.7.88–90). In a pagan world and ethos, forgiveness is often foolish, even if such folly is the wisdom of the New Testament (1 Cor. 3:19); both Lear and his daughter are destroyed irrespective of his declaration, "I'll kneel down / And ask of thee forgiveness" (5.3.10–11). His conclusion to line eleven—"So we'll live,"—end-stopped as it is by a comma—ironically fills out the line with its momentary pause and (frustrated) promise of perpetuity.

This brings us to the leitmotif of resurrection, which is intimately related to forgiveness in Christian theology and, perhaps not unsurprisingly, in Shakespeare's plays as well. Shakespeare makes the connection explicit in *Measure for Measure* when Isabella tells the unforgiving Angelo, "Why, all the souls that were forfeit once, / And He that might the vantage best have took / Found out the remedy" (2.2.78–80). This is the furthest extent of Shakespeare's didacticism; it is not remotely an attempt at proselytizing; yet in less than three lines he lays out the message of the gospel. In the theodrama to which Isabella refers, Christ's death and resurrection effects forgiveness by justifying human beings before God. It is a message that Shakespeare frequently, if more subtly, evokes. Even a tragedy such as *King Lear* is "filled," as Leithart comments, "with the unrealized possibility of restoration, redemption, resurrection, in a way that an ancient tragedy could never be."[50] The play points to forgiveness and, in Lear's final look at the dead Cordelia, the possibility of her coming back to life: "Do you see this? Look on her, look, her lips, / Look thee, look there!" (5.3.316–17). It may be delusion on his part, but the intimation of resurrection is unmistakable. Lear envisions a pagan world that can, against all reason, be redeemed.

As we saw in chapter 4, Shakespeare revisits the idea in *The Winter's Tale* with Paulina's recollection of what Apollo's oracle had declared:

That King Leontes shall not have an heir

Till his lost child be found. What that it shall

Is all as monstrous to our human reason

As my Antigonus to break his grave

And come again to me, who, on my life,

Did perish with the infant. (5.1.39–44)

For Leontes to have an heir, Paulina tells us, two resurrections must take place. First, the exposed and almost certainly (Paulina assumes) dead Perdita must return, which is as likely as the dead Antigonus breaking from his grave to return to her. Resurrection is monstrous in a pagan imaginary, conjuring as it does the idea of the purely mechanistic—and, as in *Hamlet*, soulless—reanimation of the dead. Yet Shakespeare also offers in these pagan worlds an adumbration of a more beneficent, even beatific, resurrection. As we saw in chapter 3, upon learning that Perdita is indeed alive, Leontes and Camillo "looked as they had heard of a world ransomed, or one destroyed" (5.2.15–16). Caught between on the one hand their properly pagan horror at the idea of her soulless reanimation (a world destroyed), the recognition that Perdita is alive constitutes a dramatic appropriation of the joy associated with the Resurrection, and the allusive language (a world ransomed) strengthens the association.[51] Yet as in *King Lear*, the orthodoxy of Christian resurrection is a possible world evoked and envisioned at the margins of the pagan world the characters inhabit. But those margins keep breaking into the play: Paulina also returns, fully restored, and thus the recognition scene is illuminated and understood in light of the deep comedy of the Resurrection.

It is in the comedies, and *Twelfth Night* in particular, where Shakespeare routinely reminds his audiences of the Resurrection by means of his recognition scenes. Sebastian and Viola's quasi-miraculous survival and reappearance occasions, as I discussed in chapter 1, another evocation of that earth-rending event. The language of Viola's "Do not embrace me" (5.1.247) is at once evangelical and orthodox in its conjuration of scripture, but subtle in its brevity and fluidity, which enable it to coexist with secular understandings of such joyous reunion. Yet as Balthasar remarks,

> in the remote background there are the Christian miracles of the medieval mystery plays. But Shakespeare performs a "post-figuration", transforming the Christian elements into a fluid, elusive metaphor for the grace of existence. We can hardly say whether his is fired more by themes of antiquity or by Christian themes; the atmosphere is inconceivable apart from the Christian background, but this background only diffuses an anonymous light over the miracles of earthly love. [52]

The miracle of earthly love is the same in Hermione's revivification—or is it mere reappearance?—at the end of *The Winter's Tale*. One can read it as the use of "magic" (5.3.110), as Leontes first imagines or, more prosaically and secularly, as Paulina's remarkable ability to hide her mistress for sixteen long years, even though this defies credibility. Yet Shakespeare offers a *tertium quid* by means of his evocation of the power and potential of a resurrection: "Paulina promises [Leontes] even greater things if he will rouse up his 'faith'. . . . the audience too had thought Hermione to be dead and experiences her 'resurrection' as profoundly as Leontes." [53] This is not the only way to read the scene, of course. Yet Paulina's "It is requir'd / You do awake your faith" (5.3.94–95) neatly calls to mind the good of Hermione's living whether she has been resurrected or preserved by some less miraculous means. We can have it either way, as Shakespeare allows for both supernatural and natural causality. Shakespeare's model for the scene was both the (secular) Pygmalion story as well as the Resurrection myth, although Paulina's use of "faith" suggests that the religious reading is the primary reading. [54] Nonetheless, to invoke the Resurrection as often as Shakespeare does suggests its congeniality to his thought and dramatic practice.

To be sure, there is no exact identification of his recognition scenes with the Resurrection; rather, the emotion and profundity of the recognition is brought home to us through the evocation of the Resurrection. Its power as a model, not just in Shakespeare's plays but in early modern culture as a whole, can hardly be overestimated. In the end, neither the secular nor the religious explanation of Paulina's life is wholly embraced or denied; the equipoise is omnipresent, as Christopher Baker comments:

> It is as unwise to assume that Shakespeare's works are consistently skeptical of religion as it is to presume that a religious perspective alone is the only useful vantage from which to judge them. What we do find in his plays is a religious awareness, largely Christian but not uncritically so. . . . a perceptive

religious sensibility, responsive to the impact of organized religion in society and to the presence of a spiritual reality.[55]

Shakespeare alienates no one. We are told that the happily ever after ending of *The Winter's Tale*, the deep comedy, is "almost a miracle" (4.4.537)—but not quite a miracle, apparently.

That there is, finally, in Shakespeare a willingness not simply to uphold Christian orthodoxy, but to explore its boundaries, whether from his own perspective or from those of skeptical characters, seems to me beyond doubt. At the same time, there is a pervasive religious sensibility keenly attuned to what Baker calls "the presence of spiritual reality," one that surfaces in his emphasis on forgiveness and his continual calling to mind, via his recognition scenes, the Resurrection. Shakespeare never quite breaks with orthodoxy, but he does limn its contours and ventures with gusto into both the heterodox and unorthodox. A secular understanding of life—clearly at odds with religious orthodoxy—is thus also given its advocates, as well as its due. Shakespeare's consideration of possible worlds where resurrection looks more pagan than Christian, and even where God does not exist, testifies to his intellectual and philosophical range. His enduring appeal among religious and secular audiences alike suggests that his is in a sense Pauline drama: it has become all things to all people. Even if he wished to reinforce or share the gospel in the midst of his plays (he certainly evokes its message often enough), he respected his audience's intellectual freedom and recognized that there were other, competing choices available to them. Shakespeare never shies from this pluralism.[56] And in the end, it is this irreducibility of religious and secular perspectives that suffuse the plays; to deny one in favor of the other is to overlook their interplay, which is another way of saying that Shakespeare tests the orthodox, the unorthodox, and the heterodox on his stage.

NOTES

1. Qtd. in Roy W. Battenhouse, ed., *Shakespeare's Christian Dimension: An Anthology of Commentary* (Bloomington: Indiana University Press, 1994), 2.

2. René Weis, *Shakespeare Unbound: Decoding a Hidden Life* (New York: Henry Holt, 2007), 122. On Marlowe's alleged atheism, see David Riggs, "Marlowe's Quarrel with God," in *Marlowe, History, and Sexuality: New Critical Essays on Christopher Marlowe*, ed. Paul Whitfield White (New York: AMS Press, 1998), 15–37.

3. Peter Ackroyd, *Shakespeare: The Biography* (New York: Anchor, 2006), 474.

4. Jeffrey Knapp, *Shakespeare's Tribe: Church, Nation, and Theater in Renaissance England* (Chicago: University of Chicago Press, 2002), 52.

5. Ibid., 51.

6. Ibid.

7. Ackroyd, *Shakespeare*, 474.

8. Charles Taylor, *A Secular Age* (Cambridge: Harvard University Press, 2007), 13.

9. Alison Shell, *Shakespeare and Religion* (London: Arden Shakespeare, 2010), 195.

10. Harold. Bloom, *The Western Canon: The Books and School of the Ages* (New York: Harcourt Brace, 1994), 51.

11. E. K. Chambers, *William Shakespeare: A Study of Facts and Problems*, vol. 2 (Oxford: Oxford University Press, 1951), 255.

12. Samuel Schoenbaum, *William Shakespeare: A Compact Documentary Life*, Rev. ed. (New York: Oxford University Press, 1987), 298.

13. Russ McDonald, ed., *The Bedford Companion to Shakespeare: An Introduction with Documents*, 2nd ed. (Boston: Bedford/St. Martin's, 2001), 14.

14. Park Honan, *Shakespeare: A Life* (Oxford and New York: Oxford University Press, 2000), 403.

15. Shell, *Shakespeare and Religion*, 235.

16. Taylor, *A Secular Age*, 25.

17. Ibid.

18. Qtd. in McDonald, *The Bedford Companion to Shakespeare*, 143.

19. Taylor, *A Secular Age*, 25.

20. Ibid., 25–26.

21. Ibid., 26.

22. Ibid., 25.

23. Knapp, *Shakespeare's Tribe*, 2–3.

24. Paul Collins, *The Book of William: How Shakespeare's First Folio Conquered the World* (New York: Bloomsbury, 2009), 14, 16.

25. Leonard Digges, "To the Memory of the Deceased Authour Maister W. Shakespeare," in *The First Folio of Shakespeare*, ed. Charlton Hinman, 2nd ed. (New York: W.W. Norton, 1996), 15.

26. Fintan O'Toole, "Behind 'King Lear': The History Revealed," *The New York Review of Books*, November 19, 2015, 26; James Shapiro, *The Year of Lear: Shakespeare in 1606* (New York: Simon & Schuster, 2015).

27. R. A. Foakes, *Hamlet Versus Lear: Cultural Politics and Shakespeare's Art* (Cambridge: Cambridge University Press, 2004), 211; O. J. Campbell, "The Salvation of Lear," *ELH* 15 (1948), 107; Kenneth Muir, ed., *King Lear* (London: Methuen, 1952), lix; and Sean Benson, *Shakespearean Resurrection: The Art of Almost Raising the Dead* (Pittsburgh: Duquesne University Press, 2009), 106–07.

28. Shell, *Shakespeare and Religion*, 195.

29. O'Toole, "Behind 'King Lear,'" 26.

30. Battenhouse, *Shakespeare's Christian Dimension*, 13.

31. Taylor, *A Secular Age*, 12.

32. René Descartes, *Discourse on Method and Meditations on First Philosophy*, trans. Donald A. Cress, 4th ed. (Indianapolis: Hackett Publishing Company, 1999), 91.

33. Karl Marx, "Contribution to the Critique of Hegel's Philosophy of Right," in *On Religion*, ed. Reinhold Niebuhr (Oxford: Oxford University Press, 1964), 42, italics in original; Alvin Plantinga, *Knowledge and Christian Belief* (Grand Rapids: Eerdmans, 2015), 21.

34. Shell, *Shakespeare and Religion*, 235; see also Schoenbaum, *William Shakespeare*, 178.

35. Benson, *Shakespearean Resurrection*, 4–5.

36. A. L. Rowse, *William Shakespeare: A Biography.* (New York: Harper & Row, 1963), 41.

37. See Richmond Noble, *Shakespeare's Biblical Knowledge and Use of the Book of Common Prayer* (New York: Octagon Books, 1970); Shaheen, *Biblical References in Shakespeare's Plays*; and Rowse, *William Shakespeare*, 41–47, 25.

38. Stephen Greenblatt, *Will in the World: How Shakespeare Became Shakespeare* (New York: W. W. Norton, 2005), 36; Benson, *Shakespearean Resurrection*, 9–10.

39. Rowse, *William Shakespeare*, 44.

40. Shell, *Shakespeare and Religion*, 216–7.

41. Francis Bacon, *The Essays* (New York: Heritage Press, 1944), 9.

42. Desiderius Erasmus, *Discourse on Free Will: Erasmus & Luther*, trans. Ernst F. Winter (London; New York: Continuum, 2005), 24.

43. John Donne, *Divine Poems, Sermons, Devotions, and Prayers*, ed. John E. Booty (New York: Paulist Press, 1990), 125.

44. Anthony Munday, *A Second and Third Blast of Retrait*, 91. Qtd. in Knapp, 118.

45. John Milton, "Areopagitica," in *Complete Poems and Major Prose*, ed. Merritt Yerkes Hughes (New Jersey: Prentice Hall, 1957), 727.

46. Robert G. Hunter, *Shakespeare and the Comedy of Forgiveness* (New York: Columbia University Press, 1965).

47. Hans Urs von Balthasar, *Theo-Drama: Theological Dramatic Theory*, volume 1: *Prolegomena*, trans. Graham Harrison (San Francisco: Ignatius Press, 1988), 466.

48. Peter J. Leithart, *Deep Comedy: Trinity, Tragedy, & Hope in Western Literature* (Moscow, ID: Canon Press, 2006), 3.

49. Ibid., chap. 1.

50. Ibid., 125.

51. Benson, *Shakespearean Resurrection*, 154–57.

52. Balthasar, *Theo-Drama*, 1:384.

53. Ibid.

54. See also Benson, *Shakespearean Resurrection*, 158–63.

55. Christopher Baker, *Religion in the Age of Shakespeare* (Westport, CT: Greenwood, 2007), 57–58.

56. On the era's intellectual pluralism, see Debora K. Shuger, *Habits of Thought in the English Renaissance: Religion, Politics, and the Dominant Culture* (Toronto: University of Toronto Press, 1997), 22–23, 67.

Bibliography

Ackroyd, Peter. *Shakespeare: The Biography*. New York: Anchor, 2006.

Adams, Marilyn McCord. "Horrendous Evils and the Goodness of God." In *Philosophy of Religion: Selected Readings*, edited by Michael L. Peterson, 333–42. 4th ed. New York: Oxford University Press, 2010.

Ady, Thomas. *A Perfect Discovery of Witches*. London, 1661.

Almereyda, Michael, dir. *Hamlet*, 2000.

Anderson, Anthony. *The Shield of Our Safetie*. London, 1581.

Anderson, Judith H. *Reading the Allegorical Intertext: Chaucer, Spenser, Shakespeare, Milton*. New York: Fordham University Press, 2010.

Aquinas, Thomas. "The Summa Contra Gentiles." In *Introduction to Saint Thomas Aquinas*, edited and translated by Anton C. Pegis, 429–77. New York: Modern Library, 1965.

Ariès, Philippe. *The Hour of Our Death*. Translated by Helen Weaver. New York: Knopf, 1981.

Aristotle. *On the Soul*. In *The Complete Works of Aristotle: The Revised Oxford Translation*, edited by Jonathan Barnes, translated by J. A. Smith, 1:641–92. Vol. 1. Bollingen Series 71:1. Princeton: Princeton University Press, 1995.

———. *Poetics*. In *The Complete Works of Aristotle: The Revised Oxford Translation*, edited by Jonathan Barnes, translated by I. Bywater. Vol. 2. Bollingen Series 71:2. Princeton: Princeton University Press, 1995.

Augustine. *Confessions*. Translated by R. S. Pine-Coffin. New York: Penguin, 1961.

———. *Confessions and Enchiridion*. Edited and translated by Albert Cook Outler. Vol. 7. Library of Christian Classics. Philadelphia: Westminster, 1955.

Bacon, Francis. *The Essays*. New York: Heritage Press, 1944.

Baker, Christopher. *Religion in the Age of Shakespeare*. Westport, CT: Greenwood, 2007.

Balthasar, Hans Urs von. *Theo-Drama: Theological Dramatic Theory*. Volume 1: *Prolegomena*. Translated by Graham Harrison. San Francisco: Ignatius Press, 1988.

Barish, Jonas A. *The Antitheatrical Prejudice*. Berkeley: University of California Press, 1981.

Barton, Anne. *Shakespeare and the Idea of the Play*. London: Chatto & Windus, 1962.

Bate, Jonathan. *Soul of the Age: A Biography of the Mind of William Shakespeare*. New York: Random House, 2009.

Battenhouse, Roy W., ed. *Shakespeare's Christian Dimension: An Anthology of Commentary*. Bloomington: Indiana University Press, 1994.

Belsey, Catherine. "Shakespeare's Sad Tale for Winter: Hamlet and the Tradition of Fireside Ghost Stories." *Shakespeare Quarterly* 61, no. 1 (2010): 1–27.

Benson, Sean. "'Perverse Fantasies'?: Rehabilitating Malvolio's Reading." *Papers on Language & Literature* 45, no. 3 (Summer 2009): 261–286.

———. *Shakespearean Resurrection: The Art of Almost Raising the Dead.* Pittsburgh: Duquesne University Press, 2009.

Berger, Peter L. *Redeeming Laughter: The Comic Dimension of Human Experience.* New York: Walter de Gruyter, 1997.

Berry, Lloyd E, and William Whittingham, eds. *The Geneva Bible: A Facsimile of the 1560 Edition.* Madison: University of Wisconsin Press, 1969.

Bevington, David, ed. *The Complete Works of Shakespeare.* 7th ed. Boston: Pearson, 2014.

Bevington, David. "The Debate about Shakespeare and Religion." In *Shakespeare and Early Modern Religion,* edited by David Loewenstein and Michael Witmore, 23–39. Cambridge & New York: Cambridge University Press, 2015.

Bevington, David, Lars Engle, Katharine Eisaman Maus, and Eric Rasmussen, eds. *English Renaissance Drama: A Norton Anthology.* New York: W. W. Norton, 2002.

Bishop, Kyle. "Dead Man Still Walking." *Journal of Popular Film & Television* 37, no. 1 (Spring 2009): 16–25.

Bloom, Harold. *Shakespeare: The Invention of the Human.* New York: Riverhead, 1998.

———. *The Western Canon: The Books and School of the Ages.* New York: Harcourt Brace, 1994.

Boitani, Piero. *The Gospel according to Shakespeare.* Translated by Vittorio Montemaggi and Rachel Jacoff. South Bend: University of Notre Dame Press, 2013.

Booth, Stephen. *Precious Nonsense: The Gettysburg Address, Ben Jonson's Epitaphs on His Children, and Twelfth Night.* Berkeley: University of California Press, 1998.

Boyle, Danny, dir. *28 Days Later,* 2003.

Briggs, Katharine. *The Anatomy of Puck.* New York: Arno Press, 1977.

Brook, Peter. *The Empty Space.* New York: Atheneum, 1968.

Brooke, Nicholas. *Shakespeare: King Lear.* London, 1963.

———. "The Ending of King Lear." In *Shakespeare, 1564-1964: A Collection of Modern Essays by Various Hands,* edited by Edward Alan Bloom, 71–87. Providence: Brown University Press, 1964.

Brooks, Max. *The Zombie Survival Guide: Complete Protection from the Living Dead.* Three Rivers Press, 2003.

———. *World War Z: An Oral History of the Zombie War.* Three Rivers Press, 2007.

Brown, Andrew. *Church and Society in England, 1000–1500.* Social History in Perspective. Basingstoke & New York: Palgrave Macmillan 2003.

Browne, Thomas. *Religio Medici.* In *The Major Works,* edited by C. A. Patrides. New York: Penguin Books, 1977.

Brownlow, F. W. *Shakespeare, Harsnett, and the Devils of Denham.* Lanham: University of Delaware Press, 1993.

Bruce, John, ed. *Diary of John Manningham.* London: Camden Society, 1963.

Bullough, Geoffrey, ed. *Narrative and Dramatic Sources of Shakespeare.* 8 vols. New York: Columbia University Press, 1957–71.

Calvin, John. *Institutes of the Christian Religion: The First English Version of the 1541 French Edition.* Translated by Elsie Anne McKee. Grand Rapids: Wm. B. Eerdmans Publishing, 2009.

Campbell, O. J. "The Salvation of Lear," *ELH* XV (1948): 102–113.

Camus, Albert. *The Myth of Sisyphus, and Other Essays.* Translated by Justin O'Brien. New York: Vintage Books, 1955.

Catechism of the Catholic Church. Vatican City and Washington, DC: Libreria Editrice Vaticana, 2000.

Cavell, Stanley. *Disowning Knowledge in Six Plays of Shakespeare.* Cambridge: Cambridge University Press, 1987.

Chalmers, David John. *The Conscious Mind: In Search of a Fundamental Theory.* Philosophy of Mind Series. New York: Oxford University Press, 1997.

Chambers, E. K. *The Mediaeval Stage.* Vol. 2. 2 vols. London: Oxford University Press, 1903.

———. *William Shakespeare: A Study of Facts and Problems.* Vol. 2. Oxford: Oxford University Press, 1951.

Cohen, Adam Max. *Wonder in Shakespeare*. Basingstoke & New York: Palgrave Macmillan, 2012.

Coleridge, Samuel Taylor. *Coleridge on Shakespeare: A Selection of the Essays, Notes and Lectures of Samuel Taylor Coleridge on the Poems and Plays of Shakespeare*. Edited by Terence Hawkes. New York: Penguin, 1969.

Collins, Paul. *The Book of William: How Shakespeare's First Folio Conquered the World*. New York: Bloomsbury, 2009.

Collinson, Patrick. "Antipuritanism." In *The Cambridge Companion to Puritanism*, edited by John Coffey and Paul Chang-Ha Lim, 19–33. Cambridge: Cambridge University Press, 2008.

Costa, Dennis. *Irenic Apocalypse: Some Uses of Apocalyptic in Dante, Petrarch, and Rabelais*. Saratoga CA: Anma Libri, 1981.

Critchley, Simon, and Jamieson Webster. *Stay, Illusion!: The Hamlet Doctrine*. Brooklyn, NY: Verso Books, 2013.

Dahan, Yannick, and Benjamin Rocher, dirs. *La Horde*. 2010.

Davies, J. G. *The Secular Use of Church Buildings*. London: SCM Press, 1968.

Dawson, Anthony B. "Shakespeare and Secular Performance." In *Shakespeare and the Cultures of Performance*, edited by Paul Yachnin and Patricia Badir, 83–97. Burlington, VT: Ashgate, 2008.

Delumeau, Jean. *Sin and Fear: The Emergence of a Western Guilt Culture, 13th–18th Centuries*. Translated by Eric Nicholson. New York: St. Martin's Press, 1990.

Dendle, Peter. *The Zombie Movie Encyclopedia*. Jefferson, NC: McFarland, 2010.

Denmark, Ryan, dir. *Romeo and Juliet vs. The Living Dead*, 2009.

Descartes, René. *Discourse on Method and Meditations on First Philosophy*. Translated by Donald A. Cress. 4th ed. Indianapolis: Hackett Publishing Company, 1999.

De Vries, Peter. *The Blood of the Lamb*. Signet Books. New York: New American Library, 1963.

Digges, Leonard. "To the Memory of the Deceased Authour Maister W. Shakespeare." In *The First Folio of Shakespeare*, edited by Charlton Hinman, 2nd ed. New York: W.W. Norton, 1996.

Dillard, R. H. W. "Night of the Living Dead: It's Not Like Just a Wind That's Passing Through." In *American Horrors: Essays on the Modern American Horror Film*, edited by Gregory A. Waller. Champaign: University of Illinois Press, 1987.

Dollimore, Jonathan. *Radical Tragedy*. 3rd ed. New York: Palgrave Macmillan, 2004.

Donne, John. *Divine Poems, Sermons, Devotions, and Prayers*. Edited by John E. Booty. New York: Paulist Press, 1990.

Shuger, Debora K. *Habits of Thought in the English Renaissance: Religion, Politics, and the Dominant Culture*. Toronto: University of Toronto Press, 1997.

Douglas, Audrey, and Peter Greenfield, eds. *REED. Cumberland, Westmorland, Gloucestershire*. Toronto; Buffalo: University of Toronto Press, 1986.

Duffy, Eamon. *The Stripping of the Altars: Traditional Religion in England, c.1400–c.1580*. New Haven: Yale University Press, 1992.

Dymond, David. "God's Disputed Acre." *Journal of Ecclesiastical History* 50, no. 3 (July 1999): 464–97.

Ebertz, Roger P. "Beyond Worldview Analysis: Insights from Hans-Georg Gadamer on Christian Scholarship." *Christian Scholar's Review* 36, no. 1 (Fall 2006): 13–28.

Elam, Keir, ed. *Twelfth Night*. 3rd ed. London: Arden Shakespeare, 2009.

Elliott, John R, Alan H. Nelson, Alexandra F. Johnston, and Diana Wyatt, eds. *REED. Oxford*. 2 vols. Toronto: University of Toronto Press, 2004.

Elliott, Robert C. "The Definition of Satire: A Note on Method." *Yearbook of Comparative and General Literature* 11 (1962): 19–23.

Elton, William. *King Lear and the Gods*. San Marino, CA: Huntington Library, 1966.

Emerson, Ralph Waldo. "Shakespeare; Or, the Poet." In *Shakespeare in America: An Anthology from the Revolution to Now*, edited by James Shapiro, 105–22. New York: Library of America, 2014.

Empson, William. *Seven Types of Ambiguity*. 2nd ed. New York: New Directions, 1947.

Erasmus, Desiderius. *Discourse on Free Will*. Translated by Ernst F. Winter. London & New York: Continuum, 2005.

———. *The Praise of Folly*. Translated by Clarence H. Miller. New Haven: Yale University Press, 1979.

Erler, Mary Carpenter, ed. *REED. Ecclesiastical London*. Toronto: University of Toronto Press, 2008.

Fleischer, Ruben, dir. *Zombieland*, 2009.

Fisch, Harold. *The Biblical Presence in Shakespeare, Milton, and Blake: A Comparative Study*. Oxford: Oxford University Press, 1999.

Foakes, R. A. *Hamlet versus Lear: Cultural Politics and Shakespeare's Art*. Cambridge: Cambridge University Press, 2004.

Forell, George Wolfgang. *The Protestant Faith*. Englewood Cliffs, NJ: Prentice-Hall, 1960.

Fortin, René E. "Hermeneutical Circularity and Christian Interpretations of King Lear." *Shakespeare Studies* 12 (January 1979): 113–25.

Foucault, Michel. "The Discourse on Language." In *The Archaeology of Knowledge*, translated by Rupert Sawyer, 215–37. New York: Pantheon Books, 1972.

Foxe, John. *Actes and Monuments* (1570). Edited by George Townsend. New York: AMS Press, 1965.

Frere, Walter Howard, and C. E. Douglas, eds. "An Admonition to the Parliament." In *Puritan Manifestoes: A Study of the Origin of the Puritan Revolt*. New York: Burt Franklin, 1972.

Freud, Sigmund. *The Future of an Illusion*. Edited by James. Strachey. Translated by W. D. Robson-Scott. New York: Anchor Books, 1964.

———. "The 'Uncanny'." In *The Standard Edition of the Complete Psychological Works of Sigmund Freud*, edited and translated by James Strachey, 17:217–56. London: Hogarth Press, 1953.

Frye, Northrop. *A Natural Perspective: The Development of Shakespearean Comedy and Romance*. New York: Columbia University Press, 1965.

Gadamer, Hans-Georg. *Truth and Method*. Translated by Joel Weinsheimer and Donald G. Marshall. 2nd rev. ed. New York: Continuum, 1999.

Galland, Jordan, dir. *Rosencrantz & Guildenstern Are Undead*. 2010.

Galloway, David, ed. *REED. Norwich 1540–1642*. Toronto: University of Toronto Press, 1984.

Garber, Marjorie. *Shakespeare After All*. New York: Anchor, 2005.

———. *Shakespeare's Ghost Writers: Literature as Uncanny Causality*. New York: Methuen, 1987.

Giles, Kate, and Jonathan Clark. "The Archaeology of the Guild Buildings of Shakespeare's Stratford-upon-Avon." In *The Guild and Guild Buildings of Shakespeare's Stratford: Society, Religion, School and Stage*, edited by J. R. Mulryne, 135–69. Burlington, VT: Ashgate, 2012.

Gill, Sylvia. "Reformation: Priests and People." In *The Guild and Guild Buildings of Shakespeare's Stratford: Society, Religion, School and Stage*, edited by J. R. Mulryne, 31–58. Burlington, VT: Ashgate, 2012.

Greenblatt, Stephen. *Hamlet in Purgatory*. Princeton: Princeton University Press, 2002.

———. *Renaissance Self-Fashioning: From More to Shakespeare*. Chicago: University of Chicago Press, 1984.

———. *Shakespearean Negotiations: The Circulation of Social Energy in Renaissance England*. Berkeley: University of California Press, 1988.

———. *Will in the World: How Shakespeare Became Shakespeare*. New York: W. W. Norton, 2005.

Greenfield, Peter H. "Parish Drama in Four Counties Bordering the Thames Watershed." In *English Parish Drama*, edited by Alexandra F. Johnston and Hüsken, Wim, 107–18. Amsterdam and Atlanta, GA: Rodopi, 1996.

Greer, Germaine. *Shakespeare: A Very Short Introduction*. Oxford: Oxford University Press, 2002.

Gregory of Nyssa, St. *The Soul and the Resurrection*. Translated by Catharine P. Roth. Crestwood, NY: St. Vladimir's Seminary Press, 1993.

Greif, Karen. "Plays and Playing in Twelfth Night." In *Twelfth Night: Critical Essays*, edited by Stanley Wells. New York: Garland, 1986.

Groves, Beatrice. *Texts and Traditions: Religion in Shakespeare, 1592–1604*. Oxford: Oxford University Press, 2007.

Gurr, Andrew. *The Shakespearean Stage, 1574–1642*. 4th ed. Cambridge & New York: Cambridge University Press, 2009.

———. *The Shakespearian Playing Companies*. Oxford: Oxford University Press, 1996.

Haglund, William D., and Marcella H. Sorg. "Human Remains in Water Environments." In *Advances in Forensic Taphonomy: Method, Theory, and Archaeological Perspectives*, edited by William D. Haglund and Marcella H. Sorg, 201–19. Boca Raton: CRC Press, 2002.

Hamlin, Hannibal. *The Bible in Shakespeare*. Oxford: Oxford University Press, 2013.

Handeland, Lori. *Shakespeare Undead*. New York: St. Martin's Griffin, 2010.

———. *Zombie Island: A Shakespeare Undead Novel*. New York: St. Martin's Griffin, 2012.

Hawthorne, Nathaniel. "Recollections of a Gifted Woman." In *Shakespeare in America: An Anthology from the Revolution to Now*, edited by James S. Shapiro, 148–74. Library of America 251. New York: The Library of America, 2014.

Hays, Rosalind Conklin, and C. Edward McGee, eds. *REED. Dorset*. Toronto: University of Toronto Press, 1999.

Hunter, Robert G. *Shakespeare and the Comedy of Forgiveness*. New York: Columbia University Press, 1965.

Hegel, G. W. F. "Dramatic Poetry." In *Philosophers on Shakespeare*, edited by Paul Kottman, translated by T. M. Knox, 57–85. Palo Alto: Stanford University Press, 2009.

Heidegger, Martin. *Basic Writings: From Being and Time (1927) to The Task of Thinking (1964)*. Edited by David Farrell Krell. New York: Harper & Row, 1977.

———. *Being and Time*. Translated by John Macquarrie and Edward Robinson. Oxford: Blackwell, 1967.

Heimbuch, John. *William Shakespeare's Land of the Dead*. New York: Samuel French, Inc., 2012.

Henry, Matthew. *Matthew Henry's Commentary: Matthew to John*. Vol. 5. New York: Fleming H. Revell Company, n.d.

Heywood, Thomas. *An Apology for Actors*. New York: Garland Publishing, 1973.

Hick, John. "Soul-Making Theodicy." In *Philosophy of Religion: Selected Readings*, edited by Michael L. Peterson, 316–22. 4th ed. New York: Oxford University Press, 2010.

Hill, Christopher. "Irreligion in the 'Puritan' Revolution." In *Radical Religion in the English Revolution*, edited by J. F. McGregor and Barry Reay, 191–211. Oxford: Oxford University Press, 1984.

Hobbes, Thomas. *Behemoth: The History of the Causes of the Civil Wars of England*. Edited by William Molesmith. New York: B. Franklin, 1963.

Homer, Sean. *Jacques Lacan*. London: Routledge, 2005.

Honan, Park. *Shakespeare: A Life*. Oxford and New York: Oxford University Press, 2000.

Hume, David. "Evil Makes a Strong Case Against God's Existence." In *Philosophy of Religion: Selected Readings*, edited by Michael L. Peterson, 276–81. 4th ed. New York: Oxford University Press, 2010.

Hunt, Maurice. *Shakespeare's Religious Allusiveness: Its Play and Tolerance*. Burlington, VT: Ashgate, 2003.

Ingram, R. W, ed. *REED. Coventry*. Toronto: University of Toronto Press, 1981.

Jackson, Ken, and Arthur F. Marotti. "The Turn to Religion in Early Modern English Studies." *Criticism* 46, no. 1 (Winter 2004): 167–190.

James, D. G. *The Dream of Learning: An Essay on the Advancement of Learning, Hamlet and King Lear*. Oxford: Clarendon Press, 1951.

James, M. R. "Twelve Medieval Ghost-Stories." *The English Historical Review* 37, no. 147 (July 1, 1922): 413–422.

John Paul II. *Love and Responsibility*. Translated by H. T. Willets. San Francisco: Ignatius Press, 1993.

Johnson, Samuel. *Samuel Johnson on Shakespeare*. Edited by William Kurtz Wimsatt. London: MacGibbon & Kee, 1960.

————. *The Yale Edition of the Works of Samuel Johnson*, edited by Arthur Sherbo. Vol. 7. New Haven: Yale University Press, 1968.

Johnston, Alexandra F. "Introduction." In *English Parish Drama*, edited by Alexandra F. Johnston and Wim Hüsken, 7–14. Amsterdam and Atlanta, GA: Rodopi, 1996.

————. "'What Revels Are in Hand': The Parishes of the Thames Valley." In *English Parish Drama*, edited by Alexandra F. Johnston and Wim Hüsken, 95–104. Amsterdam and Atlanta, GA: Rodopi, 1996.

Jonson, Ben. "To the Memory of My Beloved, the Author." In *The First Folio of Shakespeare*, edited by Charlton Hinman. 2nd ed. New York: W.W. Norton, 1996.

————. *The Staple of News*. Edited by Devra Rowland Kifer. Lincoln: University of Nebraska Press, 1975.

Joyce, Sally L, and Evelyn S Newlyn. *REED. Cornwall*. Toronto: University of Toronto Press, 1999.

Kastan, David Scott. *A Will to Believe: Shakespeare and Religion*. Oxford: Oxford University Press, 2014.

Kaula, David. "Hamlet and the Image of Both Churches." *Studies in English Literature, 1500–1900* 24, no. 2 (April 1, 1984): 241–255.

Keenan, Siobhan. *Travelling Players in Shakespeare's England*. Basingstoke: Palgrave, 2002.

Kempe, Margery. *The Book of Margery Kempe*. Translated by Barry Windeatt. New York: Penguin Classics, 2000.

King, Stephen. *Cell: A Novel*. New York: Scribner, 2006.

Kirk, Robert. *Zombies and Consciousness*. Oxford: Oxford University Press, 2005.

Klausner, David N. *REED. Herefordshire, Worcestershire*. Toronto & Buffalo: University of Toronto Press, 1990.

Knapp, Jeffrey. *Shakespeare's Tribe: Church, Nation, and Theater in Renaissance England*. Chicago: University of Chicago Press, 2002.

Knight, George. *The Wheel of Fire: Interpretations of Shakespearean Tragedy*. Cleveland: World Publishing, 1962.

Ko, Yu Jin. "The Comic Close of Twelfth Night and Viola's Noli Me Tangere." *Shakespeare Quarterly* 48, no. 4 (December 1, 1997): 391–405.

Kott, Jan. *Shakespeare Our Contemporary*. London: Methuen, 1967.

Lacan, Jacques. "Desire and the Interpretation of Desire in Hamlet." Edited by Jacques-Alain Miller. Translated by James Hulbert. *Yale French Studies* no. 55/56 (January 1, 1977): 11–52.

————. *The Seminar of Jacques Lacan*. Edited by Jacques-Alain Miller. Translated by Cormac Gallagher. Vol. 6. New York: W. W. Norton, 2002.

Lake, Peter. "'A Charitable Christian Hatred': The Godly and Their Enemies in the 1630s." In *The Culture of English Puritanism: 1560–1700*, edited by Christopher Durston and Jacqueline Eales, 145–83. New York: St. Martin's Press, 1996.

Lake, Peter, and Michael Questier. *The Anti-Christ's Lewd Hat: Protestants, Papists and Players in Post-Reformation England*. New Haven: Yale University Press, 2002.

Lancashire, Ian. *Dramatic Texts and Records of Britain: A Chronological Topography to 1558*. Toronto: University of Toronto Press, 1984.

Leibniz, Gottfried. "Best of All Possible Worlds Theodicy." In *Philosophy of Religion: Selected Readings*, edited by Michael L. Peterson, 282–87. 4th ed. New York: Oxford University Press, 2010.

Leithart, Peter J. *Deep Comedy: Trinity, Tragedy, & Hope in Western Literature*. Moscow, ID: Canon Press, 2006.

Levine, Jonathan, dir. *Warm Bodies*, 2013.

Lewis, Cynthia. "Soft Touch: On the Renaissance Staging and Meaning of the 'Noli Me Tangere' Icon." *Comparative Drama* 36, no. 1/2 (Summer 2002): 53.

————. "Viola's 'Do Not Embrace Me' as Icon." *Notes and Queries* 35 (233), no. 4 (December 1988): 473–474.

Linge, David E. "Editor's Introduction." In *Philosophical Hermeneutics*, edited and translated by David E. Linge. Berkeley: University of California Press, 1977.

Lodge, Thomas. *Wit's Misery, 1596*. Menston: Scolar Press, 1971.

Loewenstein, David. "Agnostic Shakespeare?: The Godless World of King Lear." In *Shakespeare and Early Modern Religion*, edited by David Loewenstein and Michael Witmore, 155–71. Cambridge & New York: Cambridge University Press, 2015.

Louis, Cameron, ed. *REED. Sussex*. Toronto: University of Toronto Press, 2000.

Lyon, Nick, dir. *Zombie Apocalypse*, 2011.

MacCulloch, Diarmaid. *The Later Reformation in England, 1547–1603*. 2nd ed. New York: Palgrave, 2001.

MacIntyre, Alasdair C. *After Virtue: A Study in Moral Theory*. 2nd ed. Notre Dame: University of Notre Dame Press, 1984.

Mack, Maynard. *King Lear in Our Time*. Berkeley: University of California Press, 1965.

Mackie, J. L. "Evil and Omnipotence." In *Philosophy of Religion: Selected Readings*, edited by Michael L. Peterson, 288–96. 4th ed. New York: Oxford University Press, 2010.

Marx, Karl. "Contribution to the Critique of Hegel's Philosophy of Right." In *On Religion*, edited by Reinhold Niebuhr. Oxford: Oxford University Press, 1964.

Mayer, Jean-Christophe. *Shakespeare's Hybrid Faith: History, Religion and the Stage*. Basingstoke & New York: Palgrave Macmillan, 2006.

Maddrey, Joseph. *Nightmares in Red, White, and Blue: The Evolution of the American Horror Film*. Jefferson, NC: McFarland, 2004.

Mallin, Eric S. *Inscribing the Time: Shakespeare and the End of Elizabethan England*. Berkeley: University of California Press, 1995.

Mann, R. W., W. M. Bass, and L. Meadows. "Time Since Death and Decomposition of the Human Body: Variables and Observations in Case and Experimental Field Studies." *Journal of Forensic Sciences* 35, no. 1 (January 1990): 103–111.

Manningham, John. *The Diary of John Manningham of the Middle Temple, 1602–1603*. Edited by Robert Parker Sorlien. Hanover, NH: University Press of New England, 1976.

Marlowe, Christopher. *Dr. Faustus: Based on the A Text*. Edited by Roma Gill. 2nd ed. New York: W. W. Norton & Company, 1990.

Marshall, Cynthia. *Last Things and Last Plays: Shakespearean Eschatology*. Carbondale: Southern Illinois University Press, 1991.

Marshall, Peter. *Beliefs and the Dead in Reformation England*. Oxford: Oxford University Press, 2002.

Maus, Katharine. *Inwardness and Theater in the English Renaissance*. Chicago: University of Chicago Press, 1995.

McCarthy, Cormac. *The Road*. New York: Vintage Books, 2007.

McCoy, Richard C. *Faith in Shakespeare*. New York: Oxford University Press, 2013.

McDonald, Russ, ed. *The Bedford Companion to Shakespeare: An Introduction with Documents*. 2nd ed. Boston: Bedford/St. Martin's, 2001.

McGee, Arthur. *The Elizabethan Hamlet*. New Haven: Yale University Press, 1987.

McMillin, Scott, and Sally-Beth MacLean. *The Queen's Men and Their Plays*. Cambridge: Cambridge University Press, 1998.

Melchert, Norman. *The Great Conversation: A Historical Introduction to Philosophy*. Vol. 2. 5th ed. Oxford and New York: Oxford University Press, 2006.

Micozzi, Marc S. "Frozen Environments and Soft Tissue Preservation." In *Forensic Taphonomy: The Postmortem Fate of Human Remains*, edited by William D. Haglund and Marcella H. Sorg, 171–80. Boca Raton: CRC Press, 1997.

Milbank, John. *Theology and Social Theory: Beyond Secular Reason*. 2nd ed. Oxford and Malden, MA: Wiley-Blackwell, 2006.

Milton, John. "Areopagitica." *Complete Poems and Major Prose*, edited by Merritt Yerkes Hughes. New Jersey: Prentice Hall, 1957.

———. *Paradise Lost*. Edited by David Scott Kastan. Indianapolis: Hackett Publishing, 2005.

———. *Complete Prose Works of John Milton*. Edited by Don M. Wolfe. Vol. 1. 8 vols. New Haven: Yale University Press, 1953.

Milward, Peter. "The Religious Dimension of Shakespeare's Illyria." In *Shakespeare and the Mediterranean*, edited by Thomas Clayton, Susan Brock, and Vicente Forés, 380–87. Newark: University of Delaware Press, 2004.

Muir, Kenneth, ed., *King Lear*. London: Methuen, 1952.

Mulryne, J. R. "Introduction." In *The Guild and Guild Buildings of Shakespeare's Stratford: Society, Religion, School and Stage*, edited by J. R. Mulryne, 1–12. London: Ashgate, 2012.

———. "Professional Players in the Guild Hall, Stratford-upon-Avon, 1568–1597." In *Shakespeare Survey*, edited by Peter Holland, 60:1–22. Cambridge: Cambridge University Press, 2007.

Munday, Anthony. *A Second and Third Blast of Retrait from Plaies and Theaters*. New York: Garland Publishing, 1973.

Nichols, Aidan. *No Bloodless Myth: A Guide Through Balthasar's Dramatics*. Washington, DC: Catholic University of America Press, 2000.

Noble, Richmond. *Shakespeare's Biblical Knowledge and Use of the Book of Common Prayer*. New York: Octagon Books, 1970.

Northbrooke, John. *A Treatise Wherein Dicing, Dauncing, Vaine Playes or Enterluds With Other Idle Pastimes Etc. Commonly Used of the Sabboth Day, Are Reproved*. Edited by Arthur Freeman. New York: Garland, 1577.

Nuttall, A. D. *Shakespeare the Thinker*. New Haven: Yale University Press, 2007.

O'Toole, Fintan. "Behind 'King Lear': The History Revealed." *The New York Review of Books*, November 19, 2015.

Palmer, Barbara D. "'Anye Disguised Persons': Parish Entertainment in West Yorkshire." In *English Parish Drama*, edited by Alexandra F. Johnston and Hüsken, Wim, 81–93. Amsterdam and Atlanta, GA: Rodopi, 1996.

———. "Playing in the Provinces: Front or Back Door?" *Medieval & Renaissance Drama in England* 22 (January 2009): 81–127.

Peterson, Michael L., editor. *Philosophy of Religion: Selected Readings*. 4th ed. New York: Oxford University Press, 2010.

Pilkinton, Mark C, ed. *REED. Bristol*. Toronto: University of Toronto Press, 1997.

Plantinga, Alvin. *Knowledge and Christian Belief*. Grand Rapids: Eerdmans, 2015.

———. "The Free Will Defense." In *Philosophy of Religion: Selected Readings*, edited by Michael L. Peterson, 297–315. 4th ed. New York: Oxford University Press, 2010.

Plato. "Phaedo." In *Plato*, translated by H. N. Fowler, 200–402. The Loeb Classical Library. Cambridge, MA: Harvard University Press, 1943.

Poole, Kristen. *Radical Religion from Shakespeare to Milton: Figures of Nonconformity in Early Modern England*. Cambridge & New York: Cambridge University Press, 2000.

Preston, John. *A Sermon Preached at the Funeral of Mr. Arthur Upton*. London, 1619.

Prosser, Eleanor. *Hamlet and Revenge*. Stanford: Stanford University Press, 1967.

Rabkin, Norman. *Shakespeare and the Common Understanding*. New York: Free Press, 1967.

Rhodes, Neil. *Shakespeare and the Origins of English*. Oxford and New York: Oxford University Press, 2004.

Rieff, Philip. *My Life Among the Deathworks: Illustrations of the Aesthetics of Authority*. Edited by Kenneth S. Piver. Vol. 1. 3 vols. Charlottesville and London: University of Virginia Press, 2006.

Riggs, David. "Marlowe's Quarrel with God." In *Marlowe, History, and Sexuality: New Critical Essays on Christopher Marlowe*, edited by Paul Whitfield White, 15–37. New York: AMS Press, 1998.

Romero, George A., dir. *Night of the Living Dead*, 1968.

Rosenberg, Marvin. *The Masks of King Lear*. Berkeley: University of California Press, 1972.

Rowse, A. L. *William Shakespeare: A Biography*. New York: Harper & Row, 1963.

Sampson, William. *The Vow Breaker or, The Faire Maide of Clifton*. Edited by Hans Wallrath. Vaduz: Kraus Reprint Ltd., 1636.

Santayana, George. "The Absence of Religion in Shakespeare." In *Interpretations of Poetry and Religion*, 147–65. The Library of Religion and Culture. New York: Harper, 1957.

Sasek, Lawrence A. *Images of English Puritanism: A Collection of Contemporary Sources, 1589–1646*. Baton Rouge: Louisiana State University Press, 1989.

Schmelling, Sarah. "Hamlet (Facebook NewsFeed Edition)." In *The Best of McSweeney's Internet Tendency*, edited by Chris Monks and John Warner, 79–81. San Francisco: McSweeney's, 2014.

Schoenbaum, Samuel. *William Shakespeare: A Compact Documentary Life*. Rev. ed. New York: Oxford University Press, 1987.

Shaheen, Naseeb. *Biblical References in Shakespeare's Plays*. Newark: University of Delaware Press, 1999.

Shakespeare, William. *The First Quarto of Hamlet*. Edited by Kathleen O. Irace. New York: Cambridge University Press, 1998.

Shapiro, James. *The Year of Lear: Shakespeare in 1606*. New York: Simon & Schuster, 2015.

Shell, Alison. *Shakespeare and Religion*. London: Arden Shakespeare, 2010.

Shuger, Debora K. *Habits of Thought in the English Renaissance: Religion, Politics, and the Dominant Culture*. Toronto: University of Toronto Press, 1997.

Sidney, Philip. "The Defence of Poesy." In *Sir Philip Sidney: A Selection of His Finest Poems*, edited by Katherine Duncan-Jones, 101–42. Oxford: Oxford University Press, 1994.

Simmons, J. L. "A Source for Shakespeare's Malvolio: The Elizabethan Controversy with the Puritans." *Huntington Library Quarterly* 36, no. 3 (May 1, 1973): 181–201.

Simpson, Jacqueline. "Repentant Soul or Walking Corpse? Debatable Apparitions in Medieval England." *Folklore* 114, no. 3 (December 1, 2003): 389–402.

Simpson, James. *Burning to Read: English Fundamentalism and Its Reformation Opponents*. Cambridge: Belknap Press of Harvard University Press, 2007.

Slack, Paul A. "Mortality and Epidemic Crisis, 1485–1610." In *Health, Medicine, and Mortality in the Sixteenth Century*, edited by Charles Webster, 9–60. Cambridge: Cambridge University Press, 1979.

Smith, Henry. *The Sermons of Master H. Smith Gathered into One Volume*. London, 1592.

Smith, Peter J. "M. O. A. I. 'What Should That Alphabetical Position Portend?': An Answer to the Metamorphic Malvolio." *Renaissance Quarterly* 51, no. 4 (1998): 1199–224.

Somerset, Alan. "'How Chances It They Travel?': Provincial Touring, Playing Places and the King's Men." In *Shakespeare Survey*, 47 (1994): 45–60.

Spivack, Bernard. *Shakespeare and the Allegory of Evil*. New York: Columbia University Press, 1958.

Spufford, Margaret. "'I Bought Me a Primer,' or, 'How Godly Were the Multitude?': The Basic Religious Concepts of Those Who Could Read in the Seventeenth Century." In *The World of Rural Dissenters, 1520–1725*, edited by Margaret Spufford, 64–85. Cambridge: Cambridge University Press, 1995.

St. John, Warren. "Market for Zombies? It's Undead (Aaahhh!)." *New York Times*, March 26, 2006, print edition, sec. 9.

Stevens, Paul. "Hamlet, Henry VIII, and the Question of Religion: A Post-Secular Perspective." In *Shakespeare and Early Modern Religion*, edited by David Loewenstein and Michael Witmore, 231–57. Cambridge & New York: Cambridge University Press, 2015.

Stiles, Chris. *Hamlet, Zombie Killer of Denmark: A Comedy in One Act*. Crystal Beach, Ontario: Theatrefolk, 2010.

Stokes, James, ed. *REED. Lincolnshire*. 2 vols. Toronto: University of Toronto Press, 2009.

Stubbes, Phillip. *The Anatomie of Abuses*. Edited by Margaret Jane Kidnie. Tempe: Arizona Center for Medieval and Renaissance Studies in conjunction with Renaissance English Text Society, 2002.

Swanson, R. N. *Church and Society in Late Medieval England*. Oxford and New York: Basil Blackwell, 1989.

Tate, Nahum. *The History of King Lear*. Edited by James Black. Regents Restoration Drama Series. Lincoln: University of Nebraska Press, 1975.

Taylor, Charles. *A Secular Age*. Cambridge: Harvard University Press, 2007.

Taylor, Gary. "Shakespeare Plays on Renaissance Stages." In *The Cambridge Companion to Shakespeare on Stage*, edited by Stanley Wells and Sarah Stanton, 1–20. Cambridge University Press, 2002.

Thompson, Ann, and Neil Taylor, eds. *Hamlet*. 3rd ed. London: Arden Shakespeare, 2006.

Tillyard, E. M. W. *The Elizabethan World Picture*. New York: The Macmillan Company, 1944.

Tiner, Elza C., ed. *Teaching with the Records of Early English Drama*. Toronto: University of Toronto Press, 2006.

Tomlins, T. Edlyn, ed. *The Statutes of the Realm*. Vol. 3. 3 vols. London: Dawsons, 1963.

Tyndale, William. *Tyndale's Old Testament: Being the Pentateuch of 1530, Joshua to 2 Chronicles of 1537, and Jonah*. Edited by David Daniell. New Haven: Yale University Press, 1992.

Wasson, John M. "A Parish Play in the West Riding of Yorkshire." In *English Parish Drama*, edited by Alexandra F. Johnston and Hüsken, Wim, 149–57. Amsterdam and Atlanta, GA: Rodopi, 1996.

———. "Professional Actors in the Middle Ages and Early Renaissance." In *Medieval & Renaissance Drama in England*, edited by J. Leeds Barroll, 1:1–11. New York: AMS Press, 1984.

———. ed. *REED. Devon*. Toronto: University of Toronto Press, 1986.

———. "The English Church as Theatrical Space." In *A New History of Early English Drama*, edited by John D. Cox and David Scott Kastan, 25–38. New York: Columbia University Press, 1998.

Weis, René. *Shakespeare Unbound: Decoding a Hidden Life*. New York: Henry Holt, 2007.

West, Robert. *The Invisible World: A Study of Pneumatology in Elizabethan Drama*. New York: Octagon Books, 1969.

Westfall, Suzanne R. "'the Useless Dearness of the Diamond': Theories of Patronage Theatre." In *Shakespeare and Theatrical Patronage in Early Modern England*, edited by Paul Whitfield White and Suzanne R Westfall, 13–42. Cambridge & New York: Cambridge University Press, 2002.

White, Paul Whitfield. *Theatre and Reformation: Protestantism, Patronage, and Playing in Tudor, England*. New York: Cambridge University Press, 1992.

Whitehead, Colson. *Zone One: A Novel*. New York: Doubleday, 2011.

Wickham, Glynne William Gladstone. *Early English Stages, 1300 to 1660*. Vol. 3. New York: Columbia University Press, 1959.

Willbern, David. "Malvolio's Fall." *Shakespeare Quarterly* 29, no. 1 (January 1, 1978): 85–90.

William of Newburgh. *The History of William of Newburgh*. Translated by Joseph Stevenson. Lampeter, Wales: Llanerch Publishers, 1996.

Williams, George Walton. "Antique Romans and Modern Danes in Julius Caesar and Hamlet." In *Literature and Nationalism*, edited by Vincent Newey and Ann Thompson, 41–55. Lanham: Rowman & Littlefield Publishers, 1991.

Wilson, F. P. *The Plague in Shakespeare's London*. Oxford: Oxford University Press, 1999.

Witmore, Michael, and David Loewenstein. "Introduction." In *Shakespeare and Early Modern Religion*, edited by David Loewenstein and Michael Witmore, 1–20. Cambridge & New York: Cambridge University Press, 2015.

Wittreich, Joseph Anthony. *"Image of That Horror": History, Prophecy, and Apocalypse in King Lear*. San Marino CA: Huntington Library, 1984.

Wright, Edgar, dir. *Shaun of the Dead*, 2004.

Index

About the Author

Sean Benson is professor of English at the University of Dubuque. He is the author of two previous books, *Shakespearean Resurrection: The Art of Almost Raising the Dead* (Duquesne, 2009), and *Shakespeare,* Othello *and Domestic Tragedy* (Bloomsbury, 2013), as well as articles on Renaissance drama and American literature and film. He has previously served as the president of the South-Central Renaissance Conference. He and his wife have two children.

Lightning Source UK Ltd.
Milton Keynes UK
UKOW03n0630060417

298426UK00002B/11/P